PRAISE FOR

LIFE-CHANGING LEADERSHIP

In a culture that revolves around the current trend and the "hottest new thing," it's empowering to know that *leadership* never goes out of style. Pastor Frank is, by all accounts, an expert in this field. He leads pastors, both young and older; churches from mega to upstarts; and, perhaps most importantly, leads his family first. This book is going to help so many *lead* better.

CARL LENTZ
Lead Pastor, Hillsong New York City

Pastor Frank Damazio's outstanding leadership skills have been proven over more than four decades as the founder and leader of City Bible Church. This book will help leaders looking to take their church to the next level by equipping them with strategies and tools for identifying and releasing the next generation of leaders within their church. Frank Damazio is well qualified to write this exceptional book on leadership.

PASTOR PHIL PRINGLE
Senior Minister, C3 Church
Author, *You the Leader*

Frank Damazio is truly a leader's leader with a ministry spanning the globe. For more than four decades he has inspired, equipped and developed multitudes. *Life-Changing Leadership* is a treasure of clear biblical principles as well as practical wisdom shared from his wealth of knowledge and experience. I know this resource will not only benefit lead pastors but their teams as well.

MIKE SERVELLO
Founding Pastor, Redeemer Church, Utica, New York
Founder and CEO, Compassion Coalition, Utica, New York

I am excited to endorse *Life-Changing Leadership*. Pastor Frank Damazio embodies the principles of integrity, purity and example in his lifestyle. You are about to receive an impartation from a deep well of knowing and following Jesus. Find a mentor like Frank and follow him . . . all the way to Jesus!

LARRY STOCKSTILL
Teaching Pastor, Bethany World Prayer Center
President, Heartbeat of Louisiana

Pastor Frank is a leader like few others I have ever known, and I respect and love him deeply. His insight in the area of leadership is extraordinary. This book will encourage you, equip you and empower you to increase your leadership capacity through the grace of God.

JUDAH SMITH
Lead Pastor, The City Church, Seattle, Washington

I can't think of anyone more qualified to write on leadership than Pastor Frank. He writes wisdom from a wealth of experience and study—which is a rare combination.

CHAD VEACH
Pastor, The City Church, Seattle, Washington
Director, Ministry Institute Program

LIFE CHA**N**GING
LEADERSHIP

IDENTIFYING AND DEVELOPING
YOUR TEAM'S FULL POTENTIAL

FRANK DAMAZIO

Regal

For more information and
special offers from Regal Books, email us at
subscribe@regalbooks.com

Published by Regal
From Gospel Light
Ventura, California, U.S.A.
www.regalbooks.com
Printed in the U.S.A.

Contents

INTRODUCTION

Life-changing leadership is the desperate need in every church worldwide. Such leadership is the key to building anything that will become life-giving and have a lasting impact. God is calling leaders today to be great leaders—not just good or average, but over-the-top—and we are committed to helping leaders grow into that calling. Together we can build great churches worldwide!

As leaders, we know that we must prepare ourselves, better ourselves, make changes and keep growing. After more than four decades of being a leader, I am convinced that leadership is the determining factor for most everything achieved in God's kingdom. I'm sure that most who pick up this book are good leaders, not weak or defective in character or ministry skills. They are most likely doing what they know to do, and doing it with all their heart. The fact is that leadership is a demanding calling, and leading Christ's Church is a high calling. The measure of a true leader is not how great the individual becomes, but how great the team becomes.

I've witnessed some great leaders in action as communicators, dreamers and highly inspirational people of influence. But what about the teams those leaders work with? Are they also great? Do team members dream big dreams? Are they world-class leaders? Our call as leaders is to build great leaders who build great churches. Great leaders are always growing—always striving to improve both their own leadership and the leaders around them. We must push the boundary lines to move beyond the normal or usual, but we don't have to do that alone. Let's push with our team and go to the next level together.

Leaders are pioneers, venturing into unexplored territory and guiding their followers to new and often unfamiliar destinations. They get people going someplace. They must take risks, rejecting the maintenance mentality.

Let us be life-changing leaders who build life-changing teams to shape life-changing churches. Let's envision what can be gained by building the greatest teams possible, using our unique gifts and strengths. We can stay on our mission, possess right motives, and give our followers a great win.

This book is about the teams we build and the church culture that supports a team-building atmosphere. Life-changing leaders are resource finders and releasers. They are focused on the future and dedicated to doing whatever it takes to get there. I've heard it said that the most significant things ever accomplished were done by people who were either too busy or too sick! Great leaders are those who, when they feel like they are pushed to their limits, push a little further.

Those who lead churches are people of amazing influence and incredible responsibility. I feel a great burden to make others great—to raise up spiritual sons and daughters who carry the vision and become the dream team we need today. Life-changing leadership identifies and develops the team's full potential.

Are you up for the challenge? We can do this! We are empowered by the Holy Spirit to lead—and to lead well. I'm praying that this book will increase your faith for the team you can build. Increase your vision for the future you can have. Increase your capacity for the greater reach God has for you. Life-changing leadership involves a collection of skills, all of which can be learned and improved: respect, experience, emotional strength, people skills, discipline, momentum and timing. Let us learn well and build wisely. The best is yet to come!

1

LIFE-CHANGING
LEADERSHIP METRONS

You are reading this book because you have answered the call to leadership—and you are serious about your call and the ministry set before you. You want to change lives. You want to be unstoppable. The reality is that great vision, great heart, great skill and great gifts aren't quite enough. It takes an unstoppable leadership spirit to make the great vision happen. The unstoppable spirit in a leader is what makes an unstoppable church. When you bump against resistance, what is your response? Every leader experiences resistance; learning how to respond to that resistance is vitally important to the health and success of your church.

What can we do to become unstoppable? Unstoppable leaders have what I call "absolutes"—principles and characteristics from which they never deviate. These absolutes are godly character, clarity of calling, development of gifting, depth of knowledge, love for the church, honoring proven principles, and being a team builder and city reacher.

Unstoppable leaders are unbeatable, relentless, unrestrainable, unyielding, never quitting—an unstoppable force. They follow the instructions found in Matthew 10:22: "But don't quit. Don't cave in. It is all well worth it in the end" (*THE MESSAGE*). Unstoppable leaders have the gift of endurance. They cannot be kept from moving forward. They are not discouraged by anything they hear. They will not be limited to the point of restraint. They have supernatural forward movement in their spirit.

We always think we've been through the worst until we experience something even more difficult. Recently, I took up the habit of bike riding. When I started, I could hardly get the bike to do what I wanted it to do. I had ridden stationary bikes in the gym, but I had never really tried to pedal a bicycle that had gears and brakes and other unfamiliar gadgets. On my first ride, I traveled four miles. That was a big deal to me! I decided that I wanted to build my endurance, so I added one mile every day to my ride.

Besides the distance, the main challenge for me was climbing hills. The hills surrounding my home are quite steep and can be intimidating to beginning cyclists. It took me a little while to realize that hills are actually not a big deal. There's a rhythm and a pace between the gears and the pedaling that propel you up the hill. As I found that rhythm, and built my stamina and knowledge, my cycling capacity expanded into arenas that I never thought I could achieve. I was riding 15 miles straight, then 20 miles, then 25, and even 30 miles. If someone had told me just 3 months ago that I would ride a bicycle from my house to the downtown area of a city 30 miles away, I would not have believed it. But as I rode and built endurance, I found that I could do more and ride farther than I ever imagined.

The key to biking is how much pain you are willing to endure. Once you realize that, you understand that pain itself is the challenge. Pain must be overcome. Pain does not limit you; it challenges you to stretch until you reach a new level and new capacity. Pain becomes what you need in order to move to the next realm. In ministry, there is a lot of pain on all levels. You cannot get to the next level of ministry without pain. It is the thing that comes to stretch you and teach you that you can go much further in ministry than you think you can go.

Painful times in ministry can be relational: people leaving the church or the team, or people spreading false reports about you. Your pain could be disappointment—in yourself or the offering or the building or the plateau, and on and on. Whatever the pain is, you need to overcome it and climb the hill. Some people will not climb the hill because they think it is too painful. They stay at the bottom with their bike, refusing to go up. But the hill is not as bad as you think it is. You just need some rhythm and a good attitude! Before you know it, you're at the top of the hill and you're wondering what was so bad about it. In ministry and in life, you are going to go up some hills—and when you've climbed them, you will say, "What was the big deal about that? I can do so much more!" That is the unstoppable spirit!

The apostle Paul was an unstoppable leader. He was beaten, stoned, publicly criticized, jailed and forsaken by his ministry companions, yet

Paul

he continued to build the Church. He witnessed to his jailers, wrote letters to strengthen local congregations, and discipled young leaders. He did not slow down! What was his ministry secret? What made him unstoppable? Paul unpacks his ministry secret in his second letter to the Corinthian church.

Second Corinthians is known as the most personal letter Paul ever wrote. It includes the most tears, most tension and most revelation of the man; it shows him at his most vulnerable moments; and it provides the most intimate description of Paul. This is his most personal epistle, and he wrote it in response to an attack from his followers—those he had raised up—in his own church plant.

Paul was attacked by critics, accused by his own church people, and demeaned by other leaders. Those who opposed him claimed that he was brave from afar but a coward face to face, and that his refusal to accept support was a sign that he was inferior. They made fun of his physical appearance and his speaking ability, even going so far as to say that Paul's relationship with Christ was not as good as theirs. Paul's greatness lies in his character and the grace he showed in getting beaten up and by responding properly. He answers his critics in this letter and reveals his secret to ministry success. In his discourse, he defends his office and his personhood. How hard is it for you to defend yourself? How do you handle attacks with humility and not just rebuke people?

Studying and imitating Paul's behavior in such a difficult situation will help us become unstoppable leaders. Let us look closely at 2 Corinthians 10:1-18. Here we find the heart of Paul's response to his critics and insight into what he considered to be his life-changing leadership "metron." A metron is the assigned scope of ministry and spiritual influence on a person or group. Let's unpack this concept as it is displayed in Paul's ministry.

PAUL'S MINISTRY SECRETS REVEALED

First, Paul clarifies his ministry identity: "Now I, Paul, myself am pleading with you by the meekness and gentleness of Christ—who in presence am lowly among you, but being absent am bold toward you" (2 Cor. 10:1). Earlier in the letter, he defended his office; now he defends and clarifies himself. This is the most personal part of the most personal letter of the apostle. His ministry identity is rooted in Christ and in the convictions by which Paul lived. I have watched leaders get sidelined because they could defend their office but not themselves. They could defend the vision, but when it came down to addressing the core of the criticism—the "This is what I think about you"—they could not defend themselves. Do I defend myself? Or do I accept people's criticism and just bow out? Here Paul defends himself in a very wise, godly and different way.

Next he explains his ministry style: "But I beg you that when I am present I may not be bold with that confidence by which I intend to be bold against some, who think of us as if we walked according to the flesh" (2 Cor. 10:2). Paul was meek, not weak. The weak do not have the strength to be meek. Meekness is strength under perfect control—strength that accommodates another's weakness. Meekness is an attitude that accepts God's dealings with us as good and does not dispute or resist. Paul responds to a view of him as walking in the flesh, or ministering on a human level. He explains that his ministry style involves meekness and gentleness. He can control his strength and his tongue under pressure.

Paul goes on to identify his weapons of warfare: "For though we walk in the flesh, we do not war according to the flesh. For the weapons of our warfare are not carnal but mighty in God for pulling down strongholds, casting down arguments and every high thing that exalts itself against the knowledge of God, bringing every thought into captivity to the obedience of Christ" (2 Cor. 10:3-5). He emphatically denies that his weapons—including any piece of his armor—for spiritual warfare were of a carnal, physical or fleshly nature. His power lay not in eloquence of speech or powers of communication or philosophical smartness. He relied on the Spirit and he was mighty in the Spirit—mighty by God, who supplied for Paul all spiritual power to pull down strongholds and deceptive reasoning and speculation.

Then Paul proves his ministry motive:

Do you look at things according to the outward appearance? If anyone is convinced in himself that he is Christ's, let him again consider this in himself, that just as he is Christ's, even so we are Christ's. For even if I should boast somewhat more about our authority, which the Lord gave us for edification and not for your destruction, I shall not be ashamed—lest I seem to terrify you by letters. "For his letters," they say, "are weighty and powerful, but his bodily presence is weak, and his speech contemptible." Let such a person consider this, that what we are in word by letters when we are absent, such we will also be in deed when we are present (2 Cor. 10:7-11).

Paul had in his heart at all times the protection of the believer and the Church. The welfare of the believer came before his own reputation, successes or rights. Paul's motive was not to protect himself, but to protect the Church. That motive had been proven, leaving him nothing to prove to them.

Finally, we come to the key to proper response to criticism. Paul defines his ministry metron:

For we dare not class ourselves or compare ourselves with those who commend themselves. But they, measuring themselves by themselves, and comparing themselves among themselves, are not wise. We, however, will not boast beyond measure, but within the limits of the sphere which God appointed us—a sphere which especially includes you. For we are not overextending ourselves (as though our authority did not extend to you), for it was to you that we came with the gospel of Christ; not boasting of things beyond measure, that is, in other men's labors, but having hope, that as your faith is increased, we shall be greatly enlarged by you in our sphere, to preach the gospel in the regions beyond you, and not to boast in another man's sphere of accomplishment. But "he who glories, let him glory in the LORD." For not he who commends himself is approved, but whom the Lord commends (2 Cor. 10:12-18).

Here Paul exposes the faulty way that ministries evaluate themselves by using the measuring rod of others. Evaluating themselves by themselves is also unwise and in fact will be harmful. Paul now introduces the pivotal ministry concept that he personally lived by—and in doing so, reveals a Kingdom secret that is true for all ministries. Paul knew his "measure"—his "rule"—using the Greek word *metron* to indicate the parameters of his ministry revelation. Ministry identity, style, warfare and motives all rest on the understanding of ministry metron. If you know your metron, no one can move you from it. If you don't know it, you are vulnerable to doubts and carnal reasoning. How do you define your ministry? How do you know where your ministry lines are, and how do you stay in your metron?

DEFINING THE METRON

"Metron" is commonly translated as "measure." It means a portioned-off section, a boundary that has been set, a parameter that should not be exceeded. A metron is a measure of capacity or limit. *It is an assigned scope of ministry grace and ministry influence within the limits of appointed lines drawn by God.*

Paul uses this word in his response to his detractors: "But we will not boast of things without our *measure* but according to the *measure* [metron] of the rule which God hath distributed to us" (2 Cor. 10:13, *KJV*, emphasis added). Here is that verse in another translation: "We will not boast about things done outside our area of authority. We will boast only about what has happened within the boundaries of the work God has given us, which includes our working with you" (*NLT*). It is a distribution from God, no matter what you say. I will lead because God has given me the capacity to lead, no matter what you say.

Every leader has a defined supernatural metron in his or her life. This metron is a limiting factor, but understand that limitations are not necessarily bad. We can get into a faith mode where we think we can do anything, go anywhere and pursue any vision. The truth is that each of us is limited by a supernatural metron. All the things that you think you can do have to fall within the present lines that God has drawn for you. If they do not fall inside those lines, you will begin to use carnal weapons against yourself: human reasoning, vain imaginations, and wrong thinking about yourself and your gifting.

Once you begin to think wrongly about your gifting and step outside the lines of your ministry metron, the enemy can take you out of the game. I have seen dozens of leaders who believed they could define their own lines, thinking that the same success they were presently enjoying in one area would follow them into another area that was not in their metron. When success in that new area did not happen, they were left discouraged, frustrated and unfulfilled. What happened? You can't blame the devil in these instances—he has nothing to do with it. It's not sin in the leader's life. It's simply a misunderstanding of his or her assignment.

One way we know we have strayed outside our metron is that we get a bad case of comparing ourselves with everyone else. Comparing metron against metron is wrong—and it is exactly what Paul means when he says that he measures according to the measure that God has given him. We should never measure our God-given assignment against someone else's assignment. We need to love the metron we have. As soon as we start comparing, we become critical: "No one is really doing a good job." Pretty soon, we're judging everyone, because we are blinded—standing in a fog outside the lines of the place where we should be standing. We become mean, critical, unfruitful, cranky and progressively angrier when things function more and more poorly. Misunderstanding of our metron throws us out of rhythm. When we are out of rhythm, things just don't work.

Every leader has an ideal, perfect measure he or she has been assigned to achieve. Paul rejects any boasting that rests on a human measure. He lives according to a "God measure"—a "God rule." His labors are constantly regulated by a "God measuring line." Within the lines of our metrons are grace, favor and everything we need to be successful in our ministry. Grace plus ministry equals influence. Influence is most effective when it is within the limits God has given us. Even if that influence looks lesser to others, it is really greater because it is the measure of influence we are supposed to have. Greatness is a direct result of our faithfulness to our divine assignments.

Abraham Lincoln, a man of persistence and an unstoppable leader, knew the power of knowing our placement. He said, "I like to see a man proud of the place in which he lives. I like to see a man live so that his place will be proud of him." When we submit to our assignments, our faults and flaws are covered by the lines. Like Moses with his stuttering speech and Peter with his anger, we can actually function in weakness and still find success in ministry, because we are operating within the lines God has assigned us.

What is your metron? It is God who holds time and chance in His hands. He is the only one who can put you in the right place at the right time with the right gifting to do the right work (see Ruth 2:2-3; Esther 4:14; Eccles. 9:11).

THE WRONG MEASURING ROD

There is a right way to measure and a wrong way to measure. Mankind's instruments of measuring can be faulty and can cause us to come to wrong conclusions. Proverbs 20:10 tells us, "Diverse weights and diverse measures, they are both alike, an abomination to the LORD." Another translation puts it this way: "A double standard of weights and measures—both are disgusting to the LORD" (GOD'S WORD). "Diverse" means not alike, separated, or turned different ways. There are wrong ways in which to measure success. The world measures success by how large the church is, how much money the congregation has, how beautiful the people are, how influential the pastor is, whether any famous people attend, and so on.

When leaders come to me to talk about planting a church, I like to ask the questions: Would you be happy and fulfilled if you had only 100 people in your church? Would you be happy if your capacity is 100? If the answer is no, then my advice is not to plant the church, because you will not be happy with 200 or 300 or 1,000 people. In this case, happiness is based on the wrong measuring line.

There will always be another conference, another way to push the limits, another creative idea. If you are operating in your metron, then you will experience fulfillment, no matter what stage of ministry you are in. If, on the other hand, you are measuring your sermon, your service, your leadership skills, or any other aspect of your ministry by the wrong weight, you can become discouraged, because there is no grace for that measurement. The Bible emphatically states, "You shall not have in your house true and false measures, a large and a small" (Deut. 25:14, *AMP*).

The wrong measuring rod is measuring the self by another. It is the self-established ruler who compares the self to someone else. Why compare yourself to others? No one in the entire world can do a better job of being you than you!

Operating outside the metron God has drawn for us is a sure way to burn out in ministry. What's more, in comparing ourselves to others, we often end up judging ourselves. There is no one worse to judge!

THE RIGHT MEASURING ROD

Paul said, in effect, "I measure by the measure God has given me." He had a standard by which his self-estimation was to be regulated. The scale is different for each person. The line between conceit and sober thinking is not the same for all. Only God has the divine measuring rod that determines our metron. Paul knew his metron, and he did not compare his with anyone else's. This is why he never gave up and never quit. He was measuring by the measuring line God had given him.

METRON DOMAINS

Metron domains are spiritual jurisdictions given to us by God. They are our places of authority, action, influence, responsibility and ownership. These domains can be described as the application of our metron applied to various circles of function. We occupy certain domains given to us by God.

If you are standing in your domain—in your place—then you can smile and not be concerned about what someone else says, because you have authority. If you are not in your domain, then you have to push, pull, manipulate, threaten and make sure everyone else knows you are the great leader. A person who has authority only has to whisper. A person who doesn't have authority has to scream. It's kind of like the Snickers commercial where the guy looks as if he is having a panic attack—wildly flailing his arms and screaming. Then he is given a Snickers bar. Once he bites into it, he smiles and calms down.

Your metron is your spiritual Snickers bar. When you start getting contorted in your leadership, you need to get back to your metron. When you're in your metron, you are sweet, relaxed and confident, and you honor other people easily. It doesn't bother you to lift up someone else because you are honoring their metron. You recognize others' metrons and can encourage them because you are secure in your own metron.

There are five metron domains that I believe apply to all leaders: grace, leadership, church, apostolic, and movements metrons. There are many more metron domains, but we will deal with these five common ones.

GRACE METRON

The grace metron is the favor of God assigned to us to be successful in a specific place. Esther lived in her grace metron: "The king loved Esther more than all the other women, and she obtained grace and favor in his sight more than all the virgins; so he set the royal crown upon her head and made her queen instead of Vashti" (Esther 2:17). Stephen operated in his grace metron: "Stephen, full of faith and power, did great wonders and signs among the people" (Acts 6:8). Success is determined by the Lord as we stay in that place and do that task that He has assigned to us. Grace, favor and everything we need to be successful in ministry are given to us for that assignment. "But to each one of us grace was given according to the measure of Christ's gift" (Eph. 4:7; see also John 1:14-18; 2 Cor. 12:6,9).

LEADERSHIP METRON

The leadership metron is the measure of influence God grants with no competition or complaining. Leaders need to understand and accept their orbit of influence. Comparing and competing are signs of not understanding and accepting one's metron. It is right to take responsibility within the metron God has given.

Sir Winston Churchill strayed outside his leadership metron when he accepted the appointment to serve as Chancellor of the Exchequer, England's chief financial officer. Churchill had never been good with math. While in office he remarked, "The higher mind has no need to concern itself with the regimentation of figures." Despite his aversion to figures, he attempted to bring Britain's budget back into balance. The result was a train wreck: hyperinflation, unemployment, and the closing of many businesses that were essential to the national life. The country was outraged. Churchill later admitted, "Everyone said I was the worst Chancellor of the Exchequer that ever was, and now I am inclined to agree with them." Churchill exceeded his metron. He was unparalleled in motivating troops, rallying a country, diplomacy and statesmanship, but he was awful in finance.

Know your metron and stay within that measure God has drawn for you. "As each one has received a gift, minister it to one another, as good stewards of the manifold grace of God" (1 Pet. 4:10; see also Acts 20:28; 1 Pet. 5:2).

CHURCH METRON

The church metron is a true and identifiable grace upon a congregation for specific influence. Churches are strategically positioned in their particular locations by the wisdom of God and are given authority and grace to occupy their assigned territory. Knowing your church metron will keep you from coveting or criticizing other churches' metrons. One great thing that is missing in teaching about church growth is the fact that what works for one leader's growth, based on his or her metron, cannot possibly work for another's. If you are doing what your metron allows, then enjoy your metron. Let God enlarge it if He wants to. Be like Barnabas: "When he came and had seen the grace of God, he was glad, and encouraged them all that with purpose of heart they should continue with the Lord" (Acts 11:23).

One of the greatest revelations you can experience is to enjoy your ministry. You have to believe that God trusts you with what He gives you. Rest in knowing that God ultimately builds the church: "If the LORD does not build the house, the work of the builders is useless; if the LORD does not protect the city, it does no good for the sentries to stand guard. It is useless to work so hard for a living, getting up early and going to bed late. For the LORD provides for those he loves, while they are asleep" (Ps. 127:1-2, GNB).

APOSTOLIC METRON

This domain activates and empowers leaders to occupy their assigned places of spiritual authority and ministry. The apostolic metron gathers, teaches, equips, assigns, targets, builds, shapes and raises spiritual sons and daughters and deploys teams. What makes a church is not the beginning, but the ending. It is a leader's mandate to train the next generation of leaders, and to equip believers to fulfill the great commission of taking the gospel to all people everywhere.

Not all leaders have apostolic metron flow. Paul writes, "Are all apostles? Are all prophets? Are all teachers? Are all workers of miracles?" (1 Cor. 12:29). We are unique individuals with unique gifts and metrons. Apostolic leaders and churches take the gospel to unreached areas (see Rom. 15:20-21); they plant churches (see 1 Cor. 3:10; Gal. 1:6-10) and appoint and train leaders for those churches (see Acts 14:21-23; Titus 1:5).

Nevertheless, all churches—even those not specifically gifted with apostolic ministry—are to be reaching and purposefully evangelizing today's world.

MOVEMENTS METRON

In this metron domain, leaders and churches strategically network the deposit God puts into that congregation to multiply Kingdom effectiveness generationally. Large-scale movements, such as Hillsong, Ministers Fellowship International (MFI), C3 or Vineyard, have a spiritual metron that is God-assigned and God-favored. We don't compete, compare or copy, nor do we fear someone else's metron. We have our own metron. Movements or defined groups of churches will keep changing, even as the word "movement" implies. Today, the emerging church, missional church and others all seek to bring clarity to the church's role in today's world. Let us each find our metron and use it to impact the world, cross-pollinating with other movements and helping one another reach the world for Christ.

EIGHT METRON ABSOLUTES

Metron living is not accidental—it is strategic. It is also not a limitation, but an enlargement; not a weakness, but a strength. David wrote, "The lines have fallen to me in pleasant places; yes, I have a good inheritance" (Ps. 16:6).

Peyton Manning may not be the fastest quarterback in the National Football League, but he is accurate! In 2009, he threw for 4,500 yards and completed 68.8 percent of his pass attempts. He operates in his metron. These eight principles about metron living will help you to lead in your metron and release others to lead in theirs.

1. KNOW YOUR GIFT METRON
In talking about spiritual gifts, Paul writes, "But to each one of us grace was given according to the measure of Christ's gift" (Eph. 4:7). Spiritual gifts are received; they are not achieved, discovered or developed. "One and the same Spirit works all these things, distributing to each one individually as He wills" (1 Cor. 12:11). Although there are some similarities, spiritual gifting and grace gifting are not the same as natural talent. Know what gift you have been given. Your spiritual gifts are important for the church to accomplish its vision. If you know that your gifts are in leadership, teaching and strategizing, then you know to add different gifts to your team.

Ministry positions may change, but our own giftedness does not. Circumstances change, but our giftedness remains the same (see Phil. 1:12-14).

2. KNOW YOUR ASSIGNMENT METRON
Understand your measure of authority. Influence is directly connected to your placement. Where God places you, you have authority. "For we are not overextending ourselves (as though our authority did not extend to you), for it was to you that we came with the gospel of Christ," writes Paul (2 Cor. 10:14). Overextending is stretching too far. That is not what God wants you to do.

Rice University conducted an "Elite Leaders Study" in which 500 elite leaders—such as the president of the United States, cabinet members, executives and other professionals—were asked, "What personal, moral and social factors have sustained you over the course of your career?" The overwhelming answer was "setting limits on ambition." Knowing your limits is essential to your success. Great leadership is the ability to limit oneself. It is a self-cultivated discipline that, if mastered, will greatly help you maintain a healthy pace. Good leaders know their values, strengths and limitations, and they are able to control their emotions and behaviors to fit their personal metron.

3. KNOW YOUR CAPACITY METRON
Capacity is the competency, fitness and potential suitability for holding, storing or accommodating the maximum amount that can be contained.

"For I say, through the grace given to me, to everyone who is among you, not to think of himself more highly than he ought to think, but to think soberly, as God has dealt to each one a measure of faith" (Rom. 12:3). Everyone has a capacity to believe for something. When you were saved, you had a measure—a capacity—of faith to believe that Jesus died for your sins and that He could save you from eternal separation from God. Since then, your faith has been stretched and increased to believe for more. Know what it is that God has built you to hold. If you know your capacity, then nothing will be impossible, because you are doing what God has stretched you to do.

In cycling, it is crucial to know the limits of your capacity. You must know when you are helping yourself, and when you are damaging your body. If you try to pace yourself with more advanced cyclists, you may push beyond your limits. You will not be able to finish your race, because you blew out by not understanding your capacity. If you know your level, you will pace yourself properly and finish strong. Great leaders know how to accurately assess themselves. They are not in self-denial about their strengths or their weaknesses.

4. KNOW YOUR LEVEL OF INFLUENCE METRON

Influence is directly related to your metron. A person of influence demonstrates character, strength, humility, integrity and vision that motivate and inspire others. Influence is when you make others successful! It is an elusive quality but a potent force for change. Influence is no mystery. God uses His favor, blessing and power to bring influence through leaders and churches. It is the Lord who raises up one and sets down another (see 1 Sam. 2:1-11).

Influence is a God-given grace that is related to your placement, your assignment, and God's good will. Influence will help you be more effective in everything you do—where you are and even outside of where you are. Influence cannot be strategized to go beyond your metron without some level of human promotion, self-marketing, and aligning with the right people mentally. To experience rest as a leader, you must let God establish your influence, let God promote, and let God make your name influential.

Secular teachers say that influence is not a genetic trait; it can be learned. Anyone can develop the skills of influence. To this I say yes, of course this is true, and it is not wrong or evil. Use all the right skills—but use them within your metron. Be strategic. If you are in need of people skills, management savvy, or drawing the best out of those greater than you, then pursue developing those skills strategically. Just don't frustrate yourself by trying to make yourself into someone God has not called you to be.

Remember what God said when He appeared to Abram: "Get out of your country, from your family and from your father's house, to a land that I will show you. I will make you a great nation; I will bless you and make your name great; and you shall be a blessing" (Gen. 12:1-2). God had a metron for Abraham that involved making his name great. This was a God work, in accordance with God's will. It was not Abraham setting out to make his name great. Rest in the influence God has allotted for you.

5. KNOW YOUR PATTERN OF SUCCESSES METRON

When you operate in your metron, there is a pattern of successes. David killed a lion, a bear, and then Goliath. Joshua claimed victory in Jericho and then moved on to 30 more cities. Mastery of a task may be a straightforward path. Mastery in leadership is a lifetime pursuit—one that is humbling and challenging as well as rewarding. When true grace is in operation upon you, whatever is supposed to happen through you will happen.

Simply put, you will be effective and see results and fruit. If you are gifted as a pastor, then your success will be found in pastoring people. They are helped, you are happy, and the result is changed lives. If you are a teacher, people will learn from you. You teach, they learn, and it is a success. If you know your pattern of success, you will find the metron God has given you.

6. KNOW YOUR RELATIONSHIP ACCOUNTABILITY METRON

Who is your direct report person in ministry? To whom are you accountable? We all need people who cover us—who can ask us the hard questions and give us true evaluations. Don't pass up the opportunity to develop covenant relationships and accountability relationships with others who will help you identify when you are straying from the lines God has drawn. All leaders need accountability built into their life and ministry. Accountability can involve a plurality of leaders who have regular and transparent communication with carefully established boundaries.

Shared responsibility in leading God's people minimizes the potential for one person to inflate pride or abuse a leadership position. Transparent communication with other trusted leaders, conducted in an atmosphere of trust and love, is great for building accountability. The best practice is not to wait for a crisis or an "as needed" moment, but to set aside regular times that include an expectation of personal accountability conversations.

The pastoral leadership ministry requires a wide range of sophisticated skills, including public speaking, intellectual ability, relational gifts, self-knowledge, theological understanding, verbal dexterity, management acumen and visioneering par excellence! It's no wonder failure in today's leaders is a reality. We can fail on so many levels! We need relational accountability in order to receive encouragement and input, and to keep us from thinking wrongly about ourselves.

If you are overworked, stressed out, and losing ground with your marriage or family, it is time to talk to those with whom you are relationally accountable. Tell them honestly, "I am tired, discouraged, and have doubts about how effective my ministry really is." If you don't already have people in your life to whom you can relate in this way, please take some time and locate those you should be accountable to.

7. KNOW HOW TO MAXIMIZE YOUR PRESENT METRON

Maximizing the metron you are in is the most strategic focus a leader can have. Stand back and take a close look at your present metron. What's going on? Think about it, question it, and imagine it being different. Remember that you don't have to just accept what is; you can create what you want rather than just accept what is—as long as it's in line with what God has called you to do.

With today's fast pace, multiple challenges and complex issues, it's easy for leaders to lose focus. In all the busyness, we have to set aside time to focus. To maintain focus is to engage in the in-depth, accurate and truthful consideration of our metron. Let us with persistence keep our focus on the field God has given us. Our priorities should be set to maximize our present metron.

Are you focused on your field? What distractions are you dealing with? Would you say, "I never used to be this way. I don't know what happened to me."? In the process of serving your entire city or reaching the nation or taking on the world's needs, have you lost focus on your field? Have you compromised your own leadership identity while trying to become something others want you to become? Your present metron deserves your full focus and an ever-increasing passion to make that metron the best metron it could possibly become.

Don't belittle today's moment—the "now"—by trying to move into another metron prematurely. Ecclesiastes tells us that God "has made everything beautiful *in its time*" (Eccles. 3:11, emphasis added). Maximize your areas of calling, your talents, or the piece of land God has given you. Leaders who live only in the future never make the most of the now. What is in your hand right now? Maximize it!

8. KNOW YOUR TIMING AND SEASON FOR ENLARGING YOUR METRON

The words and promises over your life all have designated timing for their release. Jesus came at just the right time: "But when the fullness of the time had come, God sent forth His Son, born of a woman, born under the law" (Gal. 4:4). Enlarging your metron is partly God's work and partly yours. God will allow you to stretch and to enlarge your borders. You must prepare yourself, evaluate yourself, overcome your weaknesses, and master yourself. You must also discern whether it is the right time to launch out and expand your parameters. Don't move into the next level of metron until the Lord brings clarity and release for you to step over the line. Begin now to thank God for the metron you have, and you will start thriving instead of striving!

2

LIFE-CHANGING LOCAL CHURCHES

Every local church has some form of authority, order and government. Whether it's structured with elders or a board of businesspeople, or some other form, each congregation has a group of people who organize the way the church functions. Members of this group answer the questions of who, what, when, where, why and how. They also provide pastoral covering over the congregation. These leaders have authority to give direction or management to the affairs of the church, both legal and pastoral. The authority structure determines the church's decision-making process, its growth limits, and its leadership philosophy.

Without a clearly established, biblical understanding of church government, the church will not succeed. This is why it is of utmost importance that church leaders understand organization and government—so that they can build their congregations with biblical accuracy and godly wisdom. Even if a leadership structure is ideal in theory, it can fail miserably in practice because the leaders did not know how to realistically implement the plan. Leaders, especially the lead pastor, must therefore have a solid grasp of both the spiritual and practical elements of the biblical pattern of government.

THE BIBLICAL PATTERN OF GOVERNMENT

The form of church government clearly established in Scripture is theocratic in nature. It is not autocratic, governed by one man. It is not bureaucratic, governed by a few. It is not democratic, governed by the people.

It is theocratic. In a theocracy, God chooses, calls and equips certain persons to be leaders and rulers for His people. God is the one who is in charge, and He delegates a measure of authority to His chosen leaders according to His will. The delegated leadership described in the Bible is a group of leaders referred to as "elders."

Elders are identified in the New Testament local church as a *group*, with a plural noun (see Titus 1:5; Jas. 5:14). Together, the elders pastor the congregation. Throughout the New Testament, we see demonstrations of this principle of a plural leadership body that functions and exercises authority jointly. There are 18 references to elders in the book of Acts, 10 of which relate directly to the ministry of an elder in the New Testament church. Other writers also mention eldership. Note the following Scriptures that refer to elders as the governing body of the local church (emphasis added):

- "This they also did, and sent it to the *elders* by the hands of Barnabas and Saul" (Acts 11:30).
- "So when they had appointed *elders* in every church, and prayed with fasting, they commended them to the Lord in whom they had believed" (Acts 14:23).
- "And as they went through the cities, they delivered to them the decrees to keep, which were determined by the apostles and *elders* at Jerusalem" (Acts 16:4).
- "The *elders* who are among you I exhort, I who am a *fellow elder* and a witness of the sufferings of Christ, and also a partaker of the glory that will be revealed" (1 Pet. 5:1).
- "From Miletus he sent to Ephesus and called for the *elders* of the church" (Acts 20:17).
- "Remember *those who rule over you*, who have spoken the word of God to you, whose faith follow, considering the outcome of their conduct" (Heb. 13:7).
- "Obey *those who rule over you*, and be submissive, for they watch out for your souls, as those who must give account. Let *them* do so with joy and not with grief, for that would be unprofitable for you" (Heb. 13:17).

(See also Acts 15:4-23; Titus 1:5-9; 1 Tim. 5:17-20.) Note that the plural form—*elders*—is used when referring to the ruling body. The authority structure in the church is a team concept, not a dictatorship.

Elders must qualify biblically; be knit together in one heart by the Holy Spirit; and understand their role to equip, care for and protect the flock of God—the Church. Eldership functions well when the elders love, honor and respect the lead pastor and one another, allowing unity and strength to permeate the eldership. (We'll delve more into the biblical qualifications of elders in chapter 5.)

THE LEADER AT THE FOREFRONT

Throughout history and today, we see that every government has a governing body that includes a leader at the helm, steering the ship. Without a head leader, the government and the body are crippled. There is no person giving orders on general direction, no one to keep projects in line, and no one to hold people accountable. If there is no leader at the forefront, people are lost and more vulnerable to attack.

Headship is the place of authority, and Christ is the head of the Church. Christ's headship is His authority, His lordship, His rulership and His kingship (see Isa. 9:6-7; Col. 1:15-20). Christ is also the head of the local church, which He governs through His chosen and qualified leaders whom He has ordained for that task. "And He Himself gave some to be *apostles*, some *prophets*, some *evangelists*, and some *pastors* and *teachers*, for the equipping of the saints for the work of ministry, for the edifying of the body of Christ" (Eph. 4:11-12, emphasis added).

In any given group of elders, God generally places the mantle of leadership upon one elder. Scripture recognizes this elder as the person set in place by God to be the presiding elder—or "lead pastor"—of that local church (see Acts 14:21-24; 15:6,22; 20:28-31; 21:17-18). Other names for this person could be "senior pastor," "senior minister," "general overseer," and so on. This role does not exalt this elder above the group of elders, but sets him in responsibility as "first among equals." In the Old Testament, it was the leader Moses and the elders who led the congregation of Israelites. Then came Samuel and the elders, Ezra and the elders, Jeremiah and the elders, and Joel and the elders as the delegated governing authority of God's people.

Similarly, the New Testament pattern of theocratic government mirrors the pattern set in the Old Testament. In the New Testament, the Church was led by the apostle James and the elders; Barnabas, Paul and the elders; Timothy and the elders; and Peter and the elders.

It is important to recognize that God is the one who appoints the leaders of His Church. Moses, when he was nearing the end of his ministry, asked the Lord to set a man over the congregation who would lead the people as he had done:

> Then Moses spoke to the LORD, saying: "Let the LORD, the God of the spirits of all flesh, set a man over the congregation, who may go out before them and go in before them, who may lead them out and bring them in, that the congregation of the LORD may not be like sheep which have no shepherd" (Num. 27:15-17).

The Lord selected Joshua, who was set before Eleazar the priest and the congregation as Moses transferred leadership authority to him. Joshua then functioned as the nation's leader, military commander and judge, just as Moses modeled. This is our pattern for local church government today: a leader from among the eldership who governs the people under Christ's delegated authority.

This leader is like the captain of a ship. He follows Jesus' orders to build the church and establish right principles. He keeps Christ at the center by continually remembering Jesus' death and resurrection through communion. On a naval ship, the captain is responsible for the entire vessel. That means he commands everything from operations to navigation, compliance with local and international laws, food rations and personnel, both passengers and crew. Every person is ultimately the captain's responsibility. The local church body can be imagined as the ship, and the lead pastor as the captain. The lead pastor is responsible for the soul of each crewmember who is assigned to that ship by God.

THE UNIVERSAL CHURCH
AND THE LOCAL CHURCH

The Church is a society within a society, a community within a community, a nation within a nation, and a divinely governed institution within humanly governed institutions. It is, according to the Scriptures, the vehicle for the kingdom of God, set apart as God's eternal purpose manifested in time.

God has a plan for people and for His Church, and He has set that plan in motion. The lead pastor has to totally accept the fact that the

Church was and is the eternal purpose of God. His purpose is to save everyone from an eternity separated from Him, and to establish relationship with people. To that end, the Church is God's greatest evangelistic tool:

> Now in those days, when the number of the disciples was multiplying, there arose a complaint against the Hebrews by the Hellenists, because their widows were neglected in the daily distribution. . . . Then the word of God spread, and the number of the disciples multiplied greatly in Jerusalem, and a great many of the priests were obedient to the faith (Acts 6:1,7; see also Matt. 28:18-20; Acts 7:17; 9:31; 12:24).

The Church is divinely energized in order to accomplish its God-given purpose. Further, it is divinely energized to the degree that it pursues that purpose. Lack of energy and burnout happens when the pursuit strays from its intended purpose. It is the lead pastor's responsibility to keep the church focused on its God-given purpose. That purpose is to build a community of God's people who are thinking and acting as God intended and inviting others on behalf of God to join the community.

THE UNIVERSAL CHURCH

Every government has a founder and a beginning point. The universal Church, which is the collection of all believers everywhere, was founded by Jesus Christ. Ephesians 2:20 tells us that the Church is "built on the foundation of the apostles and prophets, Jesus Christ Himself being the chief cornerstone." Christ started the Church, and today He remains busy building it. Christ in His Church is the central fact of God's will and purpose.

In the Gospels, Christ mentions the Church as two specific and identifiable entities. Once, He refers to the universal Church, and once He refers to the local, visible gathering of believers. The universal Church is often described as "mystical" or "invisible" because it refers to all people around the world who call Jesus Savior. Even if you and I do not meet each other every Sunday morning for a worship service, we are still joined by the Holy Spirit to all believers everywhere. Jesus said this about the universal Church:

> Now I tell you that you are Peter the rock, and it is on this rock that I am going to found my *Church*, and the powers of death will never prevail against it. I will give you the keys of the kingdom of

Heaven; whatever you forbid on earth will be what is forbidden in Heaven and whatever you permit on earth will be what is permitted in Heaven! (Matt. 16:18-19, *Phillips*, emphasis added).

The "Church" mentioned here is the universal Church—the fellowship of all Christians everywhere. Chuck Colson described the relationship between the believer and the universal Church this way:

> The universal church is more than simply a collection of people; it is a new community. . . . When Peter made his confession, Jesus did not say, "Good, Peter. You are now saved and will have an abundant life. Be at peace." Instead, He announced the church and established a divinely ordained pattern. When we confess Christ, God's response is to bring us into His church; we become part of His called-out people. When we become followers of Christ, we become members of His church—and our commitment to the church is indistinguishable from our commitment to Him.[1]

The word "fellowship" is often used to describe the community of the universal Church. A "fellow" was originally understood as a person who invested money in a joint venture. Members of a fellowship had a vested interest in an enterprise. Likewise, when we become part of the Christian fellowship, we commit to contributing our resources—whether time or skills or a number of other things—to other members of the fellowship. One of the most practical ways of contributing to the fellowship is in the context of a local church.

THE LOCAL CHURCH

The second way Jesus describes His Church is in the context of a local body:

> But if he will not hear, take with you one or two more, that "by the mouth of two or three witnesses every word may be established." And if he refuses to hear them, tell it to the church. But if he refuses even to hear the church, let him be to you like a heathen and a tax collector. Assuredly, I say to you, whatever you bind on earth will be bound in heaven, and whatever you loose on earth will be loosed in heaven. Again I say to you that if two of you agree on earth concerning anything that they ask, it will be done for them by My

Father in heaven. For where two or three are gathered together in My name, I am there in the midst of them (Matt. 18:16-20).

The local church as Jesus designed it consists of a group of people who share a geographical location and regularly meet to praise Jesus together and encourage one another to live a disciplined, godly lifestyle. We need both the universal Church and the local church.

The book of Acts provides evidence of a visible and practical expression of church membership and identification. It was not enough for believers to belong to the invisible, mystical Church. Membership in the fellowship was practically expressed by belonging to the local, visible church (see Luke 9:1-2; 10:1-2; Acts 1:15; 2:41,47). Just as crewmembers wear uniforms that identify them with that ship, so too do local church members demonstrate connection with their congregation.

I am not suggesting that if Joe begins attending a Foursquare church, he has to wear a tag that says, "I belong to Foursquare," or that he can never walk in the door of an Episcopal church. Local church membership means that you give your life to building godly community and relationships in that church and you commit to helping others in that community become more like Christ. It certainly does not mean that you can't minister to someone who belongs to another church. We are all part of God's Church body.

Sadly, many people today believe that they do not need the local church. Chuck Colson writes, "For we know many Christians who say they are believers but are not members of a church. By that, some mean that they are not members of a local congregation. But many mean that they do not need the church in any sense."[2] What Colson is driving at is the importance of the local church, not as a sort of club, but as a refuge—a place of multiplied resources, accountability, grace and personal transformation.

Each local church should know those for whom they are responsible. We see in the book of Acts that believers were "added" to the church. Believers were numbered and accounted for. They belonged to the Church invisible but also to a local body.

There is one church in one city, yet within the city are many congregations that are part of the whole. The responsibility of each local church is to submit to the headship of Christ and to build according to the biblical pattern (see Col. 1:16-20). Local churches must recognize one another's sovereignty under Christ's headship and not seek to dominate one another. Each church is to be self-supporting, self-governing and self-propagating.

Local churches should respect one another and flow together in unity, while maintaining their own unique personalities and callings.

In my city of Portland, Oregon, I've made it a point to develop relationship with other local pastors. Many years ago, we formed a City Pastors Network of pastors from our metro area, and we meet together periodically to pray, strategize and just keep in touch with one another. We share resources and ideas on what programs are working, what strategies are not working, what our needs are, and so on. I love meeting with this group. There is no competition among us—no pointing fingers and blaming someone for "stealing" people from our congregation—only unity and commitment to do our very best to expand God's kingdom in our city.

This is the function and the power of the dynamic between the local church and the universal Church. Everyone's goal is to win souls for Christ. We simply present the gospel in various ways that meet the needs of the variety of people in our city. Some like loud music, while others like hymns sung *a capella*. Some people like the feel of a very traditional service—maybe where the choir members wear robes and the pastor wears a three-piece suit. Others are more comfortable in jeans. These things are simply flavors—personal preferences that do not dilute the message of the gospel. Just as there are many different tastes, so too there are many local churches that are each preaching the gospel in an environment that connects authentically with the people it serves.

A GATHERING OF GOD'S PEOPLE

The Greek word translated as "church" in English is *ecclesia*, which means to call out for the purpose of gathering together as a congregation or an assembly. This word appears 114 times in the New Testament. The *ecclesia* is the assembled people of God, called together to listen to or act for God. A corporate service, such as Sunday morning worship, is this kind of gathering. It involves everyone coming together, worshiping God, and listening to what He is saying to His church.

The local church as an *ecclesia* is designed to fulfill several roles.

A DWELLING PLACE FOR GOD'S PRESENCE
The local church is a dwelling place for God's presence and a vehicle for the moving of His Holy Spirit.

There are diversities of gifts, but the same Spirit. There are differences of ministries, but the same Lord. And there are diversities of activities, but it is the same God who works all in all. But the manifestation of the Spirit is given to each one for the profit of all: for to one is given the word of wisdom through the Spirit, to another the word of knowledge through the same Spirit, to another faith by the same Spirit, to another gifts of healings by the same Spirit, to another the working of miracles, to another prophecy, to another discerning of spirits, to another different kinds of tongues, to another the interpretation of tongues. But one and the same Spirit works all these things, distributing to each one individually as He wills (1 Cor. 12:4-11).

"Diversities of gifts" means a variety of expressions of the Holy Spirit. The greater the variety of gifts being used, the more the Holy Spirit is expressed. When God's people combine their gifts to worship God together, they create a powerful atmosphere for God to move into with His presence. Just as God's presence rested as a cloud in the tabernacle of Moses and the tabernacle of David, so too can our places of worship be filled with God's presence when we gather and use our gifts to worship Him. "But You are holy, enthroned in the praises of Israel" (Ps. 22:3).

THE BODY OF CHRIST
The local church is the Body of Christ, where the members join as brothers and sisters in the commitment to fulfill their God-given ministries.

Christ gave those gifts to prepare God's holy people for the work of serving, to make the body of Christ stronger. This work must continue until we are all joined together in the same faith and in the same knowledge of the Son of God. We must become like a mature person, growing until we become like Christ and have his perfection.

Then we will no longer be babies. We will not be tossed about like a ship that the waves carry one way and then another. We will not be influenced by every new teaching we hear from people who are trying to fool us. They make plans and try any kind of trick to fool people into following the wrong path. No! Speaking the truth with love, we will grow up in every way into Christ, who is the head. The whole body depends on Christ, and all the parts of the body are joined and held together. Each part does its own work to make the whole body grow and be strong with love (Eph. 4:12-16, *NCV*).

A church body is a fellowship—a living network of interdependent relationships held together by secure connections and unconditional love. Each part relies on the others and supplies what the other parts need. Not only do others in your local church body need you, but you also need them.

I have a friend who developed appendicitis and underwent surgery to remove the inflamed appendix. The good news is that my friend went on living without the appendix. But the removed appendage did not survive. It needed the body! When a person separates himself from the local church body, he does not receive the nutrients and strength he needs to live a full and healthy life. Local churches must be the community where members give one another opportunity and resources to fulfill their unique ministry.

AN ASSEMBLY FOR CORPORATE WORSHIP

The local church is an assembly where people gather to lift up the name of Christ together through audible praise and worship.

Through him then let us continually offer up a sacrifice of praise to God, that is, the fruit of lips that acknowledge his name (Heb. 13:15, *ESV*).

True worship is a spiritual encounter with God that transforms the spirit and soul of a person. Worship creates an atmosphere where God "moves in" with His presence and power, drawing people to be touched, healed, forgiven, restored and encouraged. As God's people offer their praises to God in song, God sets up His home in their place. The local church should be marked by the powerful and transformative presence of God.

A SPIRITUAL HOSPITAL

The local church is a spiritual hospital, where ministries raise up those who are sick and diseased, not only in body, but also in soul and in spirit.

The local church is like a spiritual deliverance center for P.O.W.s. The power of the Holy Spirit in and through the local church releases and delivers people bound and kept captive by the enemy (see Luke 4:18).

GOD'S AIRCRAFT CARRIER

Let's return to our analogy of the local church as a ship. I think the ship that best represents the local church is the aircraft carrier. These ships are truly impressive. A U.S. Nimitz-class carrier stretches 1,092 feet in length, and its flight deck is 252 feet wide. That's close to four football fields long and almost one football field wide. The carrier weighs about 97,000 tons and can travel at speeds up to 34.5 miles per hour.

One of the most important functions of the aircraft carrier is providing the materials and space for aircraft to land and take off. During daylight, a flight deck crew can launch two aircraft every 37 seconds. The carrier, operated by a skilled crew, provides fuel for the aircraft and makes sure each jet is in pristine flying condition. The command crew briefs the pilots and navigators on their missions, and gives communication support to the aircraft in flight. In short, the aircraft carrier is designed to function as a launching pad for greater effectiveness and reach. A well-staffed, fully fueled and stocked aircraft does no good just sitting on the deck when its mission is to drop relief supplies in another place miles away.

The local church is the aircraft carrier that welcomes pilots returning from their mission, fuels them up with training and resources on Bible reading and prayer strategies, offers medical support for the sick and wounded, and communicates the plan for the next mission. But the church must then turn those jets around and launch them back into the sky to reach more people. That is our picture of the local church today!

The local church is a spiritual school, equipping people and releasing them into their God-given purposes (see Eph. 4:11-12). Each local church has the responsibility to train its own leaders, minister locally to its city, and be involved in God's work nationally and internationally.

This complex and impressive body called the local church is the ship you and I are called to lead! Our mission from Christ is to lead this ship in a responsible and biblical way that protects the crew, helps them become more like Christ, and invites others to jump onboard. Such a mandate would be impossible if we tried to fulfill it on our own. That is why

God has given us a great design to follow. He is the head and we are His appointed leaders, serving the church body with a team of other like-minded leaders. We'll be discussing that team in greater detail later, but first, let's look specifically at the role of lead pastor.

LIFE-CHANGING
LEAD PASTOR PROFILE

Leaders who change lives have various gifts and styles of leadership. The leadership "style" refers to the manner used to express one's values and execute ministry. A style is a person's distinctive approach. That approach is influenced by the person's gift mix and grace.

FIVEFOLD MINISTRY GIFT MIX

All leaders have been given a grace mantle to do whatever God has destined them to do. The outworking of that grace (*charis*) is *charismata* (spiritual gifts). If grace lifts, the gift loses power. Gifts operate, but it is grace that saturates and makes a corporate atmosphere. The gifts are meant to be imparted on the church.

Leaders must first understand the ministry gifts God has given them before they can release those gifts to others. The lead pastor's gift mix may be a combination of any of the five ascension gifts, along with graces and other spiritual gifts. The "ascension gifts" are those mentioned in Ephesians 4:11: "Apostles, some prophets, some evangelists, and some pastors and teachers." These are the post-ascension gift ministries. After Christ *ascended* (see Acts 1:9-11), He gave the Church these gifts. They are also referred to as the "fivefold ministry," since there are five gifts mentioned in this verse: apostle, prophet, evangelist, pastor and teacher. The gifts are given for the express purpose of perfecting, equipping and building up the Body of Christ (see Eph. 4:12). These ministry gifts are instrumental in unifying the Church and perfecting one's faith. It would be beneficial for churches to recognize and receive these ministries given to the Church by Christ.

Each gift expresses itself in leaders differently. The apostle ventures forth with authority to faithfully represent the purposes and intentions of the Sender. The prophet operates as a mouthpiece for God. The evangelist announces the good news of the gospel and equips other people to do the same. The pastor feeds and tends the sheep. The teacher instructs others, presenting truth in systematic sequences.

Lead pastors may function in some or all of these five ministry expressions. They may do some things better than others. Usually a balanced leadership team is built to strengthen the weaker side of the lead pastor. The rule of thumb is this: *Never staff your strengths; always staff your weaknesses.*

Let's take a closer look at each of these five gifts.

APOSTOLIC PASTOR

Life-changing leaders with an apostolic-pastor gift mix produce a strong apostolic foundation, an apostolic vision and an apostolic leadership team. An "apostle" is one who is sent—or simply "the sent one" (see Eph. 2:20). Apostolic gifting carries an eternal viewpoint and eternal urgency, as the apostle is sent by God. Types of ministry that are important to the apostolic pastor include planting healthy churches, pastoring other pastors, and building a strong foundation on doctrine and principles of biblical structure. The mindset of apostolic ministry is seen in Acts 1:8: "But you shall receive power when the Holy Spirit has come upon you; and you shall be witnesses to Me in Jerusalem, and in all Judea and Samaria, and to the end of the earth." This verse inspires the "apostolic mission" of the apostolic church, which involves several elements. The apostolic aspect of ministry should be a goal of every church (see Acts 2:37-47; 4:1-4; 5:12-14; 6:1-7), but some churches are especially gifted in this area.

Apostolic churches receive supernatural, miraculous power from God to fulfill the Great Commission. That power is available through the Holy Spirit; thus, apostolic churches must believe in Holy Spirit activity. They expect the Holy Spirit to empower the church, imparting strength and whatever virtue is needed. One function of the Holy Spirit that apostolic churches particularly pursue is the power to be a witness. In a historical sense, the churches whose lives and actions testified to the worth and effect of faith—and whose faith received "witness" in Scripture—were called witnesses. Believers today are witnesses of Christ through their attitudes and actions. Apostolic churches seek to encourage believers to practice this mandate.

Apostolic churches take responsibility for their city. The apostolic church sees that its mission begins with the city where God has planted them. By becoming a strong local church that experiences the power of the Holy Spirit through prayer intercession and evangelism, the church reaches into the city and serves its needs while sharing Jesus' love. *Live like Jesus, share His love.* Apostolic churches reach the regions in which God has granted them influence and favor. They aim to reach all people groups. The people-group responsibility entails more than simply building a multiethnic community. It also involves racial reconciliation. Jesus sought to reconcile Jews and Gentiles, Samaritans and outsiders. Apostolic churches recognize different ethnic groups and also realize that each is part of the human race, created and redeemed by God.

Along with taking the gospel to their city and region, apostolic churches embrace a global vision. An apostolic mission cultivates a vision that includes all nations. God has a strategy for the nations, and that strategy includes apostolic churches that are committed to raising up people and building churches that will harvest the nations.

Today's apostolic ministry expressions are various. There are apostolic ministries that are in authority over existing churches, exercising influence in any and all realms pertaining to the churches. There are also apostolic ministries that exert influence on individuals, congregations, businesses or groups of churches but do not have direct oversight. There are apostolic ministries that are identified with a local church and demonstrate balanced ministry and servanthood, respecting local church leadership and local church autonomy. These are local church builders. Apostolic ministries of all these types can touch and help the church, and we should respect the variety of models of apostolic ministries.

Apostolic pastors are life-changing leaders who highly regard, respect and esteem God and His Word. They hold proven principles in a high place in their ministry. Apostolic leaders build carefully with great vision and great faith.

PROPHETIC PASTOR

A church led by a lead pastor with a prophetic-pastor gift mix will have a strong atmosphere of inspiration, faith and the expectation that God will work. This gift mix will honor doctrine and principles and hold strong

convictions in the Word of God. Prophetic pastor-led churches are sometimes strong in vision but need help in administration. Discipleship may
happen by absorption or through a well-thought-out strategy.

Prophetic pastors have a long-range vision and minister the Word of
God with clarity and inspirational preaching. This does not imply that
they are without depth in the Word or that they lack doctrine. They preach
with a prophetic edge that inspires as well as instructs. They exhort, encourage and urge people toward set goals. Prophetic pastors correct, re-
prove, rebuke and exhort people to get back on track with regard to the
God-given goal when they have gone astray. They can see beyond the present into the future, and they equip the people to walk in faith.

Prophetic pastors preach with a prophetic unction. Prophetic preaching must address the issues of the day and offer a clear and accurate word
from the Scriptures. Prophetic preaching accurately assesses the current
human condition and offers insights into God's responses to the world
we live in. Prophetic churches usually have a strong worship atmosphere
that moves people into a prophetic realm in the presence of God. They
also often feature powerful praying.

The effective prophetic congregation holds a clear, authentic purpose
to which its members are deeply committed. It pursues that purpose
through a well-reasoned strategy. Its activities or programs are related to its
purpose through a carefully worked out rationale. Purpose functions as
the touchstone for every thought, decision, plan or action, and it provides
the overall perspective from which each of these can be viewed. Lead pastors
operating in the prophetic gift will lay out a clear vision for the church and
work with the team to build a strategy that meets the God-given vision.

EVANGELIST PASTOR

Evangelist pastors build growing churches by exercising their gift for seeing the need and exciting others to the cause of spreading the gospel. Their
gifting in evangelism and their ability to teach will produce an electrified
atmosphere of faith and spiritual expectation. The heartbeat of the evangelistic church is for the lost and unchurched people. Evangelist pastors
have a theology that compels the church to evangelize and a passion that
motivates the church into the urgency of the gospel message.

An evangelist pastor can gather many people and will need to nurture
them into a strong foundational Christianity. Evangelist pastors should
identify and surround themselves with other leaders who have apostolic

and teaching gifts to build up the church in its areas of need. Evangelist pastors know how to make the shift from a "build it and they will come" attitude to a "we must disciple people where they are" attitude. They help people embrace the idea of continually connecting to the unchurched and unsaved where they are and engaging the world with the gospel and with tools for spiritual transformation.

Churches making this shift have decided to become excellent in making disciples of both children and adults. The spirit imparted to the church is one of powerful praying. The pray-ers charge the atmosphere—the spiritual climate—with the presence of God. They lead the way into new realms where breakthroughs are possible. They hear from God in fresh and new ways, receiving open heavens, blessing, favor and the living presence of God. They see that God is enlarging their spiritual borders to reach more people.

Churches led by an evangelist pastor pray with faith, systematically and consistently, for the lost. Evangelistic churches are churches with compassion. They are connected to their community and embrace that connection with great passion.

PASTOR SHEPHERD

The combination of a dominant pastoral and motivational ministry results in well-fed, well-cared-for sheep. The pastoral gift mix operating in lead pastors will be evidenced in their caring for and maintaining of the flock. Administration, a safe budget and a well-kept flock are this leader's focus. The church is usually safe and built to last. The pastoral-dominant leader provides the congregation with qualified leaders who help the lead pastor care for the church. This is part of the pastor's assumed long-term responsibility for the spiritual health of the church. Such pastors would benefit from using the 80/20 principle: spending 80 percent of their time with 20 percent of their most influential people.

The pastoral-driven ministry usually develops a great system of small groups in the church and offers extensive training for those who do pastoral counseling. They see the small group as congruent to the *koinonia* spirit of community found in the Early Church (see Acts 2:42). A small group is a fellowship characterized by generous sharing.

Because of the great emphasis on small groups, the shepherd-led church may be one that is more in-looking than out-looking. To avoid becoming an exclusively inward-focused community, a harvesting gene must be imparted into the small groups. Small groups need to apply practically the principles of reaching the city—person by person, home by home, and neighborhood by neighborhood. Thus, through the small group, seven-day-a-week evangelism will take place, and the church will move toward outreach rather than introspection only.

TEACHING PASTOR

The teaching-pastor gift mix has the capacity to grow strong, healthy, well-balanced churches. This gifting sets in motion a powerful chemistry, which results in depth of spiritual experience and breadth of spiritual security. Teaching pastors are usually good communicators, systematic instructors, and comfortable with preaching series. This, combined with a love for people, warm personality and the ability to structure for shepherding, is a dynamic mix. Teaching and shepherding are connected and often flow together as one strong gift mix to build enduring churches—although teaching pastors may need to balance instruction with evangelism and inspiration.

The teaching-pastor gift is a grace that enables the leader to clearly understand the Word of God and to equip the church to fulfill its purpose:

> That we should no longer be children, tossed to and fro and carried about with every wind of doctrine, by the trickery of men, in the cunning craftiness of deceitful plotting, but, speaking the truth in love, may grow up in all things into Him who is the head—Christ—from whom the whole body, joined and knit together by what every joint supplies, according to the effective working by which every part does its share, causes growth of the body for the edifying of itself in love (Eph. 4:14-16).

Teaching pastors hold fast to the faithful Word, exhort their followers in sound doctrine, and refute those who contradict the truth. The Word of God is the basis of all teaching. The preacher should do the exegesis of his text carefully, using proper hermeneutics. Preaching should feed the saints and equip them to compose a strong, healthy church.

ADDITIONAL LEAD PASTOR GIFTS

Along with the fivefold ministry gift mix, there are many other gifts the lead pastor uses.

THE LEAD PASTOR AS WATCHMAN

The watchman hears the sound of the trumpet and rightly discerns the message (see Num. 10:1-10). Watchmen must respond to the warning of the trumpet if they are to deliver their own souls (see Ezek. 33:6). After the watchman hears the trumpet, he sounds the alarm and alerts the people to coming danger (see Jer. 31:6; Ezek. 3:17; 33:1-9; Acts 20:28-21; Heb. 13:17).

The watchman must be on the alert for the "little" things that can destroy a local church. The Scriptures speak of "little foxes" (Song of Songs 2:15), "little indifference" (Prov. 6:10; 24:30-33), "little folly" (Eccles. 10:1,6), "little leaven" (1 Cor. 5:6; Gal. 5:9), "little unfaithfulness" (Luke 16:10), and that "little member"—the tongue (Jas. 3:1-5). All these littles add up to one dangerous threat to the unity of the church. Lead pastors are watchmen who keep their hearts pure and encourage the leadership team and congregation to also keep their hearts pure and strong in "spiritual flow"—the ability to hear the Holy Spirit and act on what He is leading them to do.

THE LEAD PASTOR AS EQUIPPER

Lead pastors set goals for their congregations in accordance with the will of God. They work to instill those goals in the people and look for the people to embrace the goals as their own. Lead pastors then strive to motivate and equip the people to do their respective parts in accomplishing the congregational goals.

The goal of the lead pastor should be to make every Christian a minister. Elton Trueblood stated it powerfully: "If the average church should suddenly take seriously the notion that every lay member—man or woman—is really a minister of Christ, we could have something like a revolution in a very short time." Thomas Gillespie said, "Mobilization takes place if the nonclergy are willing to move up, if the clergy are willing to move over, and if all God's people are willing to move out."[1] Lead pastors set the pace for the entire church. If we wish to see our congregations and ministries flourish, we must be equippers who are willing to step aside and make room for others to use their gifts.

THE LEAD PASTOR AS VISIONARY

Lead pastors generate, communicate and sustain commonality of purpose. They can fire the imagination and create a sense of dedication to a vision that motivates followers into effective, meaningful service. They also guard the identity and direction of the congregation, clarifying and emphasizing purpose. The visionary is a spiritual pacesetter. The visionary develops strategies for implementing the mission of the church and constantly generates momentum to achieve goals.

THE LEAD PASTOR AS LEADER

Lead pastors cause the church to progress by emphasizing, clarifying and reminding people of their purpose. They keep an objective in the spotlight and show people how to merge their efforts to accomplish common goals. They are catalysts who help individuals to harmonize their abilities as the Body of Christ and to strengthen their purposefulness through a growing commitment to Christ and His kingdom.

THE LEAD PASTOR AS TEAM REFINER

Lead pastors carefully adjust those who hold a position of leadership but are not leading. A non-functioning leader transmits stagnation. This kind of "foot-dragging" may indicate that a leader secretly wants to hinder progress by quietly opposing ideas or decisions. Whether the obstruction is accidental or intentional, the lead pastor is right to deal with it. When taking decisive action like this, leadership should follow this maxim: "If you kick, be sure you kick toward the goal." Leadership must be careful to make a positive contribution to the right goal, and not to react in a counter-productive way.

THE LEAD PASTOR AS RISK TAKER AND INNOVATOR

Lead pastors welcome change and are excited about the opportunities it brings. Usually they are described as optimists; they are steadfastly hopeful about the future. Lead pastors are trailblazers, pioneers, paradigm shifters, risk takers, and of course good problem solvers. They are not content merely to imagine the future; they want to create and possess that future. Innovators seek to translate vision into reality, and they have the drive and persistence to do it. They create and implement ideas successfully. A breakthrough idea requires a stretching of a leader's abilities, skills and energies to make the idea manifest in the church or in the kingdom of God.

A businessman attended a seminar conducted by a self-made millionaire. The millionaire had made money by speculating in commodities. During the lecture, a spectator stood and asked the millionaire, "Didn't you realize all this speculation was risky and that you could have lost every penny you had?"

The millionaire said, "Why, yes, I did."

The man then asked, "Why did you continue to speculate?"

The millionaire said, "I don't know exactly why. I just know I was willing to take the risk."

The man, now a little irate, snapped, "Well, I'm not!"

The millionaire smiled and said, "That may be why I'm giving this lecture, and you're paying for it!"

THE LEAD PASTOR AS TEAM CATALYST

Lead pastors draw together a strong team of highly qualified, gifted leaders who can pull their load and a little more. As the team is being built, someone must set values, goals, standards, philosophies and vision, which are then agreed upon by the team. Team members should not all have the same gift mix; rather, the team should include people with a variety of gifts to allow for the congregation to grow in all areas. Lead pastors find and marshal resources in order to develop ways and means of organizing people and programs to achieve God-set goals and visions. They establish policies and goals, while keeping counter-productive processes from weakening the dynamics of the local church.

THE LEAD PASTOR AS CULTURE ANALYST

Lead pastors study, analyze and seek to understand the flow of culture. Understanding the moral, social, economical, political and spiritual climate is important to the leader who seeks to build a church that is in touch with society. A leadership team cannot be effective if its understanding of change is erroneous, incomplete, misinformed or outdated. The team members must know the difference between truth—which is unchangeable—and methods, procedures and programs—which are changeable.

Lead pastors must interpret culture by studying materials, people and expert opinions. Based on their study, they create and implement new ideas.

THE LEAD PASTOR AS MOTIVATOR

Lead pastors motivate others to fulfill defined tasks. They need to be adept in the art of motivating people. Motivation is a key to all activities in the church. People easily become bogged down, lose perspective, become discouraged or get sidetracked. They need motivation to keep going. An important component is keeping the vision clearly in front of the congregation. When people know where they are going, they will pursue the vision with a vengeance.

For most people, motivation is not automatic—as a matter of fact, it is downright hard. That is why lead pastors must be positive motivators to the staff, to the leadership team, and to the church as a whole—exhorting people to start where they are, use what they have, and do what they can. Paul wrote, "Let us not become weary in doing good, for at the proper time we will reap a harvest if we do not give up" (Gal. 6:9, *NIV*).

THE LEAD PASTOR AS SERVANT

Lead pastors serve others with proper motivation, seeking to develop the potential of those who have been entrusted to their care. Jesus is the model for every leader to follow. In Luke 4:1-21, we see Jesus establishing His leadership style by rejecting wrong styles and philosophies. He rejected the self-satisfying style of leadership. He decided that His ministry would not focus on providing personal pleasure.

Jesus was offered rulership over all the kingdoms by the tempter, but He rejected such a display of power. Instead, Jesus chose the style of a servant (see Matt. 20:20-28; Mark 9:35; 10:35-44; Luke 9:48; 22:24-27; John 13:3-17). Being a servant is one of the most important distinctives a lead pastor can develop. We must lead out of relationship, never by coercion. We must never demand obedience or submission, but rather demonstrate consistent concern, love and servanthood to all those with whom we work.

Lead pastors lead by support rather than by control. They give of themselves rather than take for themselves. This style of leadership develops potential in others. Servant leaders allow for a loving atmosphere to permeate the team of leaders, rejecting manipulation, exploitation or domination.

A servant leader has a life full of crosses, towels and basins. He or she never seeks position, but does seek Kingdom productivity. When lead pastors lead out of servanthood, they lead out of brokenness, not bossiness. Remember, servants are sometimes abused and insulted. They are never really appreciated to the full extent of their worth.

As the lead pastor moves into servant leadership, fear of people will be removed. Fearful leaders are likely either to dictate their wishes to people or to avoid others altogether. Let us arise with our towel, our basin of water, and a new spirit of servanthood to those around us! We'll look more closely at servant leadership in another chapter. Until then, consider these words of St. Augustine:

> *For you I am a bishop.*
> *But with you, I am a Christian.*
> *The first is an office accepted;*
> *the second a grace received.*
> *One is danger; the other safety.*
> *If then I am gladder by far*
> *to be redeemed with you*
> *than I am to be placed over you,*
> *I shall, as the Lord commanded,*
> *be mercifully your servant.*
> ST. AUGUSTINE (AD 354–430)

THE LEAD PASTOR'S UNIQUE STRUGGLES

Because of the various roles they must fill and the complex nature of their office, lead pastors face unique struggles. They wrestle continually with many opponents, who at times seem to attack from every side. We must learn to fight well, keep our footing, maintain our perspective, and persevere through prayer.

Chrysostom (AD 347–407), an Early Church father, once said, "The minister's shortcoming simply cannot be concealed. Even the most trivial ones soon become known. However trifling the offenses, these little things seem great to others, since everyone measures sin, not by the size of the offense but by the standing of the sinner." When you are in leadership, you live in a fishbowl. Everyone is watching and dissecting your every action.

Even if you are not doing anything wrong, and you are following God's instructions and biblical wisdom, you are going to rub someone the wrong way. It's a bit like driving down the road with a police car behind you. You are driving below the speed limit, your seatbelt is buckled, and both hands are on the steering wheel, but you still feel as if the police are going to pull you over for something. Lead pastors and their decisions are scrutinized to the max. I am not saying this is right; it is just reality—and this reality can cause pressure to mount on the leader.

Recognizing the pressures you face is half the battle in overcoming them. The following are 21 areas in which lead pastors may find themselves wrestling as a result of the pressure of the office:

1. THE LEAD PASTOR WRESTLES WITH IMAGE

The image of the minister held by the world around us usually is negative. The media-shaped image of the minister is quite depressing. The church-built image of the minister is one of a pious, poverty-destined, always-available doormat. The lead pastor may wrestle with ideas about who he is supposed to be, who he wants to be, and who he has to be. Perhaps no other profession finds itself so trapped by contrasting expectations and distorted stereotypes. Small wonder that many ministers succumb to the strong temptation to let the role prescribe and define their personalities and actions (see 2 Cor. 5:1-3; 10:10; 12:11).

2. THE LEAD PASTOR WRESTLES WITH RELATIONSHIPS

Pastors are tempted not to make close friends in the church. They are tempted to hide their emotions and not to be transparent. It is so easy to get hurt! But that is part of the ministry. God's healing is part of God's mercy.

Many ministers pay a heavy price for not admitting their loneliness in the ministry, and for not facing it and grappling with it honestly. They pay a price in terms of happiness and fulfillment, with their self-images, and in their professional and family lives. It is hard to overestimate the importance of sharing with one another our struggles, pains and healings. Yet it seems in the ministry that relationships are hard to develop. We have the continual pressure of others' needs upon us, busy schedules, our families, and of course church activities. Where in all of that is there time to develop true, genuine friendships that are built to last for the long haul? I am privileged to have a few very close friends with whom I can share, to whom I can be accountable, and with whom I can be real. Loneliness happens in the ministry when there is an absence of purposeful activity and meaningful relationships (see 2 Cor. 7:3).

3. THE LEAD PASTOR WRESTLES WITH RESENTMENT

When someone leaves the church, it is easy to take it personally. But remember, it is Christ's church. People do not always treat the lead pastor with respect or love. He cannot take everything to heart. The Lord will lead people out of the church for their own good—and sometimes for the church's good.

4. THE LEAD PASTOR WRESTLES WITH EXPECTATIONS

It can be difficult to tell whether the expectations to which we respond come primarily from others or from within ourselves. Most of us realize that there are things we cannot do and things we do not know, but we do not generally let this mark of humanity show. We need to shed the burden of unrealistic expectations. Spouses, children, the staff, people, sheep, goats—they all have ideas on how we should relate to them and on what we should do as lead pastors. However, only we can decide what God expects of us.

5. THE LEAD PASTOR WRESTLES WITH PRIORITIES

Like most people, pastors have priorities—a list of things we value in order of importance. But it's one thing to have the list and another thing to know how to follow it. How do we value and make time for family, friendships, God, health and recreation—to name just a few? What should be done first, today? How do we keep from overcommitting ourselves (see 2 Cor. 1:17)?

6. THE LEAD PASTOR WRESTLES WITH GUILT

At some point, all pastors have the thought, *I'm not a good pastor. If I only I had done or said something different, they wouldn't have gone through with the divorce. I'm not a good parent; I need to give my children more time. My body is really out of shape; I need to spend more time taking care of God's temple.*

7. THE LEAD PASTOR WRESTLES WITH THE FLESH

Lead pastors wrestle with the "be perfect" syndrome that is often prevalent throughout the church. Ministers usually keep up their masks of righteousness at all cost. They are expected not to have trouble with any major carnal problems. Of course this is not reality. We all battle with a carnal mind and unsubmissive flesh. A modest honesty with the congregation will help educate them and release the lead pastor from undue pressure to be perfect (see Rom. 7; 2 Cor. 7:1; Jude 24).

8. THE LEAD PASTOR WRESTLES WITH EMOTIONS

If the lead pastor interprets his leadership call as a directive to become a sort of spiritual superman, then emotions must be concealed. The pastor is expected to be tough-skinned if criticized or abused, and strong and supportive if a member of his flock is hurting. But what do ministers do with all of the emotions they suppress? Aren't they allowed to cry or get emotional once in a while (see Acts 20:17-38; 1 Cor. 2:3)?

9. THE LEAD PASTOR WRESTLES WITH PROFESSIONALISM

To be professional as a minister is not negative in itself. We should endeavor to be excellent in our letter writing, returning of phone calls, dress, appearance, and general managerial responsibilities. But let us not cease being real people and approachable as leaders. If we become too professional, we may repel people instead of drawing them (see 2 Cor. 5:12).

10. THE LEAD PASTOR WRESTLES WITH THE LIMITATIONS OF HIS CALLING

What are the limitations of our calling? How do we walk within that certain sphere? Time is so limited—how do we know if we have taken on too much? One person can't do everything! I recommend that all leaders try to discover their spiritual gifting, talents and aptitude as accurately as possible. The California Psychological Inventory (CPI) was one of the most helpful tools I found in leading me to discover my strengths and weaknesses (see 2 Cor. 10:13-16).[2]

11. THE LEAD PASTOR WRESTLES WITH REALITY

In the world of ministry, we focus a great deal on what *ought* to be. We preach with faith that all things are possible through Christ. Christ is able to break any stronghold of the devil in peoples' lives. God will answer our prayers; God is our Jehovah Jireh. Without doing harm to faith in God or the Bible, we must learn to live with unanswered prayer, people who are struggling with bad habits they can't seem to conquer, marriages that don't work, and backslidden children of wonderful Christian parents. Reality is defined by Webster's as "actual being or existence of anything, truth, fact, in distinction from mere appearance." Yes, believe that God can work supernatural turnarounds. Also rest in what is if He chooses not to change a situation into what you think it should be.

12. THE LEAD PASTOR WRESTLES WITH CONFIDENCE

Sometimes lead pastors wrestle with a lack of confidence; other times they are burdened with too much. When should they practice humility, and when should they walk in confidence of faith (see 2 Cor. 3:3-6)?

13. THE LEAD PASTOR WRESTLES WITH TIREDNESS

The continual burden of the ministry wears us down, but then we feel guilty when we get tired. We read about John Wesley and others who got by with very little sleep—who preached four times a day and wrote all night. Who can measure up (see Judg. 8:4; 2 Cor. 1:8; 2:13; 7:5)?

14. THE LEAD PASTOR WRESTLES WITH ROLE TENSION

There is role tension between pastor and prophet. The pastoral role is one of comforting and caring. During weddings, funerals and family crises, the pastor is always welcome and respected. Move, however, into the prophetic role of confronting sin in people's lives, and there is a tremendous change of attitude toward the lead pastor. Rather than polite respect, you may encounter bitter criticism and hostility. No one seems to criticize the pastoral functions of baptizing or marrying, but warning against carnality and exposing lukewarmness are not readily received!

15. THE LEAD PASTOR WRESTLES WITH GENUINE FRUITFULNESS

We live in an age of fierce competition among athletes, politicians and businesses. The minister also is affected by the competition syndrome. What are the proofs of success in the ministry? Today, the church-growth movement has raised everyone's awareness of numbers. "How many people do you have in your church?" is a question readily asked by fellow ministers, as well as by people looking for a church to attend.

This alone puts a tremendous amount of pressure on the ministry to be more "productive." Under such pressure, ministers can find their attention shifting onto external goals and away from internal fruit in lives. Achieving more visible goals is seen as being more fruitful, yet true fruitfulness is achieved in submission to the will of God. Are we pursuing true fruitfulness or mere human achievement? Let us keep Christ as our center and work toward the simplicity of the Christ-life as ministers leading others to experience Christ.

16. THE LEAD PASTOR WRESTLES WITH DISCOURAGEMENT

Lead pastors are always trying to encourage others, but who encourages them when they are at the end of their strength? Where are the Hurs and the Aarons (see Exod. 17:8-13)?

Every leader faces discouragement at some time or another. Read the Scriptures and you will encounter leader after leader who went through seasons of discouragement. Jonah, Elijah, Jeremiah, David, Peter, Paul and John Mark each left the ministry for a time because of discouragement.

William Carey, the great missionary to India, was asked, "What is the secret to your success?" He replied, "I can plod." This is the ability to keep on keeping on. Carey was known as a man who wouldn't give in to any pressure or opposition. No matter how daunting the obstacle, he expected great things and attempted great things for God. Don't let discouragement keep you from attempting great things for God. Remember, today's mighty oak is yesterday's little nut that held its ground (see 2 Cor. 4:1,8-10; 7:6).

17. THE LEAD PASTOR WRESTLES WITH JUDGING OTHERS

If someone leaves our church, we may think it is because they can't handle the flow of God in the place. We tend to think, *I am right; they are wrong* (see 2 Cor. 5:16).

18. THE LEAD PASTOR WRESTLES WITH UNANSWERED PRAYERS

It makes me irritable to pray so much and see so little happen. Sometimes I don't understand the ministry of prayer.

For 11 years my wife was barren. I prayed and prayed, but nothing happened. Once, during a meeting at another church, the Lord told me to pray for the barren women in the congregation. My response was, *You've got to be kidding!* Despite my initial resistance, I finally obeyed and issued an altar call for those who were barren. Several women responded. I prayed for each one.

A year later, some of the ones I had prayed for had babies. We had adopted two lovely daughters, but my wife was still barren. When Sharon did become pregnant many years later, I didn't believe her when she told me! Sometimes unanswered prayer is answered prayer on God's timetable!

19. THE LEAD PASTOR WRESTLES WITH THE RELENTLESS MARCH OF TIME

Time keeps going. We keep getting older, and eventually we run out of time. No matter who we are, we are allotted the same 168 hours each week as everyone else. One of the most significant measures of our spiritual commitment is what we do with discretionary or leisure time. We should not feel guilty when we use leisure time wisely by recreating, reading a book, or engaging in some chosen hobby (see Eccles. 3:1-11).

Time wasters, however, must be dealt with harshly or they may ruin our spiritual potential in God. In his book *The Time Trap*, author R. Alec McKenzie lists these time wasters for those in top management:

- Unclear objectives
- Poor information
- Postponed decisions
- Procrastination
- Lack of delegation
- Management crisis
- Inability to say no
- Snap decisions
- Low morale
- Unclear communications
- Poor physical fitness
- Lack of feedback and information

We need to get a handle on these time wasters if we are to reach our spiritual potential in God.

20. THE LEAD PASTOR WRESTLES WITH DISAPPOINTMENTS

The lead pastor hears many promises of commitment and relationship, only to be disappointed time after time. It hurts to be dropped relationally, so many choose to avoid risking the injury that comes when one depends on others. But the ministry is a place to love, trust and believe in people and in God.

21. THE LEAD PASTOR WRESTLES WITH PERSONAL LACK OF CHRISTLIKENESS

We ask ourselves, *Why am I not more like Jesus? This is my profession! I read the Bible, I pray more than most people, yet I see such a lack of Christlikeness.*

THE WINNER'S CREED

When the lead pastor deals with these unique issues, he or she should remember these words:

People are illogical, unreasonable, and self-centered. Love them anyway.

If you do good, people will accuse you of selfish ulterior motives. Do good anyway.

If you are successful, you win false friends and true enemies. Succeed anyway.

The good you do today will be forgotten tomorrow. Do good anyway.

Honesty and frankness make you vulnerable. Be honest and frank anyway.

The biggest men with the biggest ideas can be shot down by the smallest men with the smallest minds. Think big anyway.

People favor underdogs, but follow only top dogs. Fight for a few underdogs anyway.

What you spend years building may be destroyed overnight. Build anyway.

People really need help but may attack you if you do help them. Help people anyway.

Give the world the best you have and you'll get kicked in the teeth. Give the world the best you have anyway.[3]

LIFE-CHANGING
LEADERSHIP TEAMS

The team concept, or support-ministry principle, has been proven throughout Scripture and history to be one of the most effective dynamics of any healthy, successful local church or other organization. As we build strong, long-lasting churches, we want to make sure we build solid teams and learn from the mistakes of previous generations who did not place a high value on teams. One mistake that has been made repeatedly is the suppression of the laity and the exaltation of the clergy. We should give proper scriptural value to all ministries in the church, not just to the lead pastor. Joseph was never the senior leader of Egypt, yet he saved two entire nations!

TEAM DEFINITION

When various leadership ministries are harnessed together by the Holy Spirit to work in cooperation, their effectiveness is multiplied. Recognizing and submitting to one another, they work toward a common goal and truly become a leadership team.

> Two are better than one, because they have a good reward for their labor. For if they fall, one will lift up his companion. But woe to him who is alone when he falls, for he has no one to help him up. Again, if two lie down together, they will keep warm; but how can one be warm alone? Though one may be overpowered by another, two can withstand him. And a threefold cord is not

quickly broken (Eccles. 4:9-12, see also Matt. 11:29-30; Prov. 11:14; 15:22; 24:6; Ps. 133).

My family and I once vacationed at Fisherman's Wharf in San Francisco, California. The Wharf is famous for its delectable seafood and rich history, and also for its family-friendly entertainment and other attractions. During our visit to the Wharf, we saw a true one-man band. This musician was quite energetic. He played several instruments at one time, using both of his feet, both of his hands, and his mouth. He was quite amusing—an amazingly creative and talented crowd pleaser. But he was an anomaly—a unique sort of human show. He was not the norm! Generally speaking, bands function best when multiple musicians each play the instrument he or she is best gifted and trained to play.

We have the spiritual parallel to the one-man band in the modern-day pastor. In his book *The Problem of Wine Skins*, Howard Snyder includes a chapter titled "Must the Pastor Be a Super Star?" Snyder writes:

> Meet Pastor Jones, superstar. He can preach, counsel, evangelize, administrate, conciliate, communicate, and sometimes even integrate. He can also raise the budget. He handles Sunday morning better than any quiz master on weekday television. He is better with words than most political candidates. As a scholar, he surpasses many seminary professors. No church social function would be complete without him.[1]

How would you like to be Pastor Jones? Or maybe have someone on your staff be like him? It might sound enticing and cost-effective, but the reality is that one-man leadership is limited in both style and effectiveness. Even if the man is an apostle of apostles, he is still likely only in possession of one-fifth of the fivefold ministry gifts. One man is limited in his ability to minister to the whole Body of Christ. One man may fail at wisdom and judgment at times. One man cannot shepherd the flock of God biblically. He may burn out, suffer mentally, or crash morally. One man cannot possibly meet the needs of everyone. That is why the lead pastor must raise up a leadership team and not try to be a one-man band.

Ministering alone, one man has no one to adjust, correct or change his decisions or doctrine. He may become a pastor potentate, seeing himself as always right and never needing to change any of his ideas. A team brings reality to the lead pastor and to the church. A team may raise questions and bring up aspects of a doctrine or idea that the leader, by himself, would not think to ask or investigate.

One man may have a difficult time successfully hearing God for major directions or transitions in the church. Although I believe the lead pastor is a person who should hear from God and give overall direction to the church, I also believe that there are critical situations—such as buying property, developing programs and ministries, choosing staff, letting staff go, or disciplining someone in the church—where more than one opinion is needed. The whole leadership team needs to cooperate and hear from God together. One person simply cannot carry the burden of leadership alone without paying a price physically, emotionally and spiritually. Wisdom is to allow others to share the burden, as Moses learned to do:

> So Moses' father-in-law said to him, "The thing that you do is not good. Both you and these people who are with you *will surely wear yourselves out*. For this thing is too much for you; you are not able to perform it by yourself" (Exod. 18:17-18, emphasis added).

In addition to causing burnout in the lead pastor, a one-man operation destroys leadership in others, stifles creativity, and runs the risk of producing spiritual robots and ministry puppets. Don't let that happen. The cultural model of the lead pastor being the only person to do the work of pastoring or other forms of ministry produces weak churches, and weak churches do not grow. No one person is equipped to meet the needs of the entire flock single-handedly. It is obviously impossible, yet many churches still operate as if the ministry resides in one person.

So far, all of the myriad talent shows across the world have failed to produce an act where one person expertly plays every instrument in an orchestra at the same time. Sure, there are those one-man bands—like the gentleman I mentioned earlier—where the instrumentalist plays maybe three or three-and-a-half instruments simultaneously, but a single person cannot play a full orchestra. Talented as even the best musician may be, he or she can create far better music in the context of a larger group of players who are also talented and are expressing their gifts using different instruments. Those other musicians would be robbed of the chance to use their gifts if the virtuoso decided he could do everything on his own and did not need others to help him make the music more resonant. We need one another if we are to lead successfully.

Bill Hull affirms the concept of team leadership in his book *The Disciple-Making Pastor*. Hull says:

> The pastor of the church is the combined gifts, wisdom, and faith of a pastoral team, namely the elders. In most churches a full-time, paid pastor and several ministers known as laymen would compose this group. Larger churches would combine several full-time staff with the ministers, to form a pastoral team. The plural use of pastors/teachers indicates several leaders per local church, engaged in pastoring the flock. This does not preclude the role of professional clergy; in fact, it enlarges their importance and removes a great deal of triviality from their lives.
>
> The emphasis on plurality of authority and giftedness on one hand and the necessity of strong leadership from one person on the other appears contradictory. The dual emphasis is no contradiction, but rather a call to balance—the balance of a group of gifted leaders called to pastor the church and the leader of the gifted leaders to set the pace.[2]

The team context provides incredible safety and yields increased productivity. Working with a team does not take away authority; rather, it inspires loyalty in others by showing them that you trust them with a vital piece of ministry. Team members are empowered to take more ownership of the vision and work harder to reach the goal.

Let's take a closer look at the function of the team of workers who join the lead pastor in fulfilling their church's vision and destiny.

SUPPORT MINISTRY DEFINITION

A support minister is a person who functions in a leadership role as an elder, deacon, staff minister, department head or care leader, fulfilling the ministry Christ has given him or her in the local church in support of the lead pastor. All those who function on the team are to be called by the Lord and equipped with the doctrine, philosophy and vision of that congregation. The biblical pattern of the New Testament local church requires the symphonic blending of many different ministries, all of which are rooted in shared convictions that allow team members to function faithfully and yet creatively. The following are convictions that all team members should have:

GOD HAS PLACED THEM FOR HIS PURPOSE

Team members should have a conviction that God has placed them where they are for His pleasure and His purpose, and for their good. I have a friend who applied for a specific position on an event-planning team but was offered a different position instead. At first, she was devastated. Looking at the descriptions of the two positions, she thought her preference was a perfect fit; nevertheless, she accepted the offered position and joined the team. A couple of weeks into the planning and meeting process, she realized that the position she had been given was actually far more suitable to her skills and her passions, and the person who got the position she had wanted was more proficient in that area. Both new members brought strength to the team.

God knows what He is doing when He puts teams together. He knows how to draw out the gifts and skills that He put inside people. Team members must be firmly convinced of this reality.

CHRIST AND HIS PEOPLE ARE ABOVE THEIR DESIRES

Team members should have a conviction that places Christ and His people above the leader's own desires, ambitions and opinions. Team members must see the ministry as a way to serve and to give, rather than as a way to fulfill or promote themselves. The podium is a place for exalting God, not man. The platform is to promote the cause of Christ, not an opinion or a personal popularity campaign.

Our goal is to make Christ known in our city and our world. The way we can do that is by serving others and giving our lives, our resources and our time to that mission. The ministry is the battleground where we give up our lives so that others may live free in Christ.

THEY MUST ADVANCE THE TEAM'S OVERALL MISSION

Team members should have a willingness to accept any assignment necessary to advance the team's overall vision. A team member must reject position-consciousness, or an others-should-thank-me/recognize-me/reward-me attitude. A servant becomes great by making others successful. Each team member must come with a servant's spirit and a servant's heart, having the overall vision of the church in mind. He can never serve only in the areas that he likes, or the areas that he thinks will be the most fruitful or the most satisfying. He serves for the good of the whole body and the overall vision.

LOYALTY TO SAVE THE CHURCH IN TIME OF TESTING

Team members should have a conviction of loyalty that will save the church and the team in a time of testing. This conviction can be proven only when there is disagreement, disappointment or disillusionment. Loyalty keeps the larger picture in mind. It handles complaints and criticisms easily, because it understands the sad results of disunity and discord. Loyalty refuses to deny its commitment to others, regardless of the cost. In time of need, loyalty motivates the servant to stand with those in need of help.

Loyalty and service make for great team members. Those who have these convictions always seem to have a lot of responsibility and are involved in every key area of the church. Remember the adage: "The hair on the back of a good donkey is always worn thin." If you want to be a bearer of greatness, serve with humility and constancy.

FAITHFULNESS

Team members should have a conviction of faithfulness. The faithful team member understands that promotion comes from the Lord—and that the Lord promotes based on His principles. The principles of faithfulness and integrity are basic to leadership. To be faithful in something small qualifies a person to receive more. The reward of a job done well is another job. Do you want more responsibility? Do you want to make a greater contribution to the team? Perform your currently assigned tasks with excellence.

Dale Carnegie once said, "Don't be afraid to give your best to what seemingly are small jobs. Every time you conquer one it makes you that much stronger. If you do the little jobs well, the big ones tend to take care of themselves."

AVAILABILITY

Team members should have a conviction of availability. It's essential that team members recognize availability as a key ingredient to being a useful vessel to God, to other leaders, and to those being served. Being available requires disciplined stewardship of time and priorities. Available people build sufficient margins into their lives, so that if a need comes along, they have the time or resources to devote to helping solve that problem. Availability is usually much more important than capacity.

SEVEN ESSENTIALS OF A WINNING TEAM

These represent the foundational convictions each team member should have. Now let's look at the elements that build a winning team.

1. A WINNING LEADER

Winning leaders have the ability to clearly communicate a vision that excites the team to action. As the team catches a spirit of faith, excitement and enthusiasm will ensue. This will set in motion team members who will stretch out, try new things and take risks, resulting in big gains. Achieving these gains, of course, necessitates experimentation. Winning leaders have a high tolerance for experimentation and failure. Never condemn innovation, even if it doesn't always produce the right results. Big risks bring big rewards.

Team members learn about risk taking from the example of their leaders. Winning leaders push the boundary lines to move beyond what is normal or usual. They are pioneers who venture into unexplored territory. Gather your information, prepare thoroughly, envision what can be gained, understand what is at stake, risk from strength, and march forward with confidence. Leaders set the pace for the rest of the team. If you are taking risks wisely, your team will be inspired to make some adventurous moves that will result in growth and expanding reach.

Winning leaders understand that God is the source of power and authority. Based on that understanding, leaders know the proper use of their God-given authority. Power must not be abused. The key to rightly using authority is humility. A humble attitude has nothing to prove. Humble leaders do not need to wield their power over others to gain respect or to show just how great they are. Instead, they are confident that the Lord alone is their strength, and they know that their authority submits to the authority of Christ at all times. The centurion who asked Jesus to heal his servant understood this principle. His faith was called great because it emerged from his right understanding of authority (see Matt. 8:5-13). Winning leaders can carry lightly the weight of authority because they know that it belongs to God.

I once heard a pastor say, "I love the ministry, but I don't like people." If you have a similar attitude, can I ask you why you are in the ministry or why you are a leader? Winning leaders desire to respond to the needs of others. Their motto is: *People are our business.* Remember that the purpose of ministry is to serve the needs of others. Leaders who are passionate about the ministry and passionate about God are deeply compassionate toward people. They strive to meet the needs both of those in the greater body being served and of fellow ministry team members.

TEAMWORK: A LESSON WITHOUT WORDS

2. TANGIBLE GOALS

The Greek word for bishop is *episkopos*—an overseer. The word *skopos* means to see or the ability to fix one's eye on a certain mark. The very word used in the New Testament to describe the leadership of the church has to do with perception, focus and vision. A winning team must have a vision—a mark to hit—that includes tangible goals. The team must know where it is going and how it is going to get there. This is where a good vision statement becomes helpful. The vision statement is different from the mission statement. The mission statement defines why we exist. The vision statement describes where we are going. Our church recently rewrote our mission and vision statements. Here is our mission statement: *Live like Jesus. Share His love.* It's a simple statement of why we have services every Sunday, why we have small groups, why we have outreaches, and so on. Everything we do is tied to the mission.

Our vision statement is this: *To build a thriving church that impacts all people.* This is the direction we are going—toward a thriving church that influences every person to live like Jesus and share His love. The vision flows from our clearly stated mission. Now we can move forward, setting tangible goals such as starting new small groups for special interests by the next quarter, supporting a missionary from our congregation who feels called to impact people in another nation, and so on. Give the team a clear mark to reach and they will hit it. Give them no mark and they'll hit that, too.

3. ADHERENCE TO BASIC PRINCIPLES

The principle of reviewing the basics has led to many victories in sports. Great coaches have built this discipline into their teams. Why? So that in a time of crisis, a breaking point, or a moment of great emotional tension, the team will function out of principle rather than talent. The charismatic or ultra-talented player may play well when he's hot, but what about those slump times? It is unusual for the whole team to be in a slump if they are playing as a unit and obeying basic principles.

The basics for the leadership team in a local church are prayer, the Word of God, integrity, unity, respect, love, forgiveness, preferring one another, sacrifice, and the like. Basic principles and core values are biblical, easily shared and constant; they engender passion, flow with the overall vision, and are implementable. It is most important that all leaders and decision makers in every established ministry are clear about these basic values and how they make up the organization's DNA.

4. A GIVE-IT-ALL-IT-TAKES ATTITUDE

To create this kind of an attitude, there must be a clear vision with clearly articulated goals. Vision causes a person to put the needs of the group before individual needs. The key word here is *sacrifice*. Sacrifice is loyalty—being willing to lay down your life for God, His purposes and His people.

A give-it-all-it-takes attitude is contagious. This attitude will motivate the team beyond the human level of achievement.

5. THE ABILITY TO RECOVER FROM FAILURES

Don't make a big deal out of your personal failures, failures of individuals on the team, or team failures. One of the worst traps to fall into as a team is to allow criticism or blame to be cast when things go worse than expected. Examine each mistake and the results honestly, but avoid blaming others. Analyze how and why the failure occurred, learn from it, encourage one another, and go on. Concentrate on the lessons learned from mistakes, not on the failures themselves. If you focus on the future, you will put everything into perspective. Your leadership gets better as you take responsibility and learn from both the successes and the failures of the team.

6. RESPECT FOR THE VALUE OF EACH PERSON AS WELL AS FOR OTHERS' TALENTS AND GIFTS

Everyone needs to feel love and acceptance, especially from those they love and respect. Peer-level respect is worth more than silver or gold. Each team member should verbalize his love and respect to the other team members. Habitual, continual and sincere appreciation goes a long way in producing team spirit. Get into the habit of dropping one another little notes, cards and letters. Make that phone call!

7. INTENSITY AND EXCELLENCE

A winning team never allows victory to take the edge off of their spiritual hunger or alertness. Napoleon said it well: "The most dangerous moment comes with victory." The moment we reach those long-awaited goals or accomplish the most seemingly impossible task, we are in spiritual danger. We can't let our guard down after a win. A mature team maintains the tension of prayer, the need for God, and the attitude of humility after great victories.

INVESTING TIME WISELY

The ministry God has given a church expands as the congregation's leaders develop. As the church grows, multiplication on all leadership levels is needed. The larger the church becomes, the wider a leadership base must be developed. Always extend the leadership base before adding more ministries. This helps to avoid the placement of incompetent or unqualified persons in new positions.

The main focus of the lead pastor should be to equip current leaders and to develop future leaders. Doing so takes time and strategy. Like any valuable resource, time is very limited. People are constantly calling for your attention—and while you would love to meet with them all, there are simply not enough hours in a day. However, by spending quality time with a few people, you can multiply your reach so that you do in fact touch—directly or indirectly—most of the people who want to spend time with you. Here are a few priority codes that will help you make decisions about investing time with different kinds of people.

VIP: VERY INFLUENTIAL PEOPLE

Your current leaders: Spend plenty of time with this group, mentoring them and sharing the vision so deeply that these leaders turn around and impart the vision to emerging leaders. Your current leaders are vital to building the leadership base, because they must mentor other leaders with the same vision and core values.

VTP: VERY TEACHABLE PEOPLE

Your potential future leaders: Spend time with these people, who are eager to learn all they can from you. They are easily ignited by your passion and will quickly transfer your vision to others. Get to know their interests and what is happening with their families. Learn their ministry passions.

VNP: VERY NICE PEOPLE

Your encouraging sheep: Take an afternoon to write letters or emails to those who are always sending you messages of encouragement and telling you they are praying for you. Write a quick note expressing how thankful you are for their support and constant care for the church and leadership team. The smallest gesture can go a long way in saying, "I acknowledge your faithfulness and I thank you for it."

VDP: VERY DRAINING PEOPLE

Your you'll-never-solve-their-problem people: We cannot please everyone. That is the reality. As much as we try to serve every person and meet every need, someone will always be displeased by the song choice or the volume of the electric guitar or the usher who accidentally missed giving a welcome packet to a visitor. Limit your interactions with people who want to argue for the sake of arguing or who never have anything positive to say.

With whom are you investing most of your time?

TEAM WISDOM FROM NATURE

GEESE FLYING IN A V

When you see geese heading south for the winter, notice their V formation. Scientists have discovered that as each bird flaps its wings, it creates uplift for the bird immediately following it. By flying in formation, the flock has a 70 percent greater flying range than if each bird flew on its own. We can learn some useful truths from the geese.

GET TO YOUR DESTINATION WITH LESS EFFORT

People who share a common direction and a sense of community can get where they are going more quickly and easily, because they travel on the thrust of one another. Teamwork should not be forced. It should flow easily, because everyone is committed to traveling in the same direction. There is no room for personal ambition on a team. Each member must be committed to the same direction if they are to reach their destination efficiently.

STAY ON COURSE

When a goose falls out of formation, it suddenly feels the drag and resistance of trying to go it alone—and quickly gets back into formation to take advantage of the lifting power of the bird immediately in front of it. If we have as much sense as a goose, we will stay in formation with those who are headed the same way we are.

SHARE THE FRONT

When the lead goose gets tired, he moves back in the formation, and another goose flies point. It pays to build a strong team whose members can help you take turns doing hard jobs.

BE CAREFUL WITH YOUR HORN

Think about a car horn. It was intended to be an instrument for letting people know you were there if they could not see you. Using the horn is a matter of courtesy and safety, alerting other drivers to your presence. Horns can also be used to let others know of your support. Bumper stickers like "Honk if you love Jesus" call for a supportive honk, and teams holding signs for their car wash fundraiser will often get honks from drivers friendly to their cause. But probably 99 percent of the honks made on the road come from angry, frustrated and impatient drivers who just want to get to their destination rather than be stuck in traffic. If you've ever been the recipient of a honk, you probably did not feel very good after hearing it. You didn't feel as if you were being cheered on to great driving.

We each have a "horn"—and we need to be careful with how we honk from behind. The geese flying in the back of the formation honk to encourage those up front to keep up their speed. Your words are one of the most powerful instruments in building people up or tearing them down. Be careful with your words, and use them to encourage your leaders.

PROTECT ONE ANOTHER

Finally, if a goose gets sick or is wounded by a gunshot, two geese fall out of formation to help and protect the disabled bird. They stay with him until he either is able to fly again or dies. At that time, they launch out—on their own or with another formation—to catch up with their group. In the same way, we should stand by each other, protect one another, and make new friends with those who are going in our direction.

COMMON PROBLEMS IN MINISTRY

Several common problems and pitfalls show up in most, if not all, churches. Leadership teams can expect to have to deal with the following issues.

DOCTRINAL INCOMPATIBILITY

Doctrinal differences should be discussed openly as leaders are trained to be vital influences in the local church. Major doctrines established by biblical mandate should never be compromised. These include the deity of Christ, the atonement, justification, salvation, baptism in water by immersion, baptism of the Holy Spirit, and the bodily second coming of Christ. Other doctrines without clear biblical mandates may vary from church to church, but every leadership team has to unite behind the set of doctrines taught in its own local assembly.

Doctrinal incompatibility in the area of church governance, for instance, becomes an irritation among the leadership and will cause division sooner or later. Teaching on controversial subjects—such as inner healing, Christian psychology, demonology, Christian involvement in politics, and divorce and remarriage—needs to be clarified in order to avoid needless divisions.

DISLOYALTY IN ATTITUDE OR ACTION

Disloyalty does not develop suddenly one day or grow quickly in just a month. It usually begins with an unresolved offense or a philosophical difference that has not been handled properly, which causes another person to become offended. Out of this arises a spirit of criticism and ultimately disloyalty.

Disloyalty is one of the most dangerous sins in leadership—and one that can devastate the church. Disloyalty is not just an attitude of the mind; it is an attitude of the spirit and will spread throughout the congregation if not checked. All leadership teams can benefit from reading *A Tale of Three Kings* by Gene Edwards.[3]

PHILOSOPHICAL DIFFERENCES THAT DIVIDE

Most churches do not suffer division because of doctrinal incompatibility. Most eldership or leadership problems arise out of philosophical differences. We all believe in worship. But what is our philosophy concerning the mood of the church service? What are our feelings on drums, guitars, pipe organ, standing and sitting? Do we sing too many hymns, not enough hymns, too many choruses, too many long choruses, not enough Jesus choruses or too many short choruses? We face many questions of differing taste and philosophy in our life together as a church. What are the team's philosophies concerning women's ministry, evangelism, finances and decision making? Where a difference of philosophy exists, there soon will be a difference of spirit, which ultimately will divide the eldership.

JUDGING ACTIONS BY QUESTIONING MOTIVES

If we get into the habit of judging others according to our own discernment, questioning their motives and actions, it will cause many problems in the leadership team. We must, according to 1 Corinthians 13, see the good in one another and believe that others have good motives. We see people through our own eyes—questioning them because we ourselves have a problem.

ALLOWING DISCIPLES TO PRAISE SOME AND DEMEAN OTHERS

Sometimes a person in the church will become a disciple of one elder or leader and may see that leader's ministry as the greatest and most important ministry in the church. The disciple might praise the preferred leader's ministry by comparing it with another one in the church, tearing down the other ministry in the process.

Leaders can never allow anyone to tear down another leader for any reason—especially by comparison. Team members should stop the conversation immediately and not allow any leader's reputation or ministry to be pulled down through criticism.

BECOMING POSITION-MINDED

A person concerned about his prestige can be very shrewd and manipulative while trying to gain a position. His motive is not to serve the people, but to get the people to serve him and his position—to get honor from them instead of giving them the honor they need.

Position-minded leaders usually will not become involved with the menial tasks of the local church. They will not serve their way into the ministry. They will only choose leadership tasks that bring them into the limelight. These people can be dangerous, because they may often consciously or unconsciously use some form of deception or manipulation to possess a position. If a position is not handed to them, they may turn on both the church and the leadership. These ambitious leaders then may make the church appear to be at fault, when in fact the position-minded spirit of the leader caused the trouble. Many deal with this problem their entire lives.

THOSE WHO OVERESTIMATE THEIR ABILITIES AND MINISTRY

It is God who recognizes, promotes and places people in the right roles and positions in the local church. If the leadership and others in the congregation do not perceive a particular gift in a person, there is a strong possibility it is not resident. We need to be very careful to have a sober estimation of our own ministry (see Rom. 12:1-3).

If we have an overestimation of our ministry, we will become frustrated when others don't see our abilities as we do. We will become critical and ultimately bitter toward those who are over us, because they did not recognize our ministry. Occasionally a wife tells her husband that she sees him in a certain ministry (or vice versa). She praises him and lifts him up, pushing him toward a ministry God may not have given him. This is a very sensitive situation. How can you correct a man's wife without offending the man? It is almost impossible! If one spouse has a vision for the other that that person does not have for himself or herself, there will eventually be great problems in the home and in the church.

UNMET EXPECTATIONS IN RELATIONSHIPS

In the church we often use terms like *family, covenant commitment, covenant relationship*, and the like. These terms speak of our desire to be close to one another and support one another. Those desires are honest and sincere. We all want to support and encourage those we work with and others in the Body of Christ. Sometimes, in our efforts to be an encourager and a supporter, we spread ourselves too thin and are not able to develop deep relationships with many people. This may become a point of contention.

The lead pastor continually deals with people who want to be close. There is not always time, however, to develop that kind of a covenantal relationship with each person who desires it. This may eventually cause offense, if it is not handled openly and honestly with the wisdom of the Holy Spirit.

We all have a covenant in Jesus. We all are brothers and sisters in Christ and are part of the whole family of God. We all are called to *koinonia*—the kind of fellowship practiced by the church in the book of Acts. We will not all, however, be best friends with everyone in our local church. Most relationship research has discovered that a person can have only three or four very close friends with whom they spend a lot of time—and maybe only one or two.

As a leadership team grows, people will naturally be drawn into close relationships with one another. This is not a problem for the lead pastor or for the leaders. Let people grow together naturally and spiritually. Do not try to make everyone your Jonathan or your Peter, James and John.

IGNORING BASIC STANDARDS OR PHILOSOPHIES ALREADY ESTABLISHED

As the church becomes established and the leadership team begins to grow, certain basic philosophies, doctrines and vision-related values will be adopted within that team to lead the church. Once these are agreed upon, articulated and established in the local church, it is negative to try to change or ignore them, unless they are changed by the leadership team as a whole.

Problems will arise if a few leaders choose to ignore clearly established basic standards. These standards need to be respected and honored by the leadership. Things such as giving, praying, worshiping, witnessing, holiness, love and reaching out to people are basic standards for the local church. As standard bearers, leaders should lift up the basic values of the church.

I ask my leadership team to honor the following 12 basic standards:

1. Be on time for appointments.
2. Be on time for prayer before service and for prayer meetings.
3. Be on time for leadership activities.
4. Be a participator in worship, not a spectator.
5. Be involved with as many weddings and funerals as possible.
6. Be faithful to attend public worship services.
7. Be conscientious of all reports and paperwork due.
8. Be fervent and enthusiastic in prayer and worship.
9. Be an example of hospitality.
10. Be a person of faith with a positive attitude.
11. Be a support to those preaching by taking notes and saying, "Amen."
12. Be approachable and available after all church services.

Leaders must recognize and overcome these common leadership problems and other issues that may arise within their teams. To protect the vision of the church, the lead pastor should instruct the leadership team to guard against these pitfalls. Let's now look at the biblical qualifications and responsibilities of those who serve on our church leadership teams, specifically in the role of elder.

5

LIFE-CHANGING
ELDERSHIP TEAMS

Elders are to be people of character and spiritual gifting. They are called to lead the church spiritually, not necessarily administratively. Although leadership does involve paperwork and organization, there must first be a spiritual capacity to spiritually lead, feed and govern the house of God. By definition, all elders have a fivefold ministry: apostle, prophet, pastor, evangelist and teacher (see Eph. 4:11-12 and chapter 3 of this book). An elder is to rule and to pastor the souls of people. That certainly is a high standard of spiritual gifting.

Spiritual gifting is a grace or enablement from God that supersedes human ability. It is usually directed toward teaching, exhortation or other ministry that spiritually edifies the church. Gifting also serves as evidence to the church that God has chosen a person for a specific task. Because it is a *spiritual* gifting, it enables the leader to direct God's people *spiritually*. The elder leads the church first of all as a spiritual person. If the spiritual impact of an elder is non-existent or becomes administrative only, the elder loses his ability to lead and ultimately weakens the entire eldership. In the Bible, elders were never appointed on the basis of their executive abilities, social successes or public relations skills. They were chosen and appointed because of their spiritual qualifications.

Appointing an elder is not done lightly. An ordained and appointed elder is invested with authority and entrusted to fill a position. When an elder is appointed to an office, that person receives not only a title, but also the responsibility that goes with the office.

One title that illustrates the idea of receiving the responsibility of an office and not just a name is "President of the United States." Yes, the elected official is called "Mr. President," or "Madame President," but the office is not a figurehead—it is a responsibility and a function. The President is responsible for putting into operation the laws approved by Congress and for appointing cabinet members who in turn lead various agencies, such as the Department of Defense and the Social Security Administration. The President is also head of state and Commander-in-Chief of the armed forces.

The office carries much more than just a title. It makes up one of the three branches of government that together lead an entire nation. "President of the United States" is not a mere title that suggests sitting in a boardroom every month or so to listen to a brief or two on the status of education in America. The title carries the weight of an entire branch of government that has the power to shape the direction of a nation and quite possibly the world. The title of "elder" is not to be taken lightly either. This title confers responsibility to govern God's people with integrity, honor, sacrifice, and many more qualities and functions that we'll get into in this chapter.

FUNCTIONS OF THE ELDERSHIP

The New Testament lists several specific ministry functions of the eldership. Elders govern the local church in all matters of doctrine, morality, church discipline and financial integrity. Position without function or responsibility creates non-biblical eldership. Elders should be appointed to the office and the responsibility that goes with it. In the New Testament, we have evidence that elders were active: "For he [Titus] not only accepted the exhortation, but being more diligent, he went to you of his own accord. And we have sent with him the brother whose praise is in the gospel throughout all the churches, and not only that, but who was also chosen by the churches to travel with us with this gift, which is administered by us to the glory of the Lord Himself" (2 Cor. 8:17-19).

Usually, a successful local church will be established by a leader with one or more of the fivefold ministry gifts mentioned in Ephesians (apostle, prophet, evangelist, pastor, teacher), some of the spiritual gifts listed in 1 Corinthians 12 and 14, and most if not all of the leadership and government gifts mentioned in Romans 12. The lead pastor will set the vision for the church. The eldership team does not originate the vision, but they often share with the lead pastor in setting it. The lead pastor, as the presiding elder or chairperson, should also lead all eldership meetings.

The following are some of the practical matters in which the eldership should be involved as part of their function as leaders of the church:

MAINTAINING THE BUDGET

Representatives from the eldership team should sit on the trustee board, which maintains the budget and business aspects of the church. The governmental body of the church should handle these matters, not the support staff who are not involved in decision-making processes. Some church governments allow spiritual activities to be taken care of by the eldership, and practical activities—including the handling of finances—to be taken care of by the deacons or the lay ministries. This structure can create much tension and misunderstanding in the ministry. Those who govern the spiritual life of the church also should govern the financial life of the church with accountability and credibility.

The annual budget should be confirmed by the entire eldership, but the day-to-day activities can be run by a trustee board made up of elders entrusted with the ministry of finance.

PARTNERSHIP WITH STAFF

Ministries carried out by staff people of a church work in partnership with the entire eldership and are under the direct oversight of the lead pastor. The lead pastor, in conjunction with the board of trustees or board of directors, has the authority to hire or release staff ministers. Yet while the lead pastor retains this authority, he or she is wise to involve the eldership in key staff decisions in order to benefit from their wisdom and their knowledge of the people involved.

The lead pastor as overseer of staff does not have to make every hiring decision, nor should he. He or she can multiply his or her time by delegating the hiring decisions to department supervisors and trusting the team's hiring ability and insight. The lead pastor can still give input, especially when it comes to hiring other pastors, but staff positions such as maintenance workers and IT personnel should be left to the discretion of the department leaders and their teams, who can accurately assess the candidate's qualifications for the position.

If the lead pastor releases a staff minister from the staff and also from the eldership, the situation may become an eldership matter. If the staff minister feels he has a genuine grievance or has been treated unfairly, he may bring the matter to the full eldership. The elders will then consider the case and diligently carry out a biblical response that brings resolution and preserves the peace of the relationship between the minister and the lead pastor and the minister and the church. The eldership therefore acts as a check and balance against the possibility of a tyrannical ruling pastor who would hire and fire or dominate people without advice from the rest of the eldership.

DECIDING ON PROPERTY MANAGEMENT

The eldership should be the final authority in all decisions regarding the purchasing or selling of lands or buildings, as well as in new building ventures. They should make an informed decision, based on research of the current state of the property being considered and other options available.

When I consider buying or selling property, I make sure to activate several key thinkers and elders to compile a thorough report that includes cost analysis, assessment of the neighborhood community, the estimated number of people we can reach in that location, how well a church will be received in that area, and so on. The stewardship team, made up of five to seven elders and trusted businesspeople, would also review this report; discuss the benefits, potential setbacks, legal concerns and feasibility; and then recommend a course of action. If the recommendation is to move forward with the sale or purchase, then the decision goes before the entire eldership for consideration and approval.

Managing property is no small matter, especially in today's world, where so many intricate steps and legalities are involved. It is wise to use a process that thoroughly explores all options and involves the eldership. Doing so protects you from making the wrong decision as well as from accusations of heavy-handed leadership.

THIRTY MINISTRY FUNCTIONS

In broad terms, the ministry of the eldership functions in six capacities: (1) ruling, (2) teaching, (3) shepherding the flock, (4) overseeing the flock, (5) caring for them, and (6) living for them (see Ezek. 34; John 10; Acts 20:17,20,28-29; Heb. 13:7,17,24; 1 Tim. 5:17).

The following list includes ministry functions specifically given to elders in Scripture. Also listed are other functions elders perform. These other functions are found throughout the Bible.

1. AN ELDER IS TO BE AN *OVERSEER*

As we saw earlier, the Greek term we translate as "elder" describes those who were appointed to have the spiritual care of and to exercise oversight over the churches. Elders watch over the sheep. They have responsibility for the leadership and direction of the church. This means they have oversight in all levels of the church's functioning. No ministry or person is too small or too great to come under the eldership's supervision.

Elders cannot take care of that which they do not know exists. Thus the elders need to be involved in the discipleship and hands-on mentoring of new leaders. As an expression of their heart for the corporate gathering, all elders should desire to be involved in all services, and also to be in attendance at major, special meetings the church hosts whenever possible. Being involved with the various types of activity in the church broadens the elders' perspective and knowledge of what is happening in the Body of Christ they are entrusted to oversee. You can't know what you are leading if you never experience it for yourself.

> Therefore take heed to yourselves and to all the flock, among which the Holy Spirit has made you overseers, to shepherd the church of God which He purchased with His own blood (Acts 20:28; see also 1 Pet. 2:25).

2. AN ELDER IS TO BE A *RULER*

The Greek word for "ruler"—*proistemi*—means to stand before, to preside or to practice. The elder rules over a variety of bodies: the home, his or her children, and the self (see 1 Tim. 3:4,12). The indication that a person will be a good elder is that he or she has demonstrated the ability to govern his or her house, "for if a man does not know how to rule his own house, how will he take care of the church of God?" (1 Tim. 3:5).

The way you rule your own home indicates the way you will rule God's house. Is your home disorderly or neat? Is your home characterized by respect, peace and unity, or by discord? The atmosphere you cultivate at home is what you will bring into the church.

Along with ruling the home, the elder must rule his or her spirit, practicing self-control. This means regulating attitudes, passions and habits so that one is neither driven nor dominated by desires of the flesh. Self-control is not only one's own willpower, but also the product of one's relationship with God, the Holy Spirit and the Word. There is always a battle between the fleshly nature—letting impulses, thoughts and habits rule one's life—and the redeemed nature—Christ living in us. The elder must demonstrate mastery over the sinful nature through continual partnership with the Holy Spirit and faith declarations. If the elder can rule himself or herself, then he or she can be entrusted with ruling over God's people.

> Let the elders who rule well be counted worthy of double honor (1 Tim. 5:17; see also Rom. 12:8; 1 Tim. 3:4-12; 1 Thess. 5:12).

3. AN ELDER IS TO BE A *LEADER*

Elders should possess the gift of leadership. There are four different Greek terms that shape the picture of the elder as leader. First is *hegeonai*, as seen in Hebrews 13:17: "Obey those who rule over you, and be submissive, for they watch out for your souls, as those who must give account." This is leadership by virtue of esteem and respect.

The second term is *exago*, which means "to bring out," as in John 10:3: "To him the doorkeeper opens, and the sheep hear his voice; and he calls his own sheep by name and leads them out." *Exago* leadership moves people out of one geographical and/or spiritual position into another. A leader must have the gift of mobilizing congregations and individuals from the pew to the people, from church to city, from confinement to limitless feats. Every elder must be active in moving people to a higher calling and a higher vision for their lives.

Third, there is *poimano* leadership—leadership of one who goes before. This term presupposes movement and describes shepherding leadership. Elders cannot take sheep to ground that has not been scouted, prepared in prayer, and labored over. Elders go before the sheep and plug potential pitfalls. They do not lead blindly, but with divine insight and perception.

Fourth, elders must possess *episkopos*—the leadership capacity to oversee. This term can also be applied to vision perception and vision casting. The elder is a visionary. In an eldership team, the lead pastor (who is an elder) casts the vision, and the other elders support the vision. Therefore elders must be able to see the future God has planned for the people and discern how to get there.

Finally, the elder as leader must be a servant, so that "he who governs [is] as he who serves" (Luke 22:26). Elders lead from the ground level up, not from the top level down. This structure is very different from contemporary culture, which says that leadership is done from the top of the ladder to the unimportant people below. In God's system, the greatest leader is the humble one who can lead as a servant with the attitude of a servant.

> Remember those who rule over you, who have spoken the word of God to you, whose faith follow, considering the outcome of their conduct (Heb. 13:7).

4. AN ELDER IS TO BE A *FEEDER*

Elders live for God's people, continually thinking of resources that will help them grow, meeting with them regularly to offer encouragement and wisdom, and praying for them with specific prayer targets. An elder labors in the Word and doctrine, and from that labor come the insight and wisdom to share with members of the congregation (see 1 Cor. 16:16; 1 Thess. 5:12). The lead pastor functions in this role in a very pronounced way, feeding the church weekly at corporate gatherings.

> So when they had eaten breakfast, Jesus said to Simon Peter, "Simon, son of Jonah, do you love Me more than these?"
> He said to Him, "Yes, Lord; You know that I love You."
> He said to him, "Feed My lambs" (John 21:15; see also Acts 20:28).

5. AN ELDER IS TO BE A *STUDENT OF THE WORD*

Diligent Bible study is an absolute must for the elder. The Word contains God's true knowledge that forms a strong foundation for life. Elders must continually and deliberately pursue God's knowledge, which teaches correct perceptions and proven values, and leads to a life of significance. Students of the Word are educated in God's values, God's will, God's ways and God's voice. An elder strong in the Word will benefit the eldership team and the church as a whole.

> Be diligent to present yourself approved to God, a worker who does not need to be ashamed, rightly dividing the word of truth (2 Tim. 2:15; see also 2 Tim. 3:16-17; Titus 3:9).

6. AN ELDER IS TO *TEACH SOUND DOCTRINE*

As a result of being a student of the Word, the elder should have a thorough understanding of doctrine. He or she should then be able to explain sound doctrine to others, using Scripture, illustrations and real-life examples so that people can grasp the elements of doctrine and remember them. A clear teaching on doctrine will provide ample biblical basis and also demonstrate the practicality of doctrine—that it ultimately benefits God's people.

> A bishop then must be blameless, the husband of one wife, temperate, sober-minded, of good behavior, hospitable, able to teach (1 Tim. 3:2; see also 2 Tim. 2:24; Titus 1:7-9).

7. AN ELDER IS TO BE A *WATCHMAN*
The Greek word that we translate as "watch" means "to keep awake." Remember the parable of the wheat and the tares? The farmer sowed good seed and then went to sleep. While he was asleep, someone came in, sowed tares, and left. As a result, the farmer had to allow both the weeds and the wheat to grow together—or else risk tearing up the good wheat completely (see Matt. 13:24-30). It would take much longer to harvest both plants, separate the two, and risk throwing away some of the good wheat during separation than the harvesting process would have taken if the farmer had kept watch and not allowed the bad seeds to be planted. Elders must stay watchful and alert to the little foxes that try to sneak through the defenses and spoil the good work that God is doing.

> Blessed are those servants whom the master, when he comes, will find watching. Assuredly, I say to you that he will gird himself and have them sit down to eat, and will come and serve them (Luke 12:37; see also Ezek. 33:6-7; Luke 12:39; Acts 20:28-30; 1 Thess. 5:6).

8. AN ELDER IS TO *PROTECT* THE FLOCK
The shepherd lays down his *life* for the sheep. Eldership is not just a job, but a life calling. That calling involves giving one's life to keep the sheep safe from false teachings, from the enemy's attacks, and from any other strategy used against God's people. Many false ministries travel around seeking sheep to devour. The true eldership will guard the flock from false ministries and make sure that any people they allow in to minister to the church are proven and trustworthy.

You wouldn't let a perfect stranger waltz into your family room and watch your children while you went out, would you? Of course not! You would call all your friends first to see if they knew of anyone trustworthy, good with kids, punctual, and maybe even CPR certified. Then you would interview the candidate as if his or her life depended on keeping your children safe—because you do expect the sitter to make your children the top priority while you are away. Finally, after an extensive vetting process, you would feel comfortable enough to leave your children in the sitter's care for two whole hours. Gradually, you would work up to three hours—and then maybe a couple more as trust and confidence in that sitter are built.

The same care must be applied to God's children. The eldership needs to be careful to protect the flock from false teachers and unsound doctrine that threaten to choke out the good seed of truth that the Spirit is planting in the soil of your church.

Protecting the flock is a privilege. The eldership carries out this God-given mandate with diligence and joy—not grief. They are accountable to God for the people He entrusts to them, and they accept that responsibility with sincerity and delight.

> Therefore take heed to yourselves and to all the flock, among which the Holy Spirit has made you overseers, to shepherd the church of God which He purchased with His own blood. For I know this, that after my departure savage wolves will come in among you, not sparing the flock. Also from among yourselves men will rise up, speaking perverse things, to draw away the disciples after themselves. Therefore watch, and remember that for three years I did not cease to warn everyone night and day with tears (Acts 20:28-31, see also John 10:11-15).

9. An Elder Is to *Know* His or Her Grace Gift and Gift Limitations

No doubt, God has gifted leaders with grace to do many ministries. At the same time, there is a specific grace measure He gives to people for a specific purpose—a grace mantle. There are different levels of grace. Personal grace is your individual gifting—your divine deposit. Family grace is the grace on a family—such as a talent for practicing medicine, preaching, competing in athletics, and so on. There is local church grace—grace for worship, evangelism, finance, music, the poor, the city, youth, and more. The elder must know what is the grace gift deposited to him or her from God; he or she must also know what is not within that grace gift.

For instance, a successful businessperson who has the grace gift to start and build corporations uses that grace to conduct business and fund the Kingdom. Perhaps he has not been graced with the capacity to study medicine and become a physician—so he is not about to venture into the Amazon by himself, set up a medical clinic, and serve as the doctor. He might support someone else who has the gift of working with medicine—he might even help get the clinic on its feet administratively—but the tasks of operating on patients and giving diagnoses are left to the doctor. Two people, with two gifts—both using their God-given grace to build the kingdom of God. That is what makes the local church and the eldership such a dynamic force. If each person knows his or her niche and allows others to express their gifts rather than trying to do everything and dominate everyone, the Body of Christ is much more productive and fruitful.

> For I say, through the grace given to me, to everyone who is among you, not to think of himself more highly than he ought to think, but to think soberly, as God has dealt to each one a measure of faith. For as we have many members in one body, but all the members do not have the same function, so we, being many, are one body in Christ, and individually members of one another. Having then gifts differing according to the grace that is given to us, let us use them: if prophecy, let us prophesy in proportion to our faith; or ministry, let us use it in our ministering; he who teaches, in teaching; he who exhorts, in exhortation; he who gives, with liberality; he who leads, with diligence; he who shows mercy, with cheerfulness (Rom. 12:3-9; see also 1 Cor. 12:28; Eph. 4:7-11; 1 Tim. 4:14-15; 2 Tim. 1:6-7; 1 Pet. 4:10).

10. AN ELDER IS TO *SHOW COMPASSION*

Showing compassion is giving a taste of God to unsuspecting people—anyone, at any time—in your arena of influence or along your path in life. Compassion makes a difference—changing the world, one act of kindness at a time, and being Jesus to others through everyday miracles of kindness. The Greek word meaning "to be moved with compassion"—*splangchnizomai*—is used 12 times in the New Testament. This word describes something felt deep inside. It's the knot you feel in your stomach—the depth of your concern for people who have great need. Compassion for people is the outworking of passion for God. Elders are compassion conduits. They go where people are hurting; share in brokenness, fear and confusion; cry out with those in misery—and make a difference. Compassion is not only the mandate for elders, but also the call for all Christians. Elders model the compassion principle for those they lead.

> I will seek what was lost and bring back what was driven away, bind up the broken and strengthen what was sick; but I will destroy the fat and the strong, and feed them in judgment (Ezek. 34:16; see also 1 Tim. 3:2).

11. AN ELDER IS TO BE AN *EXAMPLE* IN ALL HE OR SHE IS, SAYS AND DOES

None of us lives to ourselves; we all affect others. Because the elder's function happens in front of the Body of Christ, his or her area of influence is greater than most. Elders are to be exemplary in character, lifestyle, family life, work and marriage. I once read a story of a boy who was riding in the car with his dad. At that time, the dad had a habit of spitting. On this particular car ride, the dad rolled down his window and spit onto the road. The son, wanting to be just like his dad, also turned toward the road and spit—except he missed the part about rolling down the window and left a nice wad of spit on the inside of the car. The dad broke his spitting habit after that incident.

Whether it is a young person in the church, a seasoned believer, or a community leader who never meets the elder face to face, people are watching—and they are influenced by the elder's life. If an elder models compassion, love for the Word of God and godly principles, then the people will most likely follow that example and do likewise.

> Nor as being lords over those entrusted to you, but being examples to the flock (1 Pet. 5:3; see also Phil. 3:17; 2 Thess. 3:9; 1 Tim. 4:12).

12. AN ELDER IS TO *LISTEN* TO CONSTRUCTIVE CRITICISM

Let's face it. We don't know it all. We also do not like to hear from others that we don't know everything. Listening to constructive criticism can be difficult, but it is a sign of true humility. It says that we are open to learning from anyone, because everyone has something to offer—a unique perspective or insight into a situation. It says that we are willing to develop our potential and our leadership.

I have four children, and I've walked with them through the seasons when they were deciding on a career path or a college, or making other life decisions. I often start our conversations with: "You don't have to listen to me, but I am a lot older than you, and I've seen a lot of people's lives. You might just want to do a couple things I am going to tell you." That usually causes them to pause and consider what I have to offer them.

Leaders should demonstrate that same willingness to listen. We must honor those whom God puts in our lives to teach us. Wherever you can find it, esteem the God-knowledge that, when experienced, will change your emotions, relationships and intellectual understanding. The more God-knowledge you experience, the more you can build on a solid foundation.

> Listen to counsel and receive instruction, that you may be wise in your latter days (Prov. 19:20).

13. AN ELDER IS TO *WORK HARD*

Leaders set the pace for the rest of the team and for the church. Hard-working, diligent leaders will motivate the people to work with equal diligence, both in service to God and in pursuit of Him. Working hard means giving one's full effort to whatever the task is and working as if God is the boss (because He *is* the boss!). Work, whether at a job within the church or in a position outside of the church, is a gift from God. It is also one of the greatest evangelism tools. The workplace is your mission field. How you work is a testimony to your faith. For 40 to 60 hours every week, you are divinely placed to reach the "unreached people groups" of your society. Give a testimony by your work as well as by your words.

Work becomes worship when you dedicate it to God and perform it with an awareness of His presence. Laziness and idleness are sins, and believers have a responsibility to warn, rebuke and instruct those who are lazy or idle (see Prov. 24:30-34; Eph. 4:28; 2 Thess. 3:10). Diligence is the God-ordained way to work. What you do is not as important as how you do it. Too often, people are focusing on where they can work next and how much money they can make there. But God is interested in how people work in the job they currently have—if they work wholeheartedly and with diligence. Leaders, especially elders, must be an example of hard workers.

> Because for the work of Christ he came close to death, not regarding his life, to supply what was lacking in your service to-

ward me (Phil. 2:30; see also 1 Cor. 3:13-15; Eph. 4:12; 1 Tim. 3:1;
1 Thess. 5:13).

14. An Elder Is to Be a *Team Player*

The team is made up of a small number of people, with complementary
skills, who are committed to a common purpose, performance goals
and approach, for which they hold themselves mutually accountable.
The leaders choose the team members, set specific goals, and establish
the pace. The team also paces itself, choosing the best approach to each
challenge faced. They rigorously and consistently evaluate progress and
demand that each team member have the same level of commitment.
An elder must have the attitude that *one of us is not as good as all of us.* Each
player has a place where he or she adds the most value—but that value
is most potently expressed in a team context. One is too small a number to achieve greatness. Teamwork is birthed when we concentrate on
"we" instead of "me." We will look at team leadership in greater detail in
later chapters.

> Now he who plants and he who waters are one, and each one will
> receive his own reward according to his own labor. For we are
> God's fellow workers; you are God's field, you are God's building
> (1 Cor. 3:8-9; see also Eccles. 4:9-12; Matt. 18:19-20; Rom. 12:3-5).

15. An Elder Is to *Share the Same Vision* as the Pastor and Other Elders

The lead pastor casts the vision and creates a clear purpose that provides the reason for leaders to work together. The elders, as individuals
with specific gifts and assignments, fulfill their assignments independently while working toward the overall vision. Put another way, the
leader creates a sense of unity, teamwork and accountability. The eldership team then works together to make decisions and to create better
ways to achieve, problem solve, and dispense people and methods to accomplish the overall vision. The eldership has authority of the overall vision. They do all in their power to keep the church unified in its pursuit
of that vision.

> Now I plead with you, brethren, by the name of our Lord Jesus
> Christ, that you all speak the same thing, and that there be no

divisions among you, but that you be perfectly joined together in the same mind and in the same judgment (1 Cor. 1:10; see also Ps. 133; Isa. 65:8; Zech. 4:1-6; Eph. 4:1-3).

16. AN ELDER IS TO BE *SUBMISSIVE*

Submissive leadership is the servant leadership that Jesus modeled. He taught that a leader's greatness is measured by his or her total commitment to serve others. Jesus lived "I serve" as opposed to "I lead." I am the leader; therefore I serve. It is the act of serving that leads other people to be what they are capable of becoming.

In the Bible, the Greek word *huperetes* is used to identify a servant. The term is composed of two Greek words: *hupo* (meaning "under") and *eretes* (meaning "rower"). A servant is therefore an "under-rower"—one who serves as a slave to simply move the ship in the direction the master requests, acting under another's direction. Leaders are under-rowers. They do not lead by domineering others and beating them into doing whatever is asked. Leaders are submissive, both to God and to one another. There is safety in submission.

> The elders who are among you I exhort, I who am a fellow elder and a witness of the sufferings of Christ, and also a partaker of the glory that will be revealed: Shepherd the flock of God which is among you, serving as overseers, not by compulsion but willingly, not for dishonest gain but eagerly; nor as being lords over those entrusted to you, but being examples to the flock (1 Pet. 5:1-3).

17. AN ELDER IS TO *BEAR BURDENS*

Our model for leadership is Christ, and He is a master of bearing the burdens of others. Leaders are in a unique position to bear the burdens of leading God's people together. Take Moses for example. He could not, on his own, judge every single dispute in the entire nation of Israel. So he delegated—he brought up other leaders who could help carry the burden of giving personal attention to every person who needed help and making sure each received justice. Likewise, we are to "bear one another's burdens, and so fulfill the law of Christ" (Gal. 6:2). Whether you are leading a nation, like Moses was, or a church, build your team with leaders who can help you shoulder the burden—and make sure that you are also sharing their load.

And let them judge the people at all times. Then it will be that every great matter they shall bring to you, but every small matter they themselves shall judge. So it will be easier for you, for they will bear the burden with you (Exod. 18:22; see also Deut. 1:12; Num. 11:11,17; Gal. 6:6).

18. AN ELDER IS CALLED TO *SACRIFICIAL SERVICE*

The key to leadership and depth of service is sacrifice. Sacrifice is the yardstick that measures our character and values. It's the heart of a true shepherd. Elders are willing to sacrifice their fulfillments and pleasures for those whom they are called to serve. They are willing to give up a more comfortable lifestyle for the life of a servant leader.

If anyone comes to Me and does not hate his father and mother, wife and children, brothers and sisters, yes, and his own life also, he cannot be My disciple. And whoever does not bear his cross and come after Me cannot be My disciple. For which of you, intending to build a tower, does not sit down first and count the cost, whether he has enough to finish it—lest, after he has laid the foundation, and is not able to finish it, all who see it begin to mock him, saying, "This man began to build and was not able to finish"? Or what king, going to make war against another king, does not sit down first and consider whether he is able with ten thousand to meet him who comes against him with twenty thousand? Or else, while the other is still a great way off, he sends a delegation and asks conditions of peace. So likewise, whoever of you does not forsake all that he has cannot be My disciple (Luke 14:26-33).

19. AN ELDER IS TO BE A *WISE COUNSELOR*

One of the greatest gifts to the church is a wise counselor. Elders should be adept at using basic keys for making wise decisions, and they should be able to advise others to make wise decisions using those same keys: *What does the Bible say? Do I have clear inner witness? Does this harmonize with my personal desires given by the Lord? What specific guidance can I discern? Have I sought mature counsel? Have I exercised my own common sense?*

For by wise counsel you will wage your own war, and in a multitude of counselors there is safety (Prov. 24:6; see also Ps. 16:7; Prov. 1:28-33; 11:14; 15:22; 20:18; Isa. 9:16; Mark 15:43; Luke 23:50).

20. AN ELDER IS TO BE AN *ENCOURAGER*

Encouragers inspire others with courage and hope. They fill people with strength and purpose, instilling life and new heart. Elders are to be those who refresh another's spirit—who lift up and strengthen others at all times. The Hebrew word for "encouragement" means "to fasten oneself so as to strengthen, cure, help, repair and fortify." Bible teacher Don Basham once wrote, "As our 'approval bucket' is filled, our entire personality flourishes. But if that bucket remains empty, the personality withers and suffers deprivation."[1] Elders operate in the ministry of encouragement, building up others with words of faith, approval, love and acceptance.

> A word fitly spoken is like apples of gold in settings of silver (Prov. 25:11; see also Prov. 16:24; Gal. 6:1-2; Phil. 2:25-27; 2 Tim. 1:2-4; Philem. 1:10-18).

21. AN ELDER IS TO HAVE A *POSITIVE ATTITUDE*

Attitude is everything! The most significant choice I can make on a day-to-day basis is what my attitude is going to be. Attitude influences every part of our lives. It keeps us going or cripples our progress. Attitude can be the difference between whether we are successful at life or we fail. If our attitude is right, we see opportunity in every difficulty; we move forward with a healthy, positive life-view. Leaders must commit to developing a biblically based, wholesome, positive attitude—and protect that attitude every day. A positive attitude embraces every challenge as an opportunity for growth and for God to do something previously unimagined.

Attitudes—both negative and positive—are contagious. Make sure you and your leaders have a positive attitude.

> Do all things without complaining and disputing, that you may become blameless and harmless, children of God without fault in the midst of a crooked and perverse generation, among whom you shine as lights in the world (Phil. 2:14-15; see also John 6:43; Phil. 1:27).

22. AN ELDER IS TO LEAD A *DISCIPLINED LIFESTYLE*

As I am writing this, the summer Olympics are happening, and I can't help but think of the amount of preparation these athletes put into training for these events. First Timothy 4:8 tells us, "Physical exercise has some value, but spiritual exercise is valuable in every way, because it promises life both for the present and for the future" (*GNB*). Workouts in the gym are useful, but a disciplined life in God is far more so, as it makes you fit both today and forever. Elders are committed to discipline—both physical and spiritual—undertaking godly exercises to make them capable of receiving more of Christ's life and power.

> But let each one examine his own work, and then he will have rejoicing in himself alone, and not in another (Gal. 6:4; see also Prov. 16:32).

23. AN ELDER IS TO BE *TRANSPARENT*

Elders strive to become more open people—disclosing feelings, struggles, joys and hurts when possible and appropriate. This openness on the part of the elders communicates that they cannot make it without the other party, and that they trust the other person with their problems and dreams. "Speaking the truth in love" (Eph. 4:15) is always a risk, but transparency is a key to open and honest relationships. It shows the congregation that there is no hidden agenda, only genuine concern for the growth of others.

> Open rebuke is better than love carefully concealed. Faithful are the wounds of a friend, but the kisses of an enemy are deceitful (Prov. 27:5-6).

24. AN ELDER IS TO BE A *LIBERAL GIVER*

A generous spirit is sown into the church as it is modeled by the leaders:

> Moreover, brethren, we make known to you the grace of God bestowed on the churches of Macedonia: that in a great trial of affliction the abundance of their joy and their deep poverty abounded in the riches of their liberality. For I bear witness that according to their ability, yes, and beyond their ability, they were freely willing, imploring us with much urgency that we would receive the gift and the fellowship of the ministering to the saints. And not only as we had hoped, but they first gave themselves to the Lord, and then to us by the will of God (2 Cor. 8:1-5).

The Macedonian churches had Paul's heart—his special apostolic spiritual DNA and his grace for giving, generosity and liberality. The liberality was not of themselves naturally, but of God's grace bestowed on them, enabling them to be the instruments of His grace to others. Their lack and needs had a positive effect, producing not stinted gifts, but abounding liberality. Rock-bottom destitution should not rock your world. Elders model a generous heart that abounds in liberality beyond their ability (see Mal. 3:4-12; 2 Cor. 8:8-15; 9:1-6).

25. AN ELDER IS TO BE A PERSON OF *FAITH*

Every elder must set a high value upon faith, because without faith we cannot please God or fulfill God's purposes for life. Faith is the unquestioning confidence, full persuasion and unwavering trust that what God has said, He is able to do and will perform. We all have a seed of faith deposited into our spirit at the time of salvation, but we are responsible to grow our faith, add to our faith, and live a life full of faith. Faith is to be ever increasing, expanding the elders' capacity to do great things in ministry. Faith is the power to trust God, strengthening the elders to rise to the challenges they encounter.

> Moreover David said, "The LORD, who delivered me from the paw of the lion and from the paw of the bear, He will deliver me from the hand of this Philistine." And Saul said to David, "Go, and the LORD be with you!" (1 Sam. 17:37; see also Deut. 32:20; Josh. 1:1-16; Heb. 11:6).

26. AN ELDER IS TO BE A *PRAYER WARRIOR*

God's people are encouraged to seek His face, asking for specific answers to specific prayers as an expression of faith in His willingness and ability to bring provision and reward. Many prayers are granted by God, but never received by the believers who were praying, because they abandoned their prayer before the answer came. Undelivered prayers help no one. Without the dynamic of persistence, much prayer remains unanswered. Elders must be warriors in prayer, sticking to a purpose or aim with a never-give-up attitude. There's an old saying: *Prayer demands combat to the last breath.* Prayer warriors keep praying until they have fully received the answer, and the enemy is totally defeated.

> And the prayer of faith will save the sick, and the Lord will raise him up. And if he has committed sins, he will be forgiven. Confess your trespasses to one another, and pray for one another, that you may

be healed. The effective, fervent prayer of a righteous man avails much (Jas. 5:15-16; see also Rev. 5:8; 8:3-4).

27. AN ELDER IS TO BE A *WORSHIPER*

One of the most beautiful images of the elder's function as worshiper comes from the book of Revelation: "The twenty-four elders fall down before Him who sits on the throne and worship Him who lives forever and ever, and cast their crowns before the throne, saying: 'You are worthy, O Lord, to receive glory and honor and power; for You created all things, and by Your will they exist and were created'" (Rev. 4:10-11; see also Rev. 5:1-10).

Here we see that worship is a verb, and that it is something done by us—not to us or for us. Worship builds a throne for God to sit upon. A worshiper uses the entire being—heart, soul, mind and strength—to glorify God. Notice that the elders fall to their knees and "cast their crowns" before the throne—using their strength. From their heart and soul—the inner seat of emotions and feeling—they express praise to God. Their minds recognize that God is the Creator of all things, and they worship Him because of it. The elder engages the whole personality in aspiration, intent to seek, find and express love for God. That is wholehearted worship.

28. AN ELDER IS TO BE *FILLED* WITH THE HOLY SPIRIT

Being filled with the Spirit means to be daily and continually overflowing with the presence and power of the Holy Spirit for the purpose of expanding God's kingdom with words and power. Elders filled with the Spirit live in an overflow of Holy Spirit activity. God's Word is illuminated afresh to them, a new love and desire for more of Jesus wells up within their spirit, a new sense of holiness and purity and desire to live right grips them, and a new sensitivity to the needs of others guides them. Being filled with the Spirit is vital to the elder's ministry and life. The Spirit gives power and strength—for ministry and for living an abundant life. Elders must be constantly connected to the power source.

I indeed baptized you with water, but He will baptize you with the Holy Spirit (Mark 1:8; see also Joel 2:28; Acts 2:4).

29. AN ELDER IS TO BE *MOTIVATED*

Motivated leaders are constantly reaching to improve their leadership ability and spiritual strength. They take very seriously the mandate to add to one's faith with all diligence (see 1 Pet. 2:5-7). They are initiators who go after the ways of God and the lessons He wants to teach them through His Word and through experience. That attitude will surface in the way leaders pursue the people they lead—those who need discipleship and resources to help them develop in their own faith journeys. Leaders must be self-motivated to pursue God and to help His people.

> The hand of the diligent will rule, but the lazy man will be put to forced labor (Prov. 12:24; see also Prov. 18:9; Phil. 3:13-14).

30. AN ELDER IS TO *PRACTICE LOYALTY*

Leadership loyalty is the quality of protecting others by proving your unwavering dedication to them for their good and their success. Loyal leaders inspire loyalty in others and build a culture of loyalty in the church. They are committed, even in times of difficulty, to those whom God has brought into their lives and those He has called the eldership to serve. Loyalty is the process of developing allegiance and respect for one another and not seeking to manipulate others. Loyalty resists betrayal, distrust and unforgiveness. Good leaders are loyal to God and to one another.

> A friend loves at all times, and a brother is born for adversity (Prov. 17:17).

To read more about the character qualifications of an elder, please refer to my book *The Making of a Leader.*

The calling to eldership is no light thing. It is a specific call from God to lead His people with character and vision. And the reward is priceless. But even if you are not serving in the specific capacity of elder, I encourage you to work on your leadership in these areas. Your preparation will qualify you for where you should be. Keep preparing yourself.

6

LEADERS WHO
BUILD THE CHURCH

The life-changing church leadership team has a clear and passionate vision for the church they are building. Great churches are built by great leadership teams. The leadership team that builds the church is working with Christ, the true Builder, and with all those partnering with Him in this great task of church building. Matthew 16:18-19 says, "And I also say to you that you are Peter, and on this rock I will build My church, and the gates of Hades shall not prevail against it. And I will give you the keys of the kingdom of heaven, and whatever you bind on earth will be bound in heaven, and whatever you loose on earth will be loosed in heaven." This is the leadership team's foundational biblical starting point. We are committed church builders. We are visionaries who see the church as God's plan and purpose, and we lead and equip people to build this church.

LEADERS WHO BUILD CHRIST'S CHURCH ARE FIRST COMMITTED TO CHRIST

Leaders who build the church with passion and correctness are those who first are true disciples of Christ. This may sound obvious, but there are some who seek to lead without ever having been a follower of Christ. Mark 2:14 says, "As He [Jesus] passed by, He saw Levi the son of Alphaeus sitting at the tax office. And He said to him, 'Follow Me.' So he arose and followed Him." Following Christ is first. Look at what some of the other disciples did when Jesus called them: "They immediately left their nets and followed Him" (Matt. 4:20). Leaving things behind and letting go of other endeavors is necessary when we choose to follow Christ.

Jesus said that those who do not take up their cross and follow Him are not worthy of Him (see Matt. 10:38). There is a price for leading the church, and that price includes sacrifice, dedication, pain, and living differently than you lived before. "Then Jesus said to His disciples, 'If anyone desires to come after Me, let him deny himself, and take up his cross, and follow Me'" (Matt. 16:24). To follow Christ is certainly a high calling—one that must be embraced before you can lead.

Follow first, lead second. To follow is to narrow your life before you can broaden your life. "Enter by the narrow gate; for wide is the gate and broad is the way that leads to destruction, and there are many who go in by it. Because narrow is the gate and difficult is the way which leads to life, and there are few who find it" (Matt. 7:13-14).

A disciple first, a leader second. A disciple is a fully devoted follower of Christ—someone who is becoming a person completely dedicated to Christ. Disciples submit to Jesus' lordship and imitate Him in every thought, word and deed. A disciple undergoes a changed lifestyle, manifested through biblical values, goals, perspectives and relationships. Disciples possess a resolve never to turn back. They are totally committed to living Christ's way and to building Christ's Church. These kinds of followers make great leaders, who make great leadership teams that build great churches.

William Law puts it this way: "Christianity does not consist in any partial amendment of our lives, any particular moral virtues, but in an entire change of our natural temper, a life wholly devoted to God."[1] Leaders who build the church continually develop this fully devoted life. They pursue a daily deepening of their relationship with Christ, discovering new insights into living by faith in God and His Word. Leaders who are disciples develop a relationship with the Holy Spirit and discover how to submit to and partner with the Spirit for fruitful living. A follower like this becomes a great leader who leads others into this discipleship lifestyle. We must be these leaders. We must *be* before we can *do*.

LEADERS WHO BUILD CHRIST'S CHURCH ARE PASSIONATELY COMMITTED TO THE CHURCH

You can't build what you don't love. You don't love what you say you love; you love what you give your life to. A church is built by leaders who love and live for the church. The church is the treasure in the field. It is the apple of the eye—the dream of the heart. Anything less in a leader who seeks to build the church will make for a shallow impact and a professional style of leading. Let us be careful.

Leaders who build the church have a solid theological understanding of what the church is and what the Scriptures teach about the church. These leaders understand the difference between the universal Church and the local church—and how they build the local church first. The *universal Church* speaks of the mystical union between the Body of Christ—which is all believers everywhere at all times—and the head—which is Jesus—brought about by the Spirit (see Eph. 2:19-22; Col. 1:15-20).

The *local church* speaks of the place where believers gather in true spiritual harmony, with one accord, identifying with the vision and leadership of that local church that is structured after the New Testament pattern (see Matt. 18:15-20; Acts 2:37-47).

LEADERS WHO BUILD CHRIST'S CHURCH UNDERSTAND AND BELIEVE IN THE LOCAL CHURCH

This too may sound obvious, but it is not a given in today's world of Christians. Many Christians may believe in Christ, but they do not attend, participate in or build the local church. In his book *Real Church*, Larry Crabb explains why finding a church that he would like to attend is a real challenge. Crabb says, "Church as I know it usually leaves deep parts of me dormant, unawakened, and untouched. . . . I don't much like going to church."[2] This may be a true read on why many millions choose not to go to church, much less deeply love the local church.

We must be leaders who build the kind of local church people can love and be passionate about! Crabb writes, "The church I want to be part of, a real church, will teach spiritual theology that stirs a hunger for spiritual formation that surfaces the need for spiritual community that then marshals its resources for spiritual mission."[3] Not a bad definition! This is why we need leaders who love the local church and are committed to building the church Jesus instructed His people to build.

Jesus' church is not boring. It is not shallow, unfulfilling, disappointing or dead in any way. His local church is a congregation or assembly of people in a given locality that joins to fulfill the vision to reach the lost and the unchurched with fervent prayer and worship and through giving themselves in total commitment to Christ. Jesus gave His life, not so that we could follow half-heartedly, but so that we, "speaking the truth in love, may grow up in all things into Him who is the head—Christ—from whom the whole body, joined and knit together by what every joint supplies, according to the effective working by which every part does its share, causes growth of the body for the edifying of itself in love" (Eph. 4:15-16).

The local church is a wineskin that must be kept fresh and flexible by the power of the Holy Spirit working continually within and upon the church. "Nor do they put new wine into old wineskins, or else the wineskins break, the wine is spilled, and the wineskins are ruined. But they put new wine into new wineskins, and both are preserved" (Matt. 9:17; see also Mark 2:22; Luke 5:37-38; Acts 9:31). As leaders who love and believe in the local church, we should build a church filled with a God excitement; a God presence; a heart for missions; and a buzz of people serving, loving, gathering, praying and doing church in the way Jesus meant it to be.

The local church should be constantly growing and producing disciples, as the Early Church did: "Then the word of God spread, and the number of the disciples multiplied greatly in Jerusalem, and a great many of the priests were obedient to the faith" (Acts 6:7; see also Acts 6:1). The church grows, multiplies, and challenges everyone to give their all to reaching people. Notice what Barnabas does when he finds Saul: "And when he had found him, he brought him to Antioch. So it was that for a whole year they assembled with the church and taught a great many people. And the disciples were first called Christians in Antioch" (Acts 11:26). The local church is a God idea that must be respected and protected against any and all destroyers, both human and spiritual.

The local church is a manifestation in time of God's eternal purpose, as described in Ephesians:

> To me [Paul], who am less than the least of all the saints, this grace was given, that I should preach among the Gentiles the unsearchable riches of Christ, and to make all see what is the fellowship of the mystery, which from the beginning of the ages has been hidden in God who created all things through Jesus Christ; to the intent that now the manifold wisdom of God might be made known by the church to the principalities and powers in the heavenly places, according to the eternal purpose which He accomplished in Christ Jesus our Lord (Eph. 3:8-11).

The Church is set apart as God's eternal purpose manifested in time. It is God's final instrument to fulfill His plan of the ages, which is to bring people into His family and His presence. The leader totally accepts the fact that Christ in His Church is the central fact of God's will, and that the Church was and is the eternal purpose of God—a setting forth, an intention, something determined to happen. The Church is both the product of God's purpose and the means for achieving God's purpose.

The local church, which we as leaders are building, is the greatest cause any person could ever be involved with. Whether staff or volunteer, all levels and all kinds of leaders are engaged in a God idea that produces a God result. A life-changing local church is a family that is caring; exciting; full of worship, teaching, friendship, people, serving, prayer, security, direction, healing and laughter; a place of receiving grace and giving grace—a place to call home.

The local church of the New Testament era—the local church we all can build—is described clearly in the book of Acts:

- Spirit-driven and Spirit-filled (see Acts 1:4-5; 2:1-13,33,38)
- Growing and spreading out (see Acts 1:12-14,24-26; 3:1,9-10; 4:23,31; 6:4-7; 7:55-8:1)
- Preaching and teaching full truth (see Acts 2:36-39)
- Belonging to and building fellowship together (see Acts 2:40-41; 5:14)
- Celebrating life and fulfilling purpose (see Acts 2:42-46)
- Reaching people and impacting regions (see Acts 2:47; 4:16,30-31,33; 5:12,15-16,38-39; 6:7)

LEADERS' OBVIOUS COMMITMENT TO THE LOCAL CHURCH

When leaders are in love with the church, specifically the local church they are committed to build, things happen in a marvelous way. Leaders have a deep commitment to and a deep conviction about the church. Conviction is an unshakable belief in something without need of proof or evidence. It is a strong belief that aligns everything else. Conviction is different from a bias or an opinion (see 1 Cor. 15:58; 2 Tim. 4:6).

The leader who builds the church has a chosen life value for the local church. To value something is to consider it to be of worth and critical importance. The personal core values you believe in and apply to your life will be foundational to everything you do in life and ministry. Do you value your local church? Does Matthew 13:46 reflect your heart for your church: "When he had found one pearl of great price, [he] went and sold all that he had and bought it"? Do you see the church like John's vision in Revelation 21:21: "The twelve gates were twelve pearls: each individual gate was of one pearl. And the street of the city was pure gold, like transparent glass"?

Pure gold. Valuable as pearls. It is essential that we do everything we can do to make the church of Jesus Christ glorious. Commitment to be a co-builder of this glorious and amazing church Jesus is building will result in overflowing passion—passion for the vision of the church, passion for the growth of the church.

To have passion is to be fervent in spirit. King David had a consuming passion for the church:

> Lord, I have loved the habitation of Your house, and the place where Your glory dwells (Ps. 26:8).

> Zeal for Your house has eaten me up (Ps. 69:9).

Are you passionate for and about your church? Does your heart well up with a fullness of devotion, service, zeal and intensity of spirit that enables you to leap over all obstacles in building this pearl of great price—the local church?

Leaders who build with conviction, value and passion for the local church will be filled with a God vision for the church. This vision is founded in the Word of God and is clear in the leader's mind (see Prov. 29:18; Acts 2:37-47; 26:19).

Leaders Build the Church with Intention

Leaders who build intentionally are those with heart and focus. They build with deliberate attitudes and actions. These leaders serve with design and make purposeful choices to do what is needed to build the church. The first and most important intentional action is to pray for the church consistently, specifically, passionately and with faith. Leaders fill their mouths with Scriptures to pray:

Call to Me, and I will answer you, and show you great and mighty things, which you do not know (Jer. 33:3).

And whatever you ask in My name, that I will do, that the Father may be glorified in the Son. If you ask anything in My name, I will do it (John 14:13-14).

"Sing, O barren, you who have not borne! Break forth into singing, and cry aloud, you who have not labored with child! For more are the children of the desolate than the children of the married woman," says the LORD. "Enlarge the place of your tent, and let them stretch out the curtains of your dwellings; do not spare; lengthen your cords, and strengthen your stakes. For you shall expand to the right and to the left, and your descendants will inherit the nations, and make the desolate cities inhabited" (Isa. 54:1-3).

Therefore pray the Lord of the harvest to send out laborers into His harvest (Matt. 9:38).

LEADERS PRAY WITH INTENT

Leaders who pray intentionally ask for mighty things to happen in the church and through the church. They pray for enlargement, for spiritual expansion, and for a harvest of souls. Praying leaders see more than others see, they see farther than others see, and they see before others do. Praying leaders are great builders!

Praying leaders pray specific prayers for all who are on the leadership teams that are building the house of God together. They pray for those who lead and oversee the church, as the Bible commands: "Obey those who rule over you, and be submissive, for they watch out for your souls, as those who must give account. Let them do so with joy and not with grief, for that would be unprofitable for you" (Heb. 13:17).

Pray for God to fill the church with His Spirit and to fill every leader with boldness to share the gospel.

And when they had prayed, the place where they were assembled together was shaken; and they were all filled with the Holy Spirit, and they spoke the word of God with boldness (Acts 4:31).

Pray for the Holy Spirit to strengthen every leader. Make intercession for God to do what is needed to address the weakness in the life of every person on the team.

> Likewise the Spirit also helps in our weaknesses. For we do not know what we should pray for as we ought, but the Spirit Himself makes intercession for us with groanings which cannot be uttered (Rom. 8:26).

> For we are glad when we are weak and you are strong. And this also we pray, that you may be made complete (2 Cor. 13:9).

> We give thanks to the God and Father of our Lord Jesus Christ, praying always for you (Col. 1:3).

Leaders who pray are extremely valuable to the church. They make a difference in the house they are building.

LEADERS SPEAK LIFE

Leaders intentionally speak positive words about the church. They reject negativity, critical attitudes and disloyal words that tear down the church in any way. "Now I plead with you, brethren, by the name of our Lord Jesus Christ, that you all speak the same thing, and that there be no divisions among you, but that you be perfectly joined together in the same mind and in the same judgment" (1 Cor. 1:10). Words can break into pieces the work of God in a church or a person. Words that are destructive, adverse, opposing, inflammatory or derogatory must be avoided. Proverbs 18:8 teaches that "The words of a talebearer are like tasty trifles, and they go down into the inmost body." We need to keep our spirit clean and free from any and all destructive words. We are builders, not destroyers.

Leaders are sensitive and careful not to be "snared by the words of [their] mouth" (Prov. 6:2). Leaders who build the church watch out for people who cause division and offense. They make note of these people, who may use good words and good deeds to get into places of influence where they can cause division. A minor division may result from gossip against any person in the church, but someone intent on causing dissension is more likely to speak words against a leader. We must learn to be wide awake to the divisive actions of certain people, judging them on their overall performance pattern rather than on one or two incidents.

LEADERS LOVE THE CHURCH

Leaders who build the church love the church and attend church strategically. They do not just go to church services; they go with an attitude of
ownership, helping to make the services spiritually successful by fervent
participation in prayer, worship and ministry to people. Hebrews 10:25
says that we should not be "forsaking the assembling of ourselves together,
as is the manner of some, but exhorting one another, and so much the
more as you see the Day approaching."

Leaders take responsibility for the people in and around the church
gatherings by praying for them, listening to them, reaching out to them,
and helping them to encounter God and have a positive and life-changing
experience at church. Church is to be that place where people are overtaken
by the overwhelming love of God. The church creates a genuine presence of
love. There are no feelings of pretentiousness, but a sense that every person is important. People are cared for. People thrive in this place (see Acts
2:41-47). People are looking for that place and for those people. You, as the
leader, are the builder of this atmosphere. You are the carrier of this DNA.

LEADERS CREATE A COMMUNITY SPIRIT

Leaders who build the church intentionally create a spirit of community.
People are looking for community—that emotional, spiritual atmosphere
where they can find others with whom they can do life together. In the
midst of an impersonal, demanding and driven culture, we need a safe
place where we can be connected to people. The Acts 2 church fostered
this kind of community spirit that provided relationships, purpose, security, trust, transparency, unconditional acceptance, encouragement and
connectedness. Leaders who build the church know the value of connecting people to people and building genuine community.

Community life is built by leaders who know how to love people. Jesus
gave us this command: "That you love one another; as I have loved you,
that you also love one another" (John 13:34). Leaders know how to help the
troubled person: "We then who are strong ought to bear with the scruples
of the weak, and not to please ourselves" (Rom. 15:1). The community
spirit thrives when leaders are hospitable—when they open their lives and
their homes to connect people to prayer and the love of others.

The Bible explicitly teaches this way of leading and living: "Be hospitable to one another without grumbling" (1 Pet. 4:9). Also, "Brethren, if
a man is overtaken in any trespass, you who are spiritual restore such a one

in a spirit of gentleness, considering yourself lest you also be tempted. Bear one another's burdens, and so fulfill the law of Christ" (Gal. 6:1-2). The incarnational life of God is lived out in everyday life through everyday people. When people connect to this atmosphere, their lives are transformed, and they will impact their world. Let's build the Acts 2 church atmosphere!

LEADERS DON'T BUILD ALONE

Leaders who build life-changing churches intentionally partner with other like-minded church builders. Paul had partners with whom he built the church: "Greet Priscilla and Aquila, my fellow workers in Christ Jesus" (Rom. 16.3). James and John worked with Simon: "And so also were James and John, the sons of Zebedee, who were partners with Simon" (Luke 5:10). Paul also partnered with Titus: "If anyone inquires about Titus, he is my partner and fellow worker concerning you. Or if our brethren are inquired about, they are messengers of the churches, the glory of Christ" (2 Cor. 8:23). The leader-builder joins with others in the work of the ministry as true partners with a common commitment to build the church and extend the kingdom of God. This is a companion spirit.

Life-changing churches are built by people, not by professionals. Every person is a minister of Christ and for Christ. We are all employed full-time in the ministry, because ministry is living as a specially placed person in every area of life.

> From one man he made all the nations, that they should inhabit the whole earth; and he marked out their appointed times in history and the boundaries of their lands. God did this so that they would seek him and perhaps reach out for him and find him, though he is not far from any one of us (Acts 17:26-27, *NIV*).

"You are the salt of the earth. But if the salt loses its saltiness, how can it be made salty again? It is no longer good for anything, except to be thrown out and trampled underfoot" (Matt. 5:13; see also Eph. 4:12; 1 Pet. 2:9). We are all implementers of God's plans, and we partner with all the people God is using. We build the church so that the church becomes the equipping station for people.

LEADERS CHOOSE A LIFESTYLE OF SERVICE

Leaders intentionally choose a lifestyle of service to the church. Leaders who are convinced the church is worth giving their life to will make decisions to create a lifestyle that makes room for serving. It is one thing to surrender your life at the altar or during a powerful worship service; it is quite another thing to surrender your rights, privileges, personal schedule and life itself as lived on a daily basis. To serve the church, you have to make time to serve, which necessitates a decision to change your lifestyle. Decide to take time to be trained, mentored, prepared and involved. Roy Lessin's words are to be heard and practiced:

> A godly leader finds strength by realizing his weakness, finds authority by being under authority, finds direction by laying down his plans, finds vision by seeing the needs of others, finds credibility by being an example, finds loyalty by expressing compassion, finds honor by being faithful, finds greatness by being a servant.

Leaders who are faithful and fruitful servants of the church are people who have learned sacrifice and are willing to be stretched spiritually and emotionally, allowing new capacity to increase their levels of participation (see Isa. 6:8; Matt. 6:33; Rom. 12:1-2; Phil. 3:13-14).

Do the simple things to start serving your church. Be faithful to attend and participate in services, events, projects and anywhere you see you can help. Some people underestimate the value of simply being present. Joining with others adds to the momentum and encourages people and leaders. Simply help shoulder the load of responsibility. Leaders' arms get weary. You can lift up the hands that hang down (see Exod. 17:12). It is said that 20 percent of the church does 80 percent of the work, but it doesn't have to be that way. If everyone would simply change their lifestyle to make room to pitch in and do their fair share in helping, serving and giving, then all the needs would be met, and no one would be overburdened (see Eccles. 9:10).

Life-Changing Leadership
Team Integrity

The church must be led by leaders whose character is Christ-filled and proven to be trustworthy. Serving God and the church is a high calling that should be entered into with deep conviction and commitment. It is a great and excellent thing for leaders to serve the church with integrity. It is of highest importance to have a sense of dignity and responsibility in accurately forming, carefully maintaining, and habitually exercising our service.

If you walk into a gym and ask a body builder how he got to be so strong, he will not tell you that one day he was scrawny, and the next day he was built like Superman. He had to exert great discipline to form his muscles precisely. He had to eat the right food at the right time, maintain a strict sleeping pattern, and of course lift weights. Moreover, he knows that once he builds muscle, he has to continue following a proper diet and weight-lifting regimen in order to maintain his strength.

We must approach service and leadership with the same discipline and commitment. We need to work on exercising our spiritual bodies in a way that honors God.

There are spiritual qualifications for Christian leaders, and we must be careful not to deviate from the scriptural standard. The quality of the church depends on the quality of the team that leads the church. The quality of the leader is not determined by happenstance of genetics or by the influence of environment. It is not measured by personality or social acclaim. The single most important attribute of a leader is strength of character. Integrity. There is no substitute for personal character and there never will be.

THE MEANING OF CHARACTER

Charakter, the word Aristotle used to describe moral maturity, means "enduring marks." There is something lasting about a person of character. The person of enduring character is consistent in all seasons of life for all of life. Character is not personality. A leader can have a charming personality but be utterly unreliable in the important matters of character. The truth is that we do have control over and can overcome our weaknesses of character.

You are ultimately responsible for your character. Improving your character is a decision only you can make. It is up to you.

As leaders, we must have a personal goal of developing the kind of character the Bible prescribes for us. Biblical character is outlined in some very understandable details in 1 Timothy 3:2-7 and Titus 1:6-9. In these passages, the apostle Paul explicitly speaks of the character qualifications required for leading in the church. These are the basic character standards for all leaders. The leader has a core called integrity—and from this core, all ministry flows. Let us as leaders establish a core of integrity that will not be compromised.

Let integrity and uprightness preserve me, for I wait for You (Ps. 25:21).

The LORD shall judge the peoples; judge me, O LORD, according to my righteousness, and according to my integrity within me (Ps. 7:8).

As for me, You uphold me in my integrity, and set me before Your face forever (Ps. 41:12).

Vindicate me, O LORD, for I have walked in my integrity. I have also trusted in the LORD; I shall not slip. Examine me, O LORD, and prove me; try my mind and my heart (Ps. 26:1-2).

He who walks with integrity walks securely, but he who perverts his ways will become known (Prov. 10:9).

CHARACTER QUALIFICATIONS OF LEADERS

Character as defined by the Greek word *charasso* means "a notch, indentation or writing on stone or metal." It came to mean an embosser or stamp for making coins. Character is the distinctive mark impressed upon an individual from either external or internal forces. Character involves what you are in your essence, the sum total of your habits, your personal assortment of virtues and vices. One's ethics go hand in hand with one's character. For some, being ethical means following a set of rules or laws. But one can obey laws and rules and still have a faulty character. In the deepest and most comprehensive way, ethics are a matter of personal character—of what kind of person one is inside. It is not merely a question of following rules. We do of course have rules to follow, but character goes deeper than observance of those rules. We are what we repeatedly do. Our habits—our customary behavior—ultimately define our character.

Following are 21 character qualifications that Paul outlines in 1 Timothy 3:2-7 and Titus 1:6-9. First let's read Paul's writing:

> A bishop then must be blameless, the husband of one wife, temperate, sober-minded, of good behavior, hospitable, able to teach; not given to wine, not violent, not greedy for money, but gentle, not quarrelsome, not covetous; one who rules his own house well, having his children in submission with all reverence (for if a man does not know how to rule his own house, how will he take care of the church of God?); not a novice, lest being puffed up with pride he fall into the same condemnation as the devil. Moreover he must have a good testimony among those who are outside, lest he fall into reproach and the snare of the devil (1 Tim. 3:2-7).

> If a man is blameless, the husband of one wife, having faithful children not accused of dissipation or insubordination. For a bishop must be blameless, as a steward of God, not self-willed, not quick-tempered, not given to wine, not violent, not greedy for money, but hospitable, a lover of what is good, sober-minded, just, holy, self-controlled, holding fast the faithful word as he has been taught, that he may be able, by sound doctrine, both to exhort and convict those who contradict (Titus 1:6-9).

TWENTY-ONE CHARACTER QUALIFICATIONS OF LEADERS

Based on the two Scripture passages that are quoted above, these are the character qualifications of church leaders—along with a brief description of each qualification.

1. ABOVE REPROACH
Leaders are to be blameless—having unquestionable integrity, being irreproachable, having such character that no one can rightfully take hold of the person with a charge of unfitness (the Greek word translated as "blameless" literally means "not to be taken hold of"; see 1 Tim. 3:2; Titus 1:6-7).

2. HUSBAND OF ONE WIFE
This does not mean that leaders must be married, but that if they marry, they have only one spouse. A husband of one wife is not a bigamist. Further, as "one wife's husband," he has nothing to do with any other woman in any romantic or sexual sense. Paul required married leaders to be intimately related to only one spouse, thus indicating that leaders must have a strong marriage. A husband and wife must work hard to cultivate unity and love in their marriage. They should never share their private struggles with someone of the opposite gender, only with their spouse or someone of the same gender. Single men should never share their struggles with single women, and sometimes not with some single men either (see 1 Tim. 3:2; Titus 1:6).

3. TEMPERATE
Temperance is the quality of keeping oneself in hand, self-controlled, disciplined and free from extremes. A temperate person has a clear perspective on life and a correct and fruitful spiritual orientation. Temperate leaders do not lose their physical, psychological or spiritual balance. They are stable and steadfast, always think clearly, and do not lose perspective under pressure (see 1 Tim. 3:2; Titus 1:8).

4. PRUDENT
Leaders are to be sober-minded, sensible, not given to fanciful thinking or emotional irrationality. They should always exercise sound judgment, caution, practical wisdom, and carefulness over the consequences of their actions. The prudent wisely foresee the future and plan accordingly (see 1 Tim. 3:2; Titus 1:8).

5. RESPECTABLE
A biblical leader models good behavior, having a modest, orderly, disciplined, respectable lifestyle. This leader lives a well-ordered life and maintains a well-ordered home. He or she lives out the teachings of the Bible in

speech, dress, appearance at home or office, and manner of doing business (see 1 Tim. 3:2).

6. HOSPITABLE
Showing hospitality means being fond of guests and kind to strangers. The hospitable person enjoys the company of others and seeks to make others feel comfortable and welcome in any situation (see 1 Tim. 3:2; Titus 1:8).

7. ABLE TO TEACH
A leader must be able to communicate and impart truth, resulting from having been taught. Teachers have the ability to prove the critic and unbeliever wrong. The teachable do not look for arguments or attempt to stir up disputes (see 1 Tim. 3:2; Titus 1:9).

8. NOT GIVEN TO WINE
A leader should not be a drunkard—one who loses control of his or her senses and is brought into bondage. A higher law rules us in this matter; we should not do "anything by which your brother stumbles or is offended or is made weak" (Rom. 14:21). The standard for leaders at City Bible Church is abstinence. We choose to not drink (see Prov. 20:1; 1 Tim. 3:3; Titus 1:7).

9. NOT SELF-WILLED
The biblical leader is not dominated by self-interest, self-pleasing, stubbornness or arrogance; rather, he or she is submissive to proper authority, seeking to please God and others. People who are not self-willed are not set in their own way or set on having their way. They never hesitate to lay down their desires to serve another or complain about serving someone (see Titus 1:7).

10. NOT QUICK-TEMPERED
Leaders of the church should not be quick-tempered or prone to anger. They are not cranky or irritable, not easily provoked or inflamed, and do not have a short fuse or easily fly off the handle. Leaders are capable of governing their own spirit (see Titus 1:7).

11. NOT QUARRELSOME
Leaders are not to be strikers. They should not be violent or combative, carry a chip on their shoulder, or stand always ready for a good argument (see 1 Tim. 3:3; Titus 1:7).

12. Uncontentious

The biblical leader is not quarrelsome and contentious, but peaceable and easily corrected. A contentious person domineers over others, but in reality is insecure and defensive. This person is inflexible and unwilling to bend; he or she loves controversy, strife, conflict, struggle and discord (see 1 Tim. 3:3).

13. Gentle

To be gentle is to be patient, kind, considerate and forbearing; having a mild disposition, moderation and sweet reasonableness; and not insisting on one's legal rights. A gentle person has a noble and generous spirit, such that a superior person will even yield to the lesser (see 1 Tim. 3:3).

14. Free from Love of Money

A biblical leader is not greedy for money and does not acquire money by dishonest means or acquire dishonest money by any means. Insatiable desire for wealth or readiness to obtain it by questionable means disqualifies someone from leadership (see 1 Tim. 3:3; Titus 1:7).

15. Rules His or Her Own House

Scripture requires a leader of the church to preside over and manage his or her own household in an excellent manner. The leader helps to conduct the affairs of the family, keeping children under control with dignity, respect, reverence and venerability. To truly rule our families, we must discipline them with love (see 1 Tim. 3:4; Titus 1:6).

16. Good Reputation with Those Outside the Church

A good reputation is the result of living an excellent testimony among those outside the church. A reputation may exist in the areas of business, community relations and civil law. A leader must be a respected person on the job as well as in the church (see 1 Tim. 3:7).

17. Love of Good

Loving good means being fond of good activities, things and thoughts. These leaders have desires toward the good things of God; their minds and hearts are not set on evil, questionable or less important things (see Titus 1:8).

18. JUST

To be just is to be righteous, upright, equitable in character, fair in decisions, and right in judgment. This word entails not only right standing before God, but also doing what is right and just in one's dealings with other people (see Titus 1:8).

19. DEVOUT

The biblical leader pursues holiness and pleases God; he or she is set apart. Devout leaders consistently practice righteousness and maintain moral standards (see Titus 1:8).

20. NOT A NOVICE

A church leader should not be a newly converted Christian or one who is newly planted in the local church. "Novice" refers not to age but to spiritual maturity (see 1 Tim. 3:6).

21. HOLDS FAST THE FAITHFUL WORD

The biblical leader has a firm grip and a strong hold on the Word of God; he or she knows the Scriptures and the proper teaching of sound doctrine. Leaders with character have a deep conviction of the infallibility and authority of Scripture. They are not shifty or double-talkers (see Titus 1:9).

INTEGRITY: THE CORE OF CHARACTER

Do you remember, when you were taking math in elementary school, learning about whole numbers, decimals and fractions? You probably learned back then that there was something called an "integer." An integer is a whole number—as opposed to a fraction, which is a part of the whole. There's the classic illustration of a pie: How many slices make up the whole pie? The teacher would put up a drawing of a pie cut into eight pieces, and students would eagerly count how many slices made up the whole. If one piece was missing, they would determine that only seven-eighths of the pie was there. It was not a whole unit anymore. It was fragmented.

The word "integrity" comes from "integer"—the word for a whole number. Something that is integral is complete. Every piece is present and is integrated into the whole. Integrity is the core of one's character, which is the seat of one's moral being. It is a wholeness or moral completeness that demonstrates the inner person. If your core is faulty and fragmented, the rest of your life will be imbalanced.

The Bible, using the Greek word *aphthoria*, defines integrity as the quality of moral soundness and of being uncorrupt. Integrity is the opposite of that which is destroyed, corrupted, ruined, shipwrecked or led astray. A person without integrity is one who has been seduced and corrupted away from the truth. In the Bible, a sacrifice that was without integrity was blemished and unacceptable to God. Integrity encompasses the whole moral character of purity, uprightness, honesty and genuineness. It includes having a sense of honesty and truthfulness in regard to the motivations behind one's actions. Some other words in the integrity family are righteous, upright, honesty, truthfulness, blameless, perfect, trusted, undefiled, pure heart, wholesome spirit and whole. Integrity helps you sleep great at night!

Integrity is a character virtue—it is not inherited and is not automatic because of your family tree. Integrity is not based on achievements, credentials or reputation. Integrity is not to be confused with reputation or the praise of men. A person may appear differently than they really are. Integrity is the real, inner life and secret world of the person, whereas reputation can be based on works and achievements. Many succeed momentarily by what they know, some succeed temporarily by what they do, and a few succeed permanently by what they are. Journalist Ted Koppel once said, "There's harmony and inner peace to be found in following a moral compass that points in the same direction regardless of fashion or trend." In a world that is rapidly changing on the outside, we need leaders who have a strong core on the inside. All ministry proceeds from the core. Let us establish a core of integrity that will not be compromised!

INTEGRITY IS THE CORE OF CHARACTER

The following graphic shows how each piece of life is part of the whole person. Notice that at the center—at the core—is integrity. It is like the hub of a wheel; all of the spokes are connected to it. Without an anchor point, the wheel would lose its structural stability and crumble. Integrity brings every piece together and fits them in place in order to make something whole. This is why it is so vital that we as leaders and believers live life with integrity—with undivided attention and undiminished priority given to God's Word, values and will.

Your personal life affects your authority in the public arena. If you have no integrity in your personal life, you limit your authority and influence in your public life. If you have a team with great integrity, then the people your team produces will also have sound character.

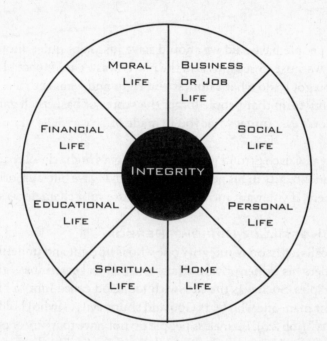

BIBLICAL UNDERSTANDING OF INTEGRITY

Now let's take a closer look at the biblical understanding of integrity. There are at least nine distinct qualities of integrity referred to in the Bible.

1. MORALLY SOUND CHARACTER

People of integrity have character that is marked by consistent, honest and moral behavior. They wholly desire to live in complete harmony with God. The word "honesty" comes from the Latin word *honestos*, which means "the state of being credible, upright and sincere, without lies, crookedness, deceit or fraud." How credible is your word? Do people believe that you will follow through with what you say you will do? Proverbs 10:9, in *THE MESSAGE* paraphrase, promises that "Honesty lives confident and carefree, but Shifty is sure to be exposed."

Several years ago, the Rockdale County (Georgia) Bulldogs won the high school state championship but later had to give it up. After the championship tournament, school officials reported that a player who played

45 seconds in the first tournament game was scholastically ineligible. The Bulldogs' coach, Cleveland Stroud, did not know at the time that the player was not qualified to play. He said this about the championship and the team:

> Some people have said we should have just kept quiet about it, that it was just 45 seconds and the player wasn't an impact player. But you got to do what's honest and right and what the rules say. I told my team that people forget the scores of basketball games; they don't ever forget what you're made of.[1]

That year, Coach Stroud was named Georgia's high school coach of the year. He had integrity in his personal life, and that gave him authority in the public sphere. If you want influence, make sure your character is sound.

2. AN UNDEFILED, UPRIGHT PERSON

The Bible calls a person of integrity one who is upright and undefiled. This person orders his or her private affairs with ethical carefulness and rock-solid principles. Such was the case with Job. God called him "a blameless and upright man, one who fears God and shuns evil . . . [who] holds fast to his integrity" (Job 2:3). Blameless people do not have to worry about being caught or exposed. They have ordered their life after biblical principles and can rest knowing that their integrity will uphold them (see Ps. 41:12).

Abraham Lincoln made a resolve never to compromise his integrity, despite errors he might make in office. He said, "I desire so to conduct the affairs of this administration that if at the end, when I come to lay down the reins of power, I have lost every other friend on earth, I shall at least have one friend left, and that friend shall be down inside me."

You might not have to live with the people in your sphere forever, but you do have to live with yourself. Make decisions that you will not regret.

3. DIVINE STANDARD FOR OUR ATTAINMENT

We must not make excuses for ourselves. We know there is a standard described in the Bible that is God's standard—and by His grace, we live up to it. Every leader chooses between being ethically complacent and caring enough about their personal integrity to strive for character improvement. We must each ask ourselves: Have I become complacent about improving my own character? Am I so concerned in my daily life with other pursuits and goals that I end up devoting little or no time and thought to how I could improve my character? Do I compromise the divine standard for my character by making excuses for my flaws? Do I say, "Oh well, I'm too set in my ways to change now" or "I'm content with the way I am, faults and all"?

Wherever we are in our character development, we can always push forward, go higher, and strive toward the divine standard that is seen in the person of Christ. We are to become like Jesus in our character. This indeed is our divine standard for attainment. One of the first—and not so pleasant—steps you and I must take is to look into the mirror and identify and acknowledge the specific things in our personal character that require improvement.

4. WHOLEHEARTED COMMITMENT TO GOD

Integrity and a heart for God go together. If our hearts are committed to God and we are passionate about pursuing Him, then our character will change. The moment we turn our lives over to Jesus and begin following Him, we start on a journey of transformation. The more we spend time in prayer, in the Word and with Jesus, the more our character is exposed to His presence and transformed into His likeness. The heart is open in the presence of God, and the voice of God is clear and strategic to our character needs. We listen and respond—and at times repent.

We must be careful not to filter what God is saying to us through our old mindsets, which will seek to make excuses or misinterpret what God is pressing upon us. We will find deep satisfaction and joy in responding to Jesus and experiencing continual personal transformation.

5. CONSISTENT SPEECH THAT IS IN COMPLETE ACCORD WITH THE TRUTH

Our words are to be trustworthy and our speech is to be accurate. According to Proverbs 12:19, "Truthful words stand the test of time, but lies are soon exposed" (NLT). Truthfulness with our words is foundational to our integrity as leaders. Truthfulness refers to someone who is honest and avoids falsehood. Leaders with integrity avoid partial truth and do not mislead others with statements that are technically accurate but not fully truthful. All partial truth communication is a form of lying—and lying is wrong.

At times, leaders may be motivated by fear or by selfish gain. Fear of what others think about them, fear of confrontation, and fear of taking responsibility for their actions cause many people to lie. Leaders of integrity understand that truthfulness builds credibility. When people find partial truth or worse in a leader's words, the leader loses credibility. Others will suspect they are being lied to even when they are being told the truth. Truthfulness deals with what is spoken, while integrity deals with the consistency between what is spoken and what is done. A good leader demonstrates consistency of words, actions, values, methods and beliefs. Good leaders know what is right and what is wrong, and they speak and act accordingly—even at personal cost—at all times.

6. FINISHED PRODUCT

"Let integrity and uprightness preserve me," wrote David (Ps. 25:21). Integrity allows for a balanced and well-rounded lifestyle that leads to wholeness. The leader who sees integrity as the core will see wholeness as the result. Integrity in the spirit, soul, mind, will and emotions of a leader will result in a complete, healthy whole. The inner wholeness of the leader begins with the solid core of integrity and then grows to affect his or her mind, will, emotions, and ultimately behavior and relationships.

The integrity core will always have authenticity as a main ingredient. Authenticity flows from an upright heart—one whose ethics are based on a dynamic relationship with God and ongoing character growth. When you have a healthy core, your wholeness is evident in the way you lead— how you deal with people, how you process your own mistakes, and how you handle shortcomings or faults. The finished product is a leader who lives a holistic life and imparts that life to others.

7. PURE MOTIVE

Whenever you deal with leadership, you deal with authority. So it's important that you ask yourself: Why do you want to have authority over people's lives? Why do you want to have this position? Why do you want to have that kind of influence? Leaders must have pure motives. They are in leadership to serve. If you have a pure motive to serve, then you willingly go where you are asked to serve. But if your motive is to use your gift in the way you want, then when you are asked to move, you become angry and dig in your heels. The motive was to elevate your gift, rather than to allow God to use your gift to serve someone else.

I dealt with a team with wrong motives several years ago in my ministry. We had a great worship team playing for one service; that particular group was full of excellent musicians and singers. I spoke with the group and asked its members to spread out and play on different teams and in different services, so that we could strengthen the overall worship team. To my surprise, almost every person in the band refused to play on a different team. They liked their group, and they liked the music they made together. Unfortunately, their motives were not right.

When I asked them to change the place where they were serving, the motive surfaced: *Where does my gift look the best?* The right heart would be: *Let's make worship best for the whole church. And if I don't get to use my creative thing the way I want to, then my creative thing dies on the Cross.*

It's important to remember that the person with the wrong attitude is the one who loses—not the church. The church belongs to Jesus, and the church will continue without all the bells and whistles we use. The musicians I just mentioned ended up leaving the worship team, but our worship stayed strong and the church continued on. If a person has a wrong attitude, deal with it. Do not try to work around it because you don't want to give offense. If they have right motives, they will adjust to serve the need best.

8. A CUT ABOVE

When we find a garment or another piece of merchandise that is outstanding and has superior excellence, we say that it is "a cut above" the rest! A person of integrity exceeds the usual limit, rises above the norm, and lives in conformity to the moral precepts of the Bible in contrast to the sinful ways of the world.

A marketing research firm conducted a survey of executives at 100 of the USA's 1,000 largest companies. They asked the question: "What qualities in employees irritate bosses most?" The number one irritant was dishonesty. "If a company believes that an employee lacks integrity," the executive who had commissioned the study explained, "all positive qualities—ranging from skill and experience to productivity and intelligence—become meaningless."[2] We as leaders are called to be a cut above—even when no one is looking. Character is what we are in the dark—those times when no one is around to see what we do. A cut above is the same in the light or in the dark.

9. CREDIBLE PEOPLE WHO LIVE BY THE RULES OF RIGHT AND WRONG

People who live by the biblical principles of upright conduct have a code of morality, a system of conduct, and a healthy conscience that serves as an inner compass. That inner compass helps them navigate all of life. Proverbs offers this wisdom: "Moral character makes for smooth traveling; an evil life is a hard life" (Prov. 11:5, *THE MESSAGE*). If you want to sail smoothly in life, make sure your inner compass firmly points to true north. Biblical integrity will never steer you wrong.

The Josephson Institute of Ethics describes right and wrong behavior like this: "Ethics is about how we meet the challenge of doing the right thing when that will cost more than we want to pay."[3] How would you rate yourself on this scale?

I am always ethical.
I am mostly ethical.
I am somewhat ethical.
I am seldom ethical.
I am never ethical.

If you live by the biblical rules of right and wrong, you will never falter. Integrity builds credibility, and credibility leads to influence. When you lose credibility, you lose influence.

FIVE BIBLICAL FACTORS OF INTEGRITY

David wrote, "The steps of a good man are ordered by the LORD, and He delights in his way. Though he fall, he shall not be utterly cast down; for the LORD upholds him with His hand" (Ps. 37:23-24). Let's consider five specific ways that integrity benefits us as we lead God's people.

1. INTEGRITY PROTECTS

God protects us as long as our hearts are committed to integrity. God can find a handle in an honest heart to keep it from sin. We have a great example of this in Genesis:

> But God came to Abimelech in a dream by night, and said to him, "Indeed you are a dead man because of the woman whom you have taken, for she is a man's wife."
> But Abimelech had not come near her; and he said, "Lord, will You slay a righteous nation also? Did he not say to me, 'She is my sister'? And she, even she herself said, 'He is my brother.' In the integrity of my heart and innocence of my hands I have done this."

And God said to him in a dream, "Yes, I know that you did this in the integrity of your heart. For I also withheld you from sinning against Me; therefore I did not let you touch her" (Gen. 20:3-6).

Abimelech had no intentional disobedience—no hidden wrong motivation. He pursued the wrong thing innocently and ignorantly. The heart was in honest error. If a person's heart is honest with God, then integrity will help prevent him or her from stumbling into error and becoming trapped by sin. God will intervene to preserve the person of integrity from failures due to ignorance. Abimelech acted upon the degree of integrity he possessed, and God honored his heart's intent.

2. INTEGRITY PROMOTES

After Solomon finished building the Temple, the Lord appeared to him and made him this promise:

> Now if you walk before Me as your father David walked, in integrity of heart and in uprightness, to do according to all that I have commanded you, and if you keep My statutes and My judgments, then I will establish the throne of your kingdom over Israel forever, as I promised David your father, saying, "You shall not fail to have a man on the throne of Israel" (1 Kings 9:4-5).

Integrity allows for promotion and prosperity without destruction. How many times have we witnessed someone who was promoted too quickly or was given too much responsibility before it was discovered that the underlying foundation—the core—was not yet strong enough to handle the responsibilities or the fame? Integrity promotes and places leaders in the right place at the right time.

3. INTEGRITY ANCHORS

An anchor is a heavy object attached to a ship. It keeps the vessel in place and restricts the motion of the ship. Vision, values and mission can be anchors in a leader, but integrity is *the* anchor. In times of perplexity and confusion, integrity anchors the soul. When Job faced the great trial of his faith, he steadfastly said, "Till I die I will not put away my integrity from me" (Job 27:5). Integrity is our anchor in times of trouble. Author Elmer Letterman wrote, "Personality can open doors, but only character can keep them open." Charisma is not equal to character. Integrity is the anchor to our heart—the commitment of being who we are deep down inside. When integrity is our anchor, we allow who we are to guide our decisions and give us hope during our suffering.

4. INTEGRITY PRESERVES

Integrity preserves the life of the leader in all seasons. David cried out to God in the psalm, "Keep my soul, and deliver me; let me not be ashamed, for I put my trust in You. Let integrity and uprightness preserve me" (Ps. 25:20-21). It is not our skills or personality that will shield us from bad reports, attacks and temptations. It is integrity. As a parent, you cannot be everywhere all the time. As a businessperson, you cannot hear every conversation of those who might try to oppose you or hurt your work. But your integrity can cover you. Integrity keeps your name clear and answers suspicions or questions. Theologian Dr. Thomas Fuller said, "Honest men fear neither the light nor the dark."

5. INTEGRITY GUIDES

Integrity is the key to making right and good decisions. It is the internal umpire that rules on what is righteous and what is ungodly. Paul reminds us to "let the peace of God rule in your hearts" (Col. 3:15). The "breastplate of righteousness" (Eph. 6:14) is a priceless gift that covers the heart and signals right and wrong to us if we accept the signals. We do have the ability to make right decisions, as we allow the Holy Spirit to fill our hearts, and as we practice listening to what He is saying. He will direct us. God does not lead us to the middle of the ocean and leave us stranded with no compass, no oars, and no way to find our bearings. He has put the Holy Spirit inside us to help us to know what the right decision is and also to have the will to make the right decision.

DECIDE TO HONOR INTEGRITY

As goes the heart, so goes the leader. "Guard your heart with all vigilance, for from it are the sources of life" (Prov. 4:23, *NET*). Integrity requires internal honesty. You cannot be honest with others unless you are honest with yourself and with God. Keep your heart clean and strong in spiritual flow.

You must choose to honor integrity as your lifetime goal, making your lifetime passion to be a person of integrity. Decide that you will make integrity the focus of your life decisions. Commit yourself to honesty, reliability and confidentiality. Make a covenant that you will never sell your integrity—not for power, revenge, pride or money. Decide to practice integrity in the little things of life. If you consistently do what is right in the little, everyday things, a life of integrity will come easy. Decide to bend your actions to conform to your principles. This is possible—in the power of the Holy Spirit! You must believe that you can become a person of integrity, no matter where you are coming from or what you have been through.

United States president Theodore Roosevelt said, "Character, in the long run, is the decisive factor in the life of an individual and of nations alike." When we look back on our lives, we will see that it was the quality of our character that adjusted the course of the lives we lived, the ministries we led, and the people we influenced.

8

LIFE-CHANGING
SERVANT LEADERSHIP

The key to any ministry is leaders who are like Jesus. Jesus was, above all else, a servant. We are all called to servanthood—to follow Jesus' example of washing His disciples' feet. Servant leadership is always popular with God, and it is always anointed by God. You might not have all the gifts you want, but if you have a servant's heart, you will have the power you need. Servanthood is at the heart of Jesus' kind of leadership.

What underpins servant leadership is the motivation behind our actions as leaders. Servant leaders—those who are serving people the way Jesus served—are a special kind of leader. They don't serve in order to get into leadership; they serve because they are servants. Leaders serve and servants lead. Once we grasp this principle, insecurity in leadership will fall off, because we are not trying to prove anything or impress anyone. Every leader has a calling, a gift, a style, distinctive strengths, and a specific depth of integrity. Out of these flow a humble spirit and a servant's heart.

Servant leadership is upside-down leadership. It is opposite of the top-down models we are so familiar with in the world today. The corporate world says that the executives at the top should be pampered, waited on, given special privileges, and treated as superiors. But the kingdom of God says that those who want to lead are those who already serve. We are called to serve God, serve God's people, serve sinners, serve servants, and serve *the* Servant, who said, "I am among you as the One who serves" (Luke 22:27). How do you know if you are functioning as a servant? By the way you react when people treat you like one!

SERVANT LEADER FOUNDATIONS

Any house worth investing in is built on a solid foundation. Let's start our study of servant leadership by establishing a biblical foundation for what it means to be a servant leader in a life-changing church. Four basic principles make up the servant leader foundation.

1. GOD SAVED ME BECAUSE HE LOVES ME

The sole reason God sent His Son to die for our sins was that He loves us. God forgives us, grants us eternal life, and helps us grow in the gift of the Holy Spirit because of His immeasurable love and grace. The Bible verse so often memorized and displayed at sporting events is essential to our understanding of servant leadership: "For God so loved the world that He gave His only begotten Son, that whoever believes in Him should not perish but have everlasting life" (John 3:16). Leaders are not above anyone else; we are all sinners saved by grace. The Father's heart is one of immeasurable love. Jesus' heart is full of love toward those He served by dying on a cross. As Jesus' followers, our heart is also to be full of love—for God and for other people.

2. GOD'S PURPOSE FOR SAVING ME WAS TO BRING HIM GLORY

God saved us so that we might be His trophies and examples to others of His love and mercy at work in and through a human life. He saved us in order that we might live every hour of every day of our lives in faithful service to Him. To the Romans, Paul wrote, "For if we live, we live to the Lord; and if we die, we die to the Lord. Therefore, whether we live or die, we are the Lord's" (Rom. 14:8). The purpose of Jesus was not just to save us, but also to invade our lives and cause us to be Jesus carriers—serving like Jesus served. We bring glory to God when we serve.

3. I AM MOST LIKE JESUS WHEN I SERVE OTHERS

The foremost characteristic of the life of Jesus was and is service. We are most like Him when we serve as He served. Our ultimate purpose in life is to go beyond—beyond ourselves, beyond position, title, praise, power, pedestals, ego, fear of being the lesser—beyond in serving others. This is to be our motive: serve because Jesus served.

How do you know if you are a good servant? Ask yourself this question: *When people treat me like a servant, how do I react?* You can determine how mature your servant heart is by examining how you serve and treat those who are "below" you—who can do nothing for you. Check your motives. Are you serving because of ambition, or are you serving because you want to be like Jesus?

4. AUTHENTIC SERVANTHOOD IS A WORK OF GOD IN US

A servant's heart does not come naturally. It is the result of a deep work of grace. We are born into a fallen humanity that does not give itself to the work of God. When Jesus saves us, He gives us a new way of life—and a renewed heart. Every virtue of Jesus flows through the servant's heart. That heart is filled with the grace of Christ; it is being shaped and transformed into feeling what Christ feels and thinking like Christ thinks. Jeremiah 24:7 says, "I will give them a heart to know Me." Only God can give us a heart to serve—and He does. We love, serve and care for others because that is normal behavior for people who are filled with God's Spirit. When Christ is in us, we cannot help but serve!

Martin Luther King Jr. said, "Everybody can be great because anybody can serve. You don't have to have a college degree to serve. You don't have to make your subject and verb agree to serve. You only need a heart full of grace and a soul generated by love." Serving is not complicated. It is the byproduct of a heart filled with love for God, which results in love for God's people.

UNDERSTANDING AND DEFINING SERVANT LEADERSHIP

Now that we have our foundation established, let's take a closer look at the way the Bible describes servant leadership. Jesus said, "Whoever wants to be great must become a servant. Whoever wants to be first among you must be your slave. That is what the Son of Man has done: He came to serve, not to be served—and then to give away his life in exchange for many who are held hostage" (Mark 10:43-45, *THE MESSAGE*). Jesus never said that a desire to be great was wrong. God puts in us desires to be great for the right reasons. It's not wrong to be great, to be successful, or to have favor and blessing. Jesus here rebukes the disciples' motive, not the desire. Our motive for serving needs to come from a servant's heart that wants to live and love like Jesus.

DEFINING THE WORD "SERVANT"

There are four different Greek words used in Scripture for "servant," also translated "minister," "attendant" and "helper." These words describe leaders who want to serve like Jesus.

1. Doulos

Doulos is the word used to describe a slave. It is most commonly translated as "bond-servant." A *doulos* was born into slavery, served for life, and usually served only one owner or family. These slaves were swallowed up by the will of others. They disregarded their own interests and were instead bound to another. But they did have positions of authority and responsibility.

A slave never had personal success. He or she served at the will and direction of someone else. As a servant leader, you have a heart and anointing to make someone else great. If people know that you have an anointing to make others great, then they will serve you. If they know your desire is to make yourself great, then they will *not* follow you. The sign of great leaders is not their own success, but the success of those they raised up. The mark of a great leader is that they enable others to be successful. That is what Jesus, Paul and the apostles did. Paul describes Jesus as a *doulos* servant: "[He] made Himself of no reputation, taking the form of a bondservant, and coming in the likeness of men" (Phil. 2:7).

Sometimes we do not want someone else to be great because we feel afraid and threatened. But if we want to be servants, our driving force must be the success of others. All the time the disciples were looking for ways to crown Jesus king, Jesus was looking for the towel. He was looking for ways to elevate others to greatness. He knew that when He was gone, the people He had trained would be those who would build His Church and represent Him to others. We must continually ask ourselves how we are elevating those around us. How are others benefitting from your leadership? Are they better leaders today because of your mentoring, or do they feel that their role is to help you satisfy your personal desires?

It is a privilege to serve God's people. John Stott once wrote, "If the church was worth His blood, is it not worth our labor? The privilege of serving it is established by the preciousness of the price paid for its purchase."[1] If we are going to serve, we must understand the preciousness of the price paid for the Church. That price is the life of a man—the Son of God. Christ gave His life for the life of others. Our serving should not be according to our need; it should be in connection to the price that was paid for our redemption. It is a privilege to pour out our life for someone else, and that is exactly what Jesus purposed for all of us.

2. Huperetes

This word is most commonly translated "servant," "minister" or "helper." It's the word we looked at earlier that describes an elder as a submissive "under-rower" who serves as a slave to move the ship in the direction the master requests. This servant acts under the direction of another, willingly learning his task and goal from the one who is over him. He rows according to the directions given him, not dictating his own course of action but yielding to another's authority for the sake of accomplishing a specific task in moving a mighty ship.

John Mark was called a *huperetes*, as was Paul (see Acts 13:5; 26:16). These are two of the church's mightiest leaders, because they followed the authority of another. All leadership starts with submission: under, not over. The more you can bend your will and make it come into submission, the greater your leadership. But if your will reacts against a person who is trying to direct you, then there is something flawed in your will. That flaw shows up dramatically when you take leadership. If you are not under authority, you will misuse your will to manipulate someone else's will. Because you do not have the patience to bring them into submission, you just bend them with your power. Let them bend themselves. Let them be the one to submit their will to your authority, as they see you submitting to authority. At times, it is easier to strong-arm someone into submission. But the servant leader exercises patience and models submission.

3. Diakonos

Diakonos can be translated as the verb "serve," and also as "servant" or "deacon." A *diakonos* was a table waiter, a server of people who hastened with focus and purpose of heart to take care of the needs of those he would serve. These were slaves with limited freedoms; they lived to meet the needs of others. Paul used this word to describe Epaphras: "our dear fellow servant, who is a faithful minister of Christ on your behalf" (Col. 1:7). Jesus said, "If anyone serves Me, let him follow Me; and where I am, there My servant will be also. If anyone serves Me, him My Father will honor" (John 12:26). If you dropped out of leadership, would the team notice? Would people miss you? Are you serving in such an indispensable way that you are meeting needs and making others successful?

Waiters at a restaurant can be the difference between a wonderful experience and a terrible experience. (Either way, the experience is memorable.) I recently stopped by a restaurant to pick up a salad to go. When I walked in, no one greeted me or offered me a menu or a seat while I waited. There were hardly any patrons in the restaurant, but there were four waiters standing there talking to one another. Finally I walked up to the host stand, took a menu, and flagged down a waiter. He came over and said, "What?" I asked if someone could take my order, and he said, "Oh yeah, someone will be with you in a minute." Then he walked away. I waited a little while longer and still no one came. The waiter who had answered me earlier came back after I waved again, looking for service. He apologized that no one had taken my order yet and offered to bring me some bread while I waited. After a while, he returned, saying "Sorry, there's no bread."

Needless to say, my experience at that restaurant was not a favorable one. The wait staff did not have a *diakonos* attitude! Servants do not wait for a request before they serve. They are intently looking for ways to take care of the needs of others. They anticipate, ask questions, check on the customer, and think of ways to make that person's experience even better. A servant leader is poised to meet someone else's needs.

4. Leitourgos

Leitourgos refers to a servant in relation to the organization that employs him. The term is used to highlight the administration of which the servant is part. This servant works for the greater good of the community. Today, we would describe public servants such as elected officials as *leitourgos*. No one forces these people to serve; they serve at their own volition. Paul, writing to the Romans, used this word to describe himself, saying that he purposed to be "a minister of Jesus Christ to the Gentiles, ministering the gospel of God" (Rom. 15:16). Servant leaders understand that they do not belong to themselves, but to God. They are owned by God, and they do whatever He wants them to do. They go wherever He directs.

This type of servanthood is not burdensome or weighty. Jesus promises that His "burden is light" (Matt. 11:30). We are told that we pay taxes because public servants "are God's ministers attending continually" to God's people (Rom. 13:6). God provides for our needs when we are doing His work. The Old Testament priests (public servants) had their needs met by God. They served the people as God commanded, and God provided for them. Servant leaders give their life to the people they are serving, knowing that God will give them all the virtue and resources they need to serve like Jesus.

JESUS REDEFINES LEADERSHIP

Even in Jesus' time, the concept of leaders serving others was not easily understood. Jesus' use of the word "servant" as a synonym for greatness was contrary to the popular opinion of the day. He taught that a leader's greatness is measured by a total commitment to serve others. Just look at these sayings of Jesus: "For who is greater, he who sits at the table, or he who serves? Is it not he who sits at the table? Yet I am among you as the One who serves" (Luke 22:27); and, "But he who is greatest among you shall be your servant" (Matt. 23:11).

Jesus took the conventional idea of leadership and totally inverted it. He said that people would follow you if you served them. The leadership standard is service. Leadership defines direction and mission, and it sets standards and values. When leaders set service as the standard, they must turn the organizational structure upside down and help other people win. Leaders identify and meet their people's legitimate needs so that others can become the best they are capable of becoming. Our goal is to help people reach their full potential. When we serve, we are paving their road to greatness.

Servant leadership achieves greater results by giving priority to the needs of those being led and served. Servant leaders understand that they are stewards of the resources of the kingdom of God—namely, people. Equipping and empowering people to accomplish God's purpose and plan, and unselfishly serving them in a way that influences and empowers them to grow in a Christ-directed, purposeful manner is servant leadership. To get to that place, one has to make a deliberate choice to serve others—to serve first and lead second. The servant leader must understand his or her self-image, moral connection and emotional stability. Servant leaders are secure in their identity. That is why they can serve humbly. They have nothing to prove. They think, speak and act as if they are personally accountable to all who may be affected by their thoughts, words and actions. Accordingly, they strive to make others great!

TWO KINDS OF LEADERS

I see two kinds of leaders in the world today and in history: the strong natural leader and the strong serving leader. Strong natural leaders are visionaries. They are energetic, action-oriented, always on the move, coura-geous, and they never lack the boldness to do the task. They are more goal/task-oriented than people-oriented. They lean toward egocentricity. Strong natural leaders tend to be intolerant of those who do not measure up to their expectations. They lead with power and ambition, and they usually believe they are indispensable. But they are super motivators.

Then there are the strong servant leaders. This kind of leader is not built by the world's spirit and is not driven by worldly standards. These leaders are different because God's standard is different. The servant leader is a paradox-ical and revolutionary new breed of leader. Whereas the world says that ser-vants don't lead and leaders don't serve, the Jesus-like leader—operating on a spiritual plane, not a natural plane—says that leaders do serve.

Strong servant leaders place:

- Character above function
- Motives above activities
- Humility above promotions
- Faithfulness above success
- Others above self

Strong servant leaders still lead, but they do so with a different spirit. They direct, delegate, preach and teach, but it is all done as an act of serv-ice. Servant leadership lifts people, grows people and loves people. Strong servant leaders have and exercise authority, but they do so with right and pure motives, values and methods that differ from those that character-ize natural leaders. The value that infuses the actions of servant leaders is the cross.

SERVANT LEADERSHIP INSIGHTS

Insights are gained over time through observation, study and practice. These are some of the insights I have learned about servant leadership.

Insight #1

Servant leadership may not be what you had in mind when you first re-sponded to God's vision.

Do you think Elisha knew what he was getting into when he followed Elijah? Look at his response to the call: "So Elisha turned back from him, and took a yoke of oxen and slaughtered them and boiled their flesh, using the oxen's equipment, and gave it to the people, and they ate. Then he arose and followed Elijah, and became his servant" (1 Kings 19:21). Elisha made a radical decision to pursue a life of service. He burned the instruments of his previous profession and followed Elijah. How is he described by his contemporaries? "Elisha the son of Shaphat is here, who poured water on the hands of Elijah" (2 Kings 3:11). Elisha is described as a servant to the prophet Elijah. In today's world, it is not a major compliment to be identified as the servant to someone great when you have your own unique set of skills. But true leadership is pouring water on the hands of someone else. Did Elisha envision himself as the one who served another when he slaughtered his oxen and burned his equipment? Maybe not. Servant leadership is usually not what you see when you begin to glimpse God's vision for your life. Be prepared to put aside your preconceived ideas of leadership and pursue God's idea of leadership.

Insight #2
Servant leadership is built by seeking the greatest good of those being led.

Servant leadership focuses on others, not on the self. Servant leaders do not place themselves at the center, but seek to place others at the center. They do not seek the attention of others, but give attention to others. They never focus on satisfying their own aims or desires, but always look for ways to respond to the needs of others. Jesus demonstrated service through washing the feet of His power-hungry disciples. The custom was for a hired servant to wash the feet of the guests. But if no servant was present, then the lowest ranking guest would do the washing. The unusual thrust of Jesus' foot-washing example redefined the meaning and function of leadership power from "power over" to "power to." It defined power as an enabling factor to choose to serve others (see John 13). Servant leadership is built by earnestly seeking the good of those being led.

Peter encourages all leaders to "shepherd the flock of God which is among you, serving as overseers, not by compulsion but willingly, not for dishonest gain but eagerly" (1 Pet. 5:2). Servant leaders are eager to elevate someone else. Understand that influence in leadership does not come from being overbearing. Influence comes from a servant heart. No one has had more influence on people than Jesus, who "made Himself of no reputation, taking the form of a bondservant, and coming in the likeness of men" (Phil. 2:7). Servant leadership pursues ways to elevate others.

Insight #3

Servant leaders have personal brokenness that makes them approachable.

Servant leaders are humble, gentle, considerate, understanding and compassionate, and many times they are marked by a personal brokenness that makes them approachable and able to be trusted. Many of us are familiar with Romans 12:1: "I beseech you therefore, brethren, by the mercies of God, that you present your bodies a living sacrifice, holy, acceptable to God, which is your reasonable service." As we present our lives to Christ, humbling ourselves, we take on an attitude of brokenness—knowing that we are no better than any other sinner saved by grace.

An attitude of personal brokenness makes a leader approachable. Actively listen to people. Empathize with them. Traditionally, leaders have been valued for their communication skills and decision-making abilities. Servant leaders must reinforce these important skills. Bring healing to hurting people. That is what servant leaders do.

Insight #4

Servant leaders always go beyond what is asked of them.

We find a great example of this kind of service in the story of Isaac's servant, who sought a wife for his master.

> "Now let it be that the young woman to whom I say, 'Please let down your pitcher that I may drink,' and she says, 'Drink, and I will also give your camels a drink'—let her be the one You have appointed for Your servant Isaac. And by this I will know that You have shown kindness to my master." . . . And when she [Rebekah] had finished giving him a drink, she said, "I will draw water for your camels also, until they have finished drinking" (Gen. 24:14,19).

A true servant goes the extra mile—beyond what is asked or required. If you were to go to a restaurant, would you like to be served by a waiter who just takes your order, never fills your water glass, brings out cold food, and has to be prompted to bring your check? Or would you rather have a waiter who attentively listens to you as you place your order, makes suggestions on what menu item you might enjoy, frequently refills your glass, and even packages your leftovers for you in a delicately folded piece of foil or in a container? Servant leaders go the extra mile to make people feel appreciated and special. They don't take shortcuts so that they can take off early. They do the inconvenient so that others can get on their way to their destination in Christ. Go beyond what men ask of you and do what God asks of you.

Insight #5

Servant leadership helps others become more than they could be on their own.

As leaders, we love to have volunteers help us. At City Bible, we could not possibly do everything we do without great volunteers. These people serve the church because they want to help others become something they could never become on their own. We as leaders need to have the same attitude. We serve others to greatness and help them become successful.

In his letter to the Colossians, Paul mentioned such a servant: "Tychicus, a beloved brother, faithful minister, and fellow servant in the Lord, will tell you all the news about me" (Col. 4:7). This man served Paul. He also took the time to talk with the Colossians and tell them what was happening with Paul—something Paul could not do at that time in his ministry. Tychicus gave of his time to visit these people, give a report about Paul's ministry, and even answer their questions. Instead of telling Paul he was on his own, Tychicus served Paul by ministering directly to the Colossians on Paul's behalf. Epaphras is another servant leader mentioned by Paul: "Epaphras, our dear fellow servant, who is a faithful minister of Christ on your behalf" (Col. 1:7). Servant leaders are aware of people. They have insight into the needs of people, and they are committed to the growth of others. They use their leadership ability to help someone else become great.

Insight #6

Servant leaders serve those above them and those below them the same.

Servant leaders will serve where there is no recognition and when there is no pressure to serve. They will serve those under them in the same manner as they serve those above them. Paul writes, "But let these also first be tested; then let them serve as deacons, being found blameless. . . . For those who have served well as deacons obtain for themselves a good standing and great boldness in the faith which is in Christ Jesus" (1 Tim. 3:10,13). Notice that before people were given a leadership position, they were tested. The test was service. Could they serve all people, regardless of station or rank, without bias? Could they serve selflessly? If they passed that test, then they were given a leadership title. But they had already proven their leadership spirit and ability by the way they served.

I mentioned earlier that our church has a great base of volunteers. Many times, when we have openings on our staff, we look first at who has volunteered. Who has given their time selflessly to make the church better? Who has proven that they can lead by serving all varieties of people? Jesus was such a leader. He served the Roman centurion by healing the man's servant (see Matt. 8:5-13). A centurion was a man in a high position of authority. He commanded 100 soldiers. He could offer Jesus protection as He traveled—or maybe give Him some money in return for healing the servant. But Jesus was not after what the centurion could offer. He served the centurion the same way He had served the leper, who was an outcast and had nothing to offer Him (see Matt. 8:1-4). Servant leaders do not consider some people more worthy to be served than others. They serve everyone with equal enthusiasm.

Insight #7
Servant leaders care for the struggling person and the gifted person the same.

We should care for the weak and struggling person just as much as we care for the strong and gifted person. Care for the underachiever, the flawed, and those quiet, hurting people. Jesus' ministry is markedly one that served both the struggling and the seemingly well off. He sat down with Nicodemus—a man who was well educated in the Law and had a high position of authority, yet was still lost when it came to understanding salvation and the new birth (see John 3:1-21). He cared for Zacchaeus—a chief tax collector who was very wealthy. Jesus did not pass by Zacchaeus, but stopped what He was doing to serve a man who seemed to have it all together (see Luke 19:1-10). He cared about Saul—a very gifted leader who was well educated and prominent among the Jewish leadership. But Saul's theology was deeply flawed, and it took a divine encounter with Jesus and the service of Ananias to set Paul on the track to greatness in God's kingdom.

Jesus served the seemingly well off, and also the broken and the sick: "Then Jesus went about *all* the cities and villages, teaching in their synagogues, preaching the gospel of the kingdom, and healing *every* sickness and *every* disease among the people" (Matt. 9:35, emphasis added). No sickness was too small to be treated, and no person was so insignificant that Jesus did not take notice and serve. Leadership is caring for every need in every place.

Insight #8

Servant leadership transforms the way people think about themselves.

Our goal is to get people to think more highly of themselves, not more highly of us as leaders. So we must learn to mentor people; to influence people to be more intentional about their spiritual state; to encourage them to see themselves as God sees them. Servant leaders are like the parents on the sidelines cheering on their kids in a soccer game. At the end of the game, they give their kids a pat on the back and tell them, "Great job! You were the best one out there!" They don't say, "Did you see me leading the cheer? Wasn't I great? I am the best parent on this entire team." No, they lift up their kids and encourage them to develop the gift within them. They point out good plays their kids made and affirm that they are skilled at kicking the ball in just the right place. Those words build confidence and help the kids think of themselves as some of the best soccer players around! Be the leader who helps people see themselves as who they really are in Christ: accepted, loved and valued.

HINDRANCES TO BECOMING A SERVANT LEADER

In Mark's gospel, we read about an interesting interaction between the disciples and Jesus; the conversation relates to servant leadership. Jesus, with these brief words, makes a clear distinction between self-centered leadership and others-centered leadership—and lets His followers know they are to be different from worldly leaders.

> James and John, Zebedee's sons, came up to him. "Teacher, we have something we want you to do for us."
>
> "What is it? I'll see what I can do."
>
> "Arrange it," they said, "so that we will be awarded the highest places of honor in your glory—one of us at your right, the other at your left."
>
> Jesus said, "You have no idea what you're asking. Are you capable of drinking the cup I drink, of being baptized in the baptism I'm about to be plunged into?"
>
> "Sure," they said. "Why not?"
>
> Jesus said, "Come to think of it, you will drink the cup I drink, and be baptized in my baptism. But as to awarding places

of honor, that's not my business. There are other arrangements for that."

When the other ten heard of this conversation, they lost their tempers with James and John. Jesus got them together to settle things down. "You've observed how godless rulers throw their weight around," he said, "and when people get a little power how quickly it goes to their heads. It's not going to be that way with you" (Mark 10:35-43, *THE MESSAGE*).

This passage points out two main hindrances to becoming a servant leader: the self and the sinful nature.

1. THE "SELF" HINDRANCE

Your biggest hindrance is usually yourself. James and John told Jesus, "Do for us whatever we ask" (v. 35). The Greek word used here is *aiteo*, meaning "to request or demand." Someone in a lower position would use this word when speaking to one with more authority—as in a child asking for something from a parent. The word is usually used for a request that will benefit the self. In effect, James and John were saying, "We know it is possible for You to do this thing, and we really want You to do it, but we aren't sure if You will." Then they defined their request: "Give us a position of power and prestige." Sitting on the right and left hand of the person in charge were the two most prominent positions. James and John had been lured into the carnal "power for self" trap. They wanted power "over" people—power to tell others what to do. They wanted Jesus to assign them to a position of authority over everyone else.

James and John's request was not entirely out of the blue. In Matthew 19:28, Jesus told His disciples that they would sit on 12 thrones judging the 12 tribes of Israel. Immediately after that is when Matthew records James and John's petition—although he credits the actual asking of the question to the brothers' mother (see Matt. 20:21). Either way, the request to Jesus was to let these particular disciples hold the top two positions. They were not content with being put in a position of leadership—they wanted top billing! They had the "terrible twos" syndrome: *Me first! My needs! My wants! My desires! My issues! Me!* The disciples' attitude then is no different from many leaders' attitude today. We live in a culture that stresses the individual's need to be more confident and assertive, to fight for his or her rights, and not to let anyone tell him or her what to do. But that philosophy is dealt a devastating blow when it meets the Cross, which says, "Lay down your life for the life of someone else." Yes, we can be confident—but confident in Christ. Yes, we can be assertive—but in pursuit of godly things. If we are going to change lives with our leadership, we need to move beyond our selves and humbly pick up the towel to serve someone else.

2. THE SINFUL NATURE HINDRANCE

Because each of us has a sinful nature, we are bent to a sinful pattern of thinking and living. When we gave our lives to Christ, we took on the Christ nature and began a lifelong project of amplifying that nature within us in order that we might live like Jesus. Even so, we are often hindered from serving like Jesus because of our lingering sinful nature. These are some flaws that must be overcome if we are to be true servant leaders:

- Manipulation: using one's influence through shrewd and devious means in order to gain personal advantage

- Control: exerting power and authority over someone, overpowering and restraining them

- Self-centeredness: putting oneself at the center, as the fixed and stationary point around which all else turns

- Exploitation: selfishly using others and taking the greatest possible advantage of them for selfish purposes

- Strong-willed: being determined to do something one wants to do, or to behave in a particular way, even when there are good reasons for not doing so, including the advice of others

- Stubbornness: being tenaciously unwilling to yield, difficult to deal with, inflexible, unreasonable, obstinate and headstrong

- Dominance: exercising the most influence or control, and maintaining a position of prominence

- Dictatorial: expecting unquestioning obedience; being dogmatic, overbearing and tyrannical

If you observe any of these flaws in yourself, it is vital that you face them honestly and sincerely. Don't excuse yourself or make things look better than they are. Pray, renounce, repent, cleanse and rebuild. Choose to be someone different from who you are today.

SERVING LIKE JESUS

The good news is that you can overcome these hindrances and become a servant leader! It starts with presenting your life as a living sacrifice—and taking on the life of Jesus. You receive forgiveness and you pass on that forgiveness. You receive hope and you pass that on as well. When you begin to live a life like Jesus did, you learn to live outside yourself. It is not about your problems and concerns or what you face. The sooner you start helping someone else, the sooner your problem will get helped. Don't wait until you are perfect and free and have everything together before you serve—it will never happen!

When I started my journey in the Jesus People Movement, I did not know much about the Bible or Christianity—and neither did the guys I was with. I did have a background in Baptist theology, my father being a Baptist minister, so I perhaps knew a little more than the others. One evening, we were sitting in a massive house with about 100 young people who had come to learn more about Jesus—and there was no leader there. We were the leaders and we were not leaders. We were just freshly delivered people who had a past—and who now had a present and a future—and we were talking to a bunch of young people who asked us how our lives had been radically changed.

At that first meeting, I spoke up and said, "Men and brethren," and then read a long passage of Scripture from the *Amplified* translation. I learned very quickly that the *Amplified* translation is the best translation, because it has so much explanation that you hardly have to say anything else. So I would read chapters to the kids who came to our meetings, and that is how I got started with teaching the Bible. Others in the group would share testimonies, and we would pray for people and answer questions as best we could. We had no idea what we were doing, but people were getting saved, healed, filled with the Holy Spirit and excited about Jesus! Out of our weakness came the strength of God. We were still barely in formation, but Jesus said, "I don't need perfect people; I need available people. I'll use you." We had a desire to serve—and from that foundation, Jesus was able to shape us into servant leaders.

It's important that we establish a right focus on leadership function. God has "made us sufficient as ministers of the new covenant, not of the letter but of the Spirit; for the letter kills, but the Spirit gives life" (2 Cor. 3:6). Of course, if there is a right focus, then there is also a wrong focus. Let's look briefly at both.

LEADING WITH THE WRONG FOCUS

Concentrating on:

- Bottom line rather than the horizon
- Mistakes rather than possibilities
- Control rather than confidence
- Reputation rather than relationships

LEADING WITH THE RIGHT FOCUS

Believing that:

- Coaching is more productive than controlling
- Mentoring is just as important as managing
- Strengthening others is as valuable as supervising people's work
- Empowering people is more profitable than employing them
- Creating ownership is more important than your success record

Serving with the right focus is a process that starts with a spiritual experience. We encounter Jesus and are saved by grace. Then a spiritual transformation takes place. We change into a person who lives by grace. We become the person Jesus wants us to become, not the person we in our flesh want to become. From that transformation flow new spiritual desires to live like Jesus. We cultivate love for people and concern for their situations. The next step is in the area of spiritual disciplines—applying our heart and soul to living by biblical principles. Finally we arrive at our spiritual mission—we believe we are created with a purpose. Each of us does have a purpose, and that purpose is to bring God glory.

SEVEN ACTIONS FOR SERVING LIKE JESUS

There are seven actions you should do if you want to take on the mission to serve like Jesus.

1. LOOK FOR OPPORTUNITIES TO SERVE

Pay attention to needs and always be on the lookout for ways to help others. You will be amazed at all the opportunities to serve you will discover around you. Start with the little things. John Wesley said, "Do all the good you can, by all the means you can, in all the ways you can, in all the places you can, at all the times you can, to all the people you can, as long as you can." Do you get the idea? Start with the smallest thing you see where you can move in and help, and go from there.

2. BE WILLING AND AVAILABLE

It is really that simple. Proverbs 3:28 advises us to "Never tell your neighbors to wait until tomorrow if you can help them now" (*GNB*). A willing heart is a moldable heart. You don't need skill to serve. You need feet that are ready to run where Jesus asks you to go.

3. BE GRATEFUL AS YOU SERVE

Consider it a privilege to serve. Don't murmur the entire time you are serving. If you are going to serve, do it with a smile and be grateful for the opportunity you have been given. The psalmist invites us to "serve the LORD with gladness" (Ps. 100:2). Let's serve the Lord and His people with a great attitude!

4. BE FAITHFUL

If you commit to doing something, do it. If you commit to a person, be there. Look at how "faithful" and "servant" are connected in these verses: "Moreover it is required in stewards [servants] that one be found faithful" (1 Cor. 4:2); and, "Well done, good and faithful servant" (Matt. 25:21). A good servant is faithful and always goes beyond what is asked.

5. BE PASSIONATE AS YOU SERVE

Passion is a matter of the heart. It is an internal fire that motivates us and energizes us to fulfill a purpose. If you are passionate about the purpose of serving like Jesus, your passion will show in the way you serve others. I love it when I go into a coffee shop, and the barista is passionate about my drink—when I place my order, and he or she says, "Oh that's a great drink! This is going to be the best one you have ever had. If you don't like it, I'll make you another one." I would much rather be served by someone with passion than someone who lazily talks to other servers while I am waiting for my order.

6. BE FULL OF GOD AS YOU SERVE

Sustained servanthood flows out of spiritual fullness. We need to be properly fueled with prayer, the Word and the presence of God if we want to serve—and keep serving. The Bible exhorts us, "Do not grow weary in doing good" (2 Thess. 3:13). Let's not let ourselves burn out or get drained. Busyness is not godliness! Don't live on the edge of exhaustion. Fill yourself with the Word of God and with Holy Spirit anointing. From that surplus will come the strength to serve.

7. BE READY FOR A SURPRISE

Sometimes we look at service with resentment: It is too hard or we are sacrificing too much. But there is a wonderful surprise in store for those who lose their life. When we step in and choose to live for others and give our life away, an amazing thing happens: we receive life. "He who loses his life for My sake will find it," Jesus assures us (Matt. 10:39). We think we are going to lose our life, but Jesus says we will gain more than we ever thought we could. We will find life in a way we never thought we would. Ralph Waldo Emerson said, "It is one of the most beautiful compensations of this life that no man can sincerely try to help another without helping himself." We rob ourselves of this beautiful compensation if we never serve—if we are unwilling to pay the price sacrificially.

We lead from the inside out. Whatever is in our heart will overflow into the way we do ministry. If your heart is full of love for the church and love for God, then your actions as a leader will reflect that love. Understand that our mission is more than managing results. It is leading, serving and developing people. Servant leaders simply love people and seek to be with people. Walk slowly through the foyer after the church service. Talk, initiate, and show love and concern. Servant leaders will see the need, seize the opportunity, and serve without expecting anything in return. True influence with people comes from serving them. No person had greater influence on the world than Jesus did. He had influence because He put others ahead of His needs and personal desires. People were His ministry, His agenda and His joy. If we want to have influence on others and change lives, we will serve like Jesus.

9

LEADERSHIP TEAMS GUARD THE ATMOSPHERE

As church builders, our vision is to build a life-giving and life-changing church. Every church has its own culture, its own feel—or what I call spiritual atmosphere. The church culture is made up of its members' behaviors, values, beliefs and principles as applied in that local church setting. Together these elements build an identifiable atmosphere in the church. People who are part of the congregation are affected by this atmosphere, and they become its carriers.

Atmosphere in the church is felt more than explained. Atmosphere is a powerful shaper of those who dwell within it, and this is why each church's spiritual atmosphere should be built well and guarded carefully. The spiritual atmosphere is established by the lead pastor and the leadership team. As goes the leadership team, so goes the church. Leadership team members are the primary implementers of the desired atmosphere envisioned by the lead pastor and leadership team.

Atmosphere is a feeling, a mood, an impression, a climate, an emotion, an experience. What do you want people to experience when they enter your church services—your place of creating a specific atmosphere that reflects your biblical values and DNA? A church's atmosphere is built through strategic preaching; strategic structures; and strategic leaders who implement, nurture and work toward the atmosphere they want to see among those they lead.

The atmosphere of a life-changing church is filled with the living and powerful presence of God. This is a church that encounters the Holy Spirit regularly—and has developed an atmosphere where Jesus is the center and hope, where He brings healing and help, and where transformation is always present and possible. We can build an atmosphere of faith, of belief that the supernatural is possible, of lifting up our head to see the mighty plans of God for our life. Let's look at these atmospheres described in the Bible:

> Indeed it came to pass, when the trumpeters and singers were as one, to make one sound to be heard in praising and thanking the LORD, and when they lifted up their voice with the trumpets and cymbals and instruments of music, and praised the LORD, saying: "For He is good, for His mercy endures forever," that the house, the house of the LORD, was filled with a cloud, so that the priests could not continue ministering because of the cloud; for the glory of the LORD filled the house of God (2 Chron. 5:13-14).

> For where two or three are gathered together in My name, I am there in the midst of them (Matt. 18:20).

> When the Day of Pentecost had fully come, they were all with one accord in one place. And suddenly there came a sound from heaven, as of a rushing mighty wind, and it filled the whole house where they were sitting. Then there appeared to them divided tongues, as of fire, and one sat upon each of them. And they were all filled with the Holy Spirit and began to speak with other tongues, as the Spirit gave them utterance (Acts 2:1-4).

I believe that where the Holy Spirit is, there is freedom, as Paul wrote, "Now the Lord is the Spirit; and where the Spirit of the Lord is, there is liberty. But we all, with unveiled face, beholding as in a mirror the glory of the Lord, are being transformed into the same image from glory to glory, just as by the Spirit of the Lord" (2 Cor. 3:17-18). It is possible for anyone to change and find God in their moment of need. This is the attitude of our leadership team; as a result, it is a true felt atmosphere in our church services as well as in small groups, conferences and prayer meetings. The atmosphere is a Jesus-in-the-house kind of excitement: "And again He entered Capernaum after some days, and it was heard that He was in the house. Immediately many gathered together, so that there was no longer room to receive them, not even near the door. And He preached the word to them" (Mark 2:1-2). When Jesus is in the house, things happen—good things!

The atmosphere that develops when Jesus is in the house is one that is full of the Holy Spirit's presence—where the love of God is evident in our words, our worship and our preaching. Luke 7:16-17 in *THE MESSAGE* paraphrase says it so well: "They were quietly worshipful—and then noisily grateful, calling out among themselves, 'God is back, looking to the needs of his people!' The news of Jesus spread all through the country." Or consider this description in Genesis of an atmosphere we should all want: "Then Jacob awoke from his sleep and said, 'Surely the LORD is in this place, and I did not know it.' And he was afraid and said, 'How awesome is this place! This is none other than the house of God, and this is the gate of heaven!' " (Gen. 28:16-17). Surely, without a doubt—absolutely—Jesus is in the house and the Lord is in this place! This is the right atmosphere for any and every church.

Science teaches us that there are five principal layers in the earth's physical atmosphere: troposphere, stratosphere, mesosphere, thermosphere and exosphere. In the spiritual realm, the atmosphere of the church has layers of prayer intercession, praise and worship, the presence of God, hunger for the Holy Spirit, powerful faith, the Word of God, unity, integrity of heart, leaders with godly character, and Jesus in the house. Leaders are the builders and guardians of the church's atmosphere. The leadership team on all levels must implement these atmospheric layers and then protect the atmosphere they have nurtured into being.

GUARDING THE
ATMOSPHERE WITH UNITY

If we are to build an enduring church that changes lives, we must build with the dynamic vital principle called unity. The unity principle is God's weapon against the kingdom of darkness. God is a God of unified order. He created a uni-verse, not a multi-verse. God works from harmony to harmony, and He created man to work in unity. The Bible teaches that God's "hands have made me and fashioned me, an intricate unity" (Job 10:8). We, as the leaders who set the spiritual atmosphere, must understand and honor this vital principle and work to build and guard the atmosphere with unity.

A church with an atmosphere of unity is a place where people harmonize, agree together, cooperate and work together with one heart, one soul, one vision and one spirit to achieve great things for God's kingdom. The Early Church in Acts was a unified church. They met at the temple every day, ate together, worshiped together and met one another's needs (see Acts 2:42-47). It was in the context of this atmosphere of unity that the apostles laid hands on people and released miracles (see Acts 5:12). Chrysostom said, "What we cannot obtain by solitary prayer, we may by unified prayer because where our individual strength fails, there union and concord are effectual." Unity is the core. As integrity is the core of ministry, unity is the core of local church function. We cannot have a healthy and effective local church if there is division within the body.

The atmosphere of unity is the power to overcome the insurmountable and reach the unachievable. Think about the Israelites rebuilding the wall in Jerusalem. In Nehemiah's day, there were no semi-trucks to transport supplies, and no automated cranes that could pour ready-made concrete or hoist massive bricks with the push of a lever or click of a button. The people had to work—hard! We read in Nehemiah: "We built the wall, and the entire wall was joined together up to half its height, for the people had a mind to work" (Neh. 4:6). Not only was the task of rebuilding the wall physically challenging, but the builders also faced verbal and physical assaults.

Many people sought to discourage the Israelites and spread rumors about the leadership. At one point, things got so bad that workers had to hold their construction tool in one hand and a weapon in the other hand. But after 52 days, the wall was built. Nehemiah recorded this testimony: "And it happened, when all our enemies heard of it, and all the nations around us saw these things, that they were very disheartened in their own eyes; for they perceived that this work was done by our God" (Neh. 6:16). The atmosphere of unity releases power to overcome seemingly impossible obstacles.

Unity is the power to reach out and fulfill impossible dreams, increase and release powerful anointing in your life, and win battles against all your enemies. By yourself you cannot do it. If there is division, then you will never do it; but when there is unity, impossible dreams become reality. Unity is the power to see the manifested glory of God.

LEADERS WHO GUARD THE UNITY

The atmosphere of unity is guarded by leaders walking in harmony. If you've been in leadership for more than five minutes, you've probably noticed that there are many opportunities for divisiveness, criticism, or being out of step with one another for a variety of reasons. We must not let any of those things happen. Paul, writing to the Corinthians, begs them to walk in unity: "Now I plead with you, brethren, by the name of our Lord Jesus Christ, that you all speak the same thing, and that there be no divisions among you, but that you be perfectly joined together in the same mind and in the same judgment" (1 Cor. 1:10).

Notice how often the word "same" is used: speaking the same thing, having the same mind, and having the same judgment. Paul wouldn't have insisted on all that sameness if it were not possible. We *can* have unity in speech, mind and judgment—but maintaining that unity requires vigilance and strategic action on the part of the leadership team.

LEADERS ARE SENSITIVE AND ALERT TO ANY LEVEL OF DIVISION

A schism does not just suddenly appear. It is the result of a smaller crack that was not addressed. Long before an earthquake is felt in the home, tectonic plates are moving beneath the earth's surface—shifting, cracking and rubbing against each other. When there is division, nothing seems to fall in the right order. There cannot be health in the local church if there is discord. The divided church will have problems from every angle.

Any level of division has to be stopped. A level of division could be established by a gossiper—one who speaks half-truths or says things that harm another person's reputation without facts. That person is a dangerous person, and if the gossiper is a leader, he or she is even more dangerous, because we have given leaders authority over people—and told those people to follow their leaders. If one or more leaders have a divisive tongue against ministry, leadership or church philosophy, and they sow discord when they lead, then the people who are with them will pick up the same mindset of divisiveness, and they will pass it on without ever proving it or questioning its truth. Gossiping is sowing doubt in the leadership.

If you have a problem with a leader or with a decision, how do you handle it? How do you have clean leadership? The biblical response is to go to the person and talk with him or her (see Matt. 18:15). If someone comes to you with a doubt or a question about another leader, don't sit and listen to the complaint, thereby allowing yourself to get emotionally attached to that person's perspective. Bring in the other party and get the full story rather than half of the story. Go to the source and talk face to face. Leaders must be shoulder to shoulder, mind to mind, spirit to spirit, clean and healthy.

LEADERS ARE SPIRITUALLY READY TO RESIST ANY FORM OF CARNALITY

Call it what it is. If people are commenting about what they think another person did, politely say, "Have you talked to the other person about that?" More than likely, the answer will be no—and you can then respond by directing the commenter to get clarity about the other person's actions by talking with him or her. If you let people continue with their carnality, you are teaching them that division can be handled by hearsay or half-truth. It cannot. It has to be handled by light and truth.

I can't count the dozens of times I have told someone to just talk to the other person—and the response after that discussion was, "I am so glad I talked to him. It was not at all what I thought." The devil works best in darkness. Jesus works best in light. If you know how to bring things to light, it will be hard for the devil to wound you. Any level of carnality must be addressed; it cannot be allowed to gain a foothold in the church or in our leadership.

LEADERS ARE COMMITTED TO WALKING IN HARMONY WITH THE LEADERSHIP TEAM

Walk in harmony with those God has joined to you to lead His church. If something is in harmony, it is in agreement. It fits together. Harmony is bringing together separate parts and connecting them to form a unified whole. In music, harmony is what happens when different sounds are in union. The music we make as a leadership team can be sweet and inspiring to all who listen. Walking in harmony is a decision to love and honor all leaders on the team.

The difficulty lies in the reality that team members who work closely together see one another's flaws, mistakes and carnal attitudes. We can allow a critical perspective to shroud our minds and cause us to begin to see our own team leaders and team players in a negative way. Harboring this attitude in our heart will ruin the harmony of the team. We all must forgive, see the best in those we partner with, and build a spirit of faith for one another. Champion other team players with encouragement, and help them achieve all they can in life and ministry.

LEADERS ARE MATURE AND WISE IN REMOVING
ALL UNRESOLVED OFFENSES

The responsibility to resolve is upon both the hurting and the hurter. "If your brother sins against you, go and tell him his fault between you and him alone. If he hears you, you have gained your brother" (Matt. 18:15). If you have been hurt, Jesus calls you to forgive. If you have hurt someone else, "be reconciled to your brother, and then come and offer your gift" (Matt. 5:24).

Wisdom is needed in this process, because some offenses can be resolved without going to the other person. Sometimes, a person offends out of immaturity. There is no wrong intention; the offender simply acted out of ignorance. Sometimes it is an isolated instance—not likely to be repeated—and affects only us individually. Sometimes, the offense is a personality thing; the person is just different—with different humor, different drives and a different sense of friendship. How they treated you may not be wrong to them. In cases like these, we need to forbear, and we need to forgive quietly. We need the wisdom to understand the other person's point of view, and we need to take an attitude of forgiveness.

A forgiving spirit is the willingness to let go of things you have nurtured for a long time. It is also the willingness to confess—to own up to a fault that is laid to your charge. Francis Schaeffer said, "When the world can turn around and see a group of God's people exhibiting substantial healing in the area of human relationships in their present life, then the world will take notice."

A leadership team with resolved offenses has strong relationships that enable people to work together in a spirit of unity. Team members have less reason to gossip, murmur, criticize or tear down others. This creates an atmosphere of encouragement and positive reinforcement for a unified church. A church with resolved offenses has the capacity to focus energy on serving others, reaching others, healing the broken, and lifting up the downcast.

LEADERS ARE CAREFUL AND DISCIPLINED NOT TO
LISTEN TO ANY EVIL REPORTS

Learn how to process the things people say to you. Be prepared to respond to evil reports so that you do not get drawn into something you should not be involved in solving.

When people come to me with a heavy accusation, I ask them to write it down and sign it. I tell them, "If I am going to confront this person, I want to make sure I have all the details right, so please write down everything you just told me." When people have to put their name on an accusation that is a half-truth, they will usually retract their statement.

Don't listen to gossip. You can be the atmosphere changer who stops division from spreading. Don't listen to evil reports—and don't start them either.

GUARDING THE ATMOSPHERE WITH PRAYER

The leader who guards spiritual atmosphere is a person of prayer who understands the power of gap-standing, hedge-building, intercessory prayer. This kind of prayer stops hell's worst, unlocks prison doors, and shatters the chains the enemy uses to bind his victims. Every leader should have a prayer team. Accountability to a group that prays for you has influence on your inner spirit. Every service I lead is covered in prayer. While I preach, there is a team praying. When I travel, my prayer team activates a larger group of intercessors to pray for me as I travel and speak.

Find the prayer warriors in your church. You as the leader should know how to stand in the gap, and you should have others who stand in the gap with you.

The leader is a carrier of the prayer atmosphere and a motivator who encourages others to pray. Prayer is an atmosphere that is built by strong teaching and strong praying. The leader is to be a strong pray-er. A person strong in fervent prayer is marked by wholeheartedness, passion and a great intensity of spirit. This is not a shallow or lazy type of praying. This kind of praying boils over with red-hot intensity—no lukewarmness allowed. The prayer atmosphere of the church is guarded by leaders who carry a spirit of prayer intensity. This atmosphere lifts up the greatness of God, who gives strength to the weak and upholds those who fall—who makes a way when there is no way. It is the Romans 12:11 spirit: "not lagging in diligence, fervent in spirit, serving the Lord."

Leaders cultivate the atmosphere of prayer first in our own heart. We "break up [our] fallow ground, for it is time to seek the LORD" (Hos. 10:12). To "break up" means a shattering or penetrating—to split something apart. We lay our hearts open before the Lord and cultivate a depth of prayer—engaging our heart, not just our head, in praying with deep feeling. To break up our heart and prepare the self for prayer is a work of labor, intensity and a decisive move toward God. This is the leader's work of sacrifice and perseverance: plowing the heart and doing the work of renovation. The soil of the heart may initially be unfit to produce the powerful prayers the leader needs to pray in order to build a prayer atmosphere. It has to be in you before it can go through you.

God searches for a leader—a real-life person—to stand in the gap, just as He looked in Ezekiel's day: "So I sought for a man among them who would make a wall, and stand in the gap before Me on behalf of the land, that I should not destroy it; but I found no one" (Ezek. 22:30). You as the leader must enter into a covenant to seek the Lord as the people of God did long ago: "Then they entered into a covenant to seek the LORD God of their fathers with all their heart and with all their soul" (2 Chron. 15:12).

We are to be praying people: "praying always with all prayer and supplication in the Spirit, being watchful to this end with all perseverance and supplication for all the saints" (Eph. 6:18). We must be the kind of praying leaders who create and guard this prayer atmosphere in the church. We need more prayer, more God, more power, and more of the Holy Spirit. The Lord wants to give us more of His Spirit. He is the good Father: "If you then, being evil, know how to give good gifts to your children, how much more will your heavenly Father give the Holy Spirit to those who ask Him!" (Luke 11:13). Let our praying be effectual, infused with active zeal and made energetic by the Spirit working in us. Prayer intensity involves depth of feeling, force, power, passion and excitement—and this reproduces itself!

James 5:16 commands: "Confess your trespasses to one another, and pray for one another, that you may be healed. The effective, fervent prayer of a righteous man avails much." Prayer expands one's ability to see what the Lord wants to do. Be the leader who expands the faith borders for all who are under your influence. Zechariah 4:7 depicts the attitude leaders should have: "Who are you, O great mountain? Before Zerubbabel you shall become a plain! And he shall bring forth the capstone with shouts of 'Grace, grace to it!'" Prayer moves the leader from one realm to another. A leader must visualize through prayer and see by faith. Faith that creates powerful praying is the faith that centers itself on powerful persons who believe in Christ's ability to do and do greatly.

GUARDING THE ATMOSPHERE
AS A GATEKEEPER

The church is ours to build and to protect from anything that would erode its health. Leaders are gatekeepers of the church. A gatekeeper stands at the entrance and is committed to keeping out all things that could harm or destroy the work of God. Gatekeepers guard all that God has given to the church. In Judges, we read that Gideon "took the elders of the city, and thorns of the wilderness and briers, and with them he taught the men of Succoth" (Judg. 8:16). With our weapons of prayer, unity and the Word of God, we do as these elders did and stand in our place to guard the house of God and His people. This is a sacred duty and not one to be taken lightly. "For in this trusted office were four chief gatekeepers; they were Levites. And they had charge over the chambers and treasuries of the house of God" (1 Chron. 9:26). Guarding the gate is our charge, our privilege, as leaders. It is not some heavy burden. It is a privilege. David wrote, "For a day in Your courts is better than a thousand. I would rather be a door-keeper in the house of my God than dwell in the tents of wickedness" (Ps. 84:10). People are looking for the opportunity we have to be ministers in God's house! Let's embrace our responsibility as gatekeepers with delight and gratitude that God has chosen us to protect His treasures.

Gatekeepers were responsible for the security of the worship space, both in a practical and a spiritual sense. They made sure that only those who were ready to serve and worship God could come to the Temple and its associated building. The work had to be organized and arranged just as precisely as the work of the priests who officiated at the sacrifices. Essentially, the gatekeepers' duty was to make ordinary people aware of the practical limits of holiness so that they would not enter God's house or presence when they shouldn't.

These gatekeepers were described as able leaders, with the strength and ability to guard the house of God. They were overseers of the treasuries of the house of God and the treasuries of the dedicated items. As church leaders today, we are similarly given the great honor to serve and do all we can to ensure that the work of God is strong and that the people are encouraged to worship and serve in ways that are pleasing to God.

Gatekeepers were assigned to the four directions: east, west, north and south (see 1 Chron. 9:22-25). They were to watch all entry points at all times. Nehemiah was such a gatekeeper—a builder and protector of the work of God, the city, the Temple, the people and the gates. The gatekeepers under Nehemiah had a definite commitment to the house of God: "For the children of Israel and the children of Levi shall bring the offering of the grain, of the new wine and the oil, to the storerooms where the articles of the sanctuary are, where the priests who minister and the gatekeepers and the singers are; and we will not neglect the house of our God" (Neh. 10:39). We as leaders must be committed to guarding the house we serve. We want the Lord's house to be holy, filled with God's presence, and saturated with powerful prayer. The gatekeeper protects the house, all the while being full of God's Word and overflowing with the Holy Spirit.

KNOW YOUR GATE

Gatekeepers know the gates they are responsible to watch over and keep strong. The gates mentioned in the book of Nehemiah point to the gates we as leaders are to protect and maintain today.

- Sheep Gate (3:1)—Shepherding the people
- Fish Gate (3:3)—Equipping for evangelism
- Old Gate (3:6)—Value of unchanging truth
- Valley Gate (3:13)—Trials and suffering
- Dung or Refuse Gate (3:13)—Refining and cleansing
- Fountain Gate (3:15)—Living water of the Holy Spirit
- Water Gate (3:26)—Drinking in the Holy Spirit
- Horse Gate (3:28)—Spiritual warfare
- East Gate (3:29)—Vision for the future
- Inspection Gate (3:31)—Living in light of eternity

We work together with all the gatekeepers to repair and restore all the gates in the church we love. Every leader can be a gatekeeper. As we fulfill this role, the house of God will be protected, and we will see the church filled with God's glory. Psalm 87:2 says, "The LORD loves the gates of Zion more than all the dwellings of Jacob." God loves His house, and God loves all the gates of the house. Be a gatekeeper today and every day.

GUARDING THE ATMOSPHERE BY STAYING STRONG SPIRITUALLY

Strong leaders build strong churches. Strength is God's power and ability imparted to us so that we may accomplish something beyond ourselves—

meeting the challenges and completing the vision God has given us. God commands leaders to be strong: "And let us not grow weary while doing good, for in due season we shall reap if we do not lose heart" (Gal. 6:9). When we sustain our own strength, we are able to strengthen the people of God and other leaders as well. Notice how Jesus strengthened Peter: "And the Lord said, 'Simon, Simon! Indeed, Satan has asked for you, that he may sift you as wheat. But I have prayed for you, that your faith should not fail; and when you have returned to Me, strengthen your brethren'" (Luke 22:31-32). Jesus operated out of the virtue He had to strengthen Peter—and then He directed Peter to pass his strength on to others. Leaders who build God's house and guard the dynamic atmosphere of His church continually give out spiritual virtue. They are suppliers, not consumers. As a leader, you must guard your virtue levels and keep your spiritual flow strong. God commands leaders to be strong!

JOSHUA

Then Moses called Joshua and said to him in the sight of all Israel, "Be strong and of good courage, for you must go with this people to the land which the LORD has sworn to their fathers to give them, and you shall cause them to inherit it. And the LORD, He is the One who goes before you. He will be with you, He will not leave you nor forsake you; do not fear nor be dismayed" (Deut. 31:7-8).

Be strong and of good courage, for to this people you shall divide as an inheritance the land which I swore to their fathers to give them. Only be strong and very courageous, that you may observe to do according to all the law which Moses My servant commanded you; do not turn from it to the right hand or to the left, that you may prosper wherever you go.... Have I not commanded you? Be strong and of good courage; do not be afraid, nor be dismayed, for the LORD your God is with you wherever you go.... Whoever rebels against your command and does not heed your words, in all that you command him, shall be put to death. Only be strong and of good courage (Josh. 1:6-7,9,18).

SOLOMON

I go the way of all the earth; be strong, therefore, and prove yourself a man (1 Kings 2:2).

"Consider now, for the LORD has chosen you to build a house for the sanctuary; be strong, and do it." . . . And David said to his son Solomon, "Be strong and of good courage, and do it; do not fear nor be dismayed, for the LORD God—my God—will be with you. He will not leave you nor forsake you, until you have finished all the work for the service of the house of the LORD" (1 Chron. 28:10,20).

HEZEKIAH
Be strong and courageous; do not be afraid nor dismayed before the king of Assyria, nor before all the multitude that is with him; for there are more with us than with him (2 Chron. 32:7).

ZERUBBABEL
"Yet now be strong, Zerubbabel," says the LORD; "and be strong, Joshua, son of Jehozadak, the high priest; and be strong, all you people of the land," says the LORD, "and work; for I am with you," says the LORD of hosts (Hag. 2:4).

ZECHARIAH
Thus says the LORD of hosts: "Let your hands be strong, you who have been hearing in these days these words by the mouth of the prophets, who spoke in the day the foundation was laid for the house of the LORD of hosts, that the temple might be built" (Zech. 8:9).

BELIEVERS
Finally, my brethren, be strong in the Lord and in the power of His might (Eph. 6:10).

Be strong! Don't give up; don't walk in weakness. Don't allow your virtue barrel to run dry. The church must have strong leaders. As leaders, our concern is not the devil, the darkness of our culture, or the pressures of life and ministry. Our concern is the potential for becoming empty in spirit and having a lack of sufficient virtue—a lack of spiritual overflow. Simply put, we need to be concerned about ministering out of lack instead of surplus. Paul states his spiritual health as a leader in Romans 15:29: "But I know that when I come to you, I shall come in the fullness of the blessing of the gospel of Christ." Paul ministered out of fullness, not lack.

Jesus also demonstrates this principle: "And of His fullness we have all received, and grace for grace. For the law was given through Moses, but grace and truth came through Jesus Christ" (John 1:16-17). Out of Jesus' fullness, He gave to everyone who needed more life, more power, more miracles. We are called to be leaders with a surplus—full to the brim, abundant, overflowing, a fountain filled and flowing out to all.

LEADERS OF SURPLUS

Surplus means having more than enough, extra, over the top. Surplus is the space between yourself and your limit. When you reach the limit of your spiritual resources, you will begin to lead out of emotions. This is a sure way to burn out. We lead as spiritual leaders, leading out of our spiritual overflow (see John 7:37-38).

Surplus can be emptied through a flood of challenging circumstances, crises and pressures. Matters beyond your control can create overload—a continual drain that causes a no-margin, no-surplus ministry. Effective leaders have learned to minister out of surplus not minus, functioning with spiritual flow and more than enough virtue. Diminished leaders never have enough. Plus leaders have just enough. Surplus leaders have more than enough. Super surplus leaders have abundantly more, excessively beyond enough!

Fullness is stretchability. Full leaders have allowed the Holy Spirit to renew the wineskins of their soul, to expand their vision and understanding, to enlarge their hearts and to extend their reach. Guard your heart so that you can guard the heart of the church. What is in your heart will flow into the life of the church, as the Scriptures remind us:

> Keep your heart with all diligence, for out of it spring the issues of life (Prov. 4:23).

> How can you, being evil, speak good things? For out of the abundance of the heart the mouth speaks (Matt. 12:34).

> A good man out of the good treasure of his heart brings forth good; and an evil man out of the evil treasure of his heart brings forth evil. For out of the abundance of the heart his mouth speaks (Luke 6:45).

Your heart is your treasure. It is the measuring rod for all you do as a leader. It's a simple question: How full are you of God, the Holy Spirit, goodness, knowledge, kind words and encouragement? We can't give people what we don't have. The church deserves full leaders.

SURPLUS DECLARATIONS

Be a surplus leader—start today. The church will love you and respond to you (see Ps. 45:1). Here are 11 surplus decisions you can make right now:

1. I will remove all hindrances to receiving surplus (see Pss. 51:2,7; 66:18; Matt. 5:8; Jas. 4:8).

2. I will increase my surplus with God-words and God-thoughts (see Ps. 40:5; Jer. 29:11; Luke 1:38).

3. I will increase my surplus with more of God's presence (see Pss. 16:11; 23:5-6; 31:20; Acts 3:19).

4. I will increase my surplus by renewing my mind (see Ps. 26:2; Rom. 6:14; 12:2; Eph. 4:23).

5. I will increase my surplus with new, deeper praying (see Pss. 19:14; 49:3; 104:34; Jer. 33:3).

6. I will increase my surplus with renewed vision (see Ps. 30:5; Lam. 3:22-25; Gal. 2:20).

7. I will increase my surplus with an overflowing heart (see Ps. 45:3; John 2:6-10; 7:37-39; Acts 6:3; Eph. 3:19).

8. I will increase my surplus with the full favor and blessing of God (see Num. 6:25-26; Deut. 33:23; Ps. 5:12; Eph. 1:3; 3:19).

9. I will increase my surplus by receiving from others (see Prov. 27:17; 1 Cor. 15:3; Titus 2:3-5).

10. I will increase my surplus with more laughter and joy (see Job 8:21; Pss. 16:11; 126:2; Prov. 15:13; 17:22).

11. I will increase my surplus with more anointing (see 1 Sam. 16:13; Isa. 10:27; Luke 4:18; 1 John 2:27).

Surplus is possible and it is for every leader! Let us make room for more of what God wants to pour into us.

LEADERSHIP TEAMS HONOR LEADERSHIP COVENANTS

"Covenant" is not a word we often use today. It is one of those Bible words that seems unrelated to the reality of today's world. After all, who is going to sacrifice a live animal or build an altar out of stones or do some of those other strange things we associate with the biblical concept of a covenant? PETA would be knocking at the church door in no time!

But what does it really mean to make a covenant with someone? The English definition has to do with a bland legal concept of a mutual understanding between two individuals, in which each person binds himself or herself to the agreement with a commitment to fulfill the specified obligations. The biblical definition of a covenant adds a cultural component of symbolic ceremonial acts that are wrought with great meaning, promises and warnings. To really understand the term, we need to look at the Old Testament concept of a covenant.

THE BIBLICAL CONCEPT OF COVENANT

In biblical times, making a covenant with someone was serious business. It was considered one of the strongest bonds between two people, and the covenant affected their lives from that point forward. The first thing the two parties did was to sacrifice several animals, cutting their bodies in half and then dragging the pieces apart to make a path between the bloody carcasses. To begin the covenant-making process, the two men walked that bloody path with the understanding that each person was pledging to give up his own life to keep the terms of the covenant. If either party violated this agreement, his body would be ripped asunder in the same way that the animals had been torn apart. This was not a lightly made promise of convenience. It was a life-changing commitment that carried serious consequences for not fulfilling agreed-upon obligations.

After sacrificing the animals, the men made a series of exchanges—trading outer garments to signify that everything each owned now belonged to the other person as well, and exchanging weapons to signify that all of one's power and strength were now at the disposal of the other. The next step was to cut their wrists and then join their right hands and forearms together in a bloody handshake that mixed their blood, making this relationship one that was even stronger than family—as they were now one blood and thus irrevocably committed to each other. From that day on, the scar on their wrist served as a sign to anyone who saw them that they were not alone, but were part of a blood covenant—so if you messed with one, you had to take on both.

After all of this, the two men sat down to share a ceremonial meal, as their culture believed that eating from the same loaf of bread and drinking from the same flask of wine bound the participants together. Finally, they built a monument to stand as a reminder of their covenant—a symbol of the fact that they no longer stood alone, but were unequivocally bound to another person. Their lives were now dependent upon each other.

So what does a covenant relationship look like today? It is still a deliberate commitment between two people to lay down their lives for each other, to each give everything he or she possesses to serve the other, to passionately defend and look out for each other, and to commit themselves to stand behind each other. It is a life-long commitment to a friendship that surpasses differences that may arise and distance that may intervene.

FOUR ASPECTS OF RELATIONSHIP

How do covenant relationships relate to life-changing leaders? No leader can exist in isolation. A man or woman who desires to be a godly leader must value relationships and be committed to them. Great leadership teams that build great churches are teams that are covenanted together in deep and abiding relationships. Ecclesiastes 4:9-12 states:

Two are better than one, because they have a good reward for their labor. For if they fall, one will lift up his companion. But woe to him who is alone when he falls, for he has no one to help him up. Again, if two lie down together, they will keep warm; but how can one be warm alone? Though one may be overpowered by another, two can withstand him. And a threefold cord is not quickly broken.

There are four types of relationships that leaders should be intentional about developing. First there is fellowship interaction. These are people you interact with in your local church. They are people you know and love, and with whom you share important things in common: a love for Jesus and a love for the church. You join together in prayer, worship and communion. Fellowship interaction is living out Acts 2:42: "And they continued steadfastly in the apostles' doctrine and fellowship, in the breaking of bread, and in prayers."

Second are Kingdom partnerships. These are relationships built around your ministry involvement as you work together with other leaders or other people who are in the same area of ministry. Paul often referred to Kingdom partners—for instance, in the long list seen in Romans 16: Priscilla and Aquila, Mary, Andronicus and Junia, Urbanus, Tryphena and Tryphosa, and others. These are the people you work alongside and with whom you serve.

Every leader must also have personal friendships. These are people you choose to be with because you like them. You have developed a friendship that is built around mutually sharing your lives, with each person contributing to the success of the relationship (see Prov. 18:24; Rom. 12:10).

Finally, there are covenant relationships that are rooted in a commitment to another person and a knitting together of your lives. These are life-long relationships that weather trials, hurts, misunderstandings and change, and they are built on principles of integrity and trust (see Prov. 27:17; John 15:12).

I AM COMMITTED TO COVENANT RELATIONSHIPS

I personally have made covenant relationships a core value of my life, and I have committed myself to cultivating, guarding and sustaining these relationships. It has not always been easy, but I have the deep satisfaction of knowing that I have kept lifetime covenant relationships through the good, the bad and the ugly. It has been a journey of deep sorrow, as I have let some relationships slip by or have been unable to fix some that were broken. It has also been a journey of learning and changing, as I have realized how supremely important life-long relationships are.

The impact of these covenant relationships has changed my life. I have made my most important life decisions based on the value of covenant relationships. At pivotal points in my life, I have been given courage and have been lifted up by those with whom I am in covenant relationship. I have also been hurt the most deeply and discouraged the most severely by troubles I have encountered in my covenant relationships. But I have made a life decision not to break covenant. I will work through differences, fight for the relationship, and do all within my power to keep my covenants.

COVENANT BREAKERS

Before looking at the areas in which we can be covenant makers, let's consider what it means to break covenant. A covenant breaker is one who violates a covenant relationship by spirit, word or actions. As we look at several individuals whose actions are described in Scripture, don't think about people who you feel have broken covenant with you, but instead ask yourself, *Are there any seeds of this in my life that I must root out so that I do not break covenant with others?*

GEHAZI: STEALING REWARD (2 KINGS 5:20-27)

Gehazi was Elisha's servant and betrayed Elisha's trust in him in order to gain a material reward. After Naaman, the Syrian leper, had been healed, he came to give gifts of appreciation to Elisha, but Elisha refused them. As Gehazi watched Naaman drive off, the bitterness of serving without receiving what he considered his just due overtook him, and he chased after Naaman to collect. Instead of getting great riches, he ended up being afflicted with the same disease Naaman had just been healed from. Do you feel your friend is being honored and you are not? Do you feel you are serving and yet receiving nothing for your troubles? Take those frustrations to God and do not allow them to turn bitter within you.

ABSALOM: STEALING LOYALTY (2 SAM. 15:1-6)

Absalom is a prime example of a covenant breaker. As his father, King David, sat ruling on his throne, Absalom stood at the city gate, looking for those who were upset and stealing their allegiance away from the king to himself.

If you have the Absalom spirit, you exploit the apparent flaws or weaknesses of those in leadership in order to garner loyalty to yourself. You listen to people's grievances and hurts, and then use that information to woo their hearts to love you more, to value you more, to seek you out first. The Absalom spirit puts you first in the hearts of the people instead of encouraging their loyalty to the senior leader. It sows discord and disloyalty (see v. 2) and can lead to rebellion against the senior leader, resulting in division.

ALEXANDER: CONFRONTATIONAL ATTITUDE (2 TIM. 4:14-16)

Paul says of Alexander the coppersmith, "He has greatly resisted our words" (v. 15). Alexander fought against Paul and his authority—always challenging everything Paul said and did. He was never willing to work with Paul, but was always confrontational. This is the attitude of "I'm right and I must be heard." There may be times when your lead pastor makes decisions you are not in agreement with. How do you handle that?

BECOME A COVENANT MAKER

God created us with the ability and the deep need to be in relationship, both with Him and with other people. Covenant makers are those who view relationships as something that is life-long, with a permanent commitment. The classic example we see in Scripture is Jonathan and David: "The soul of Jonathan was knit to the soul of David, and Jonathan loved him as his own soul. . . . Then Jonathan and David made a covenant, because he loved him as his own soul. And Jonathan took off the robe that was on him and gave it to David, with his armor, even to his sword and his bow and his belt" (1 Sam. 18:1,3-4). Even though Jonathan knew that David was destined for Jonathan's father's throne, that did not affect his covenant commitment to David's well-being.

MENTORING RELATIONSHIPS

There are four different types of people with whom you make covenant relationships. First there are mentors—the spiritual fathers and mothers who pastor you. This is the type of relationship Elisha had with Elijah. This relationship must be built on respect for the more mature person God has placed in your life. Without respect, you will be unable to receive and learn from their input. You must also have a hunger to learn and an attitude of receptiveness.

LOCAL CHURCH LEADERSHIP TEAM RELATIONSHIPS

The second type of relationship is with other members of your local church leadership team. These are people you have joined with in order to fulfill vision together. For these relationships to succeed, there must be four *P*s in place: principles, performance, process and personality. First, there must be clearly stated biblical principles of relationship and leadership. Good relationships do not happen by chance or accident; they must be deliberately cultivated according to biblical principle. They also cannot happen based solely on a secular perspective of what makes a good relationship, as the world's perspective is flawed and therefore cannot lead to the desired result.

There must also be performance—within the parameters of clearly stated expectations and job description. Sometimes teams grow without purposeful planning. This creates a challenge when a person is called upon to fill a position without knowing what is expected of him or her. In this type of situation, rifts can form in a relationship, as one party can feel that the other is not fulfilling their obligations—yet it is hardly the other person's fault if the obligations have not been clearly stated.

The next *P* is process. This refers to clearly stated procedures and policy. Even if performance expectations are clearly stated, there can be problems if there are not clear guidelines regarding how those expectations can be fulfilled. Unfortunately, it is common to have many unwritten policies in church settings. This leaves a new person facing the difficult challenge of discerning why one decision made was acceptable and another was not.

Finally, there must be a clear understanding of personality style. There are numerous tools that a pastor can use to discern the personality traits of leadership team members. It is good to find one, and to study your team to understand them better. Each person will have strengths and weaknesses. Through understanding your team members, you will discover which ones can work well together, and which ones can better handle stressful situations. This understanding can also help in resolving communication difficulties.

Two leaders were butting heads on an issue, and things seemed to be at a stalemate. As they pondered how to proceed, one leader said, "My personality profile says I am . . ." The other leader immediately responded by sharing his personality profile, and they were able to see how they had been looking at the issue from different perspectives. Armed with that awareness, they returned to their discussion and quickly found a resolution.

POTENTIAL RELATIONSHIP PROBLEMS

In all relationships, certain areas can be a potential source of challenges. The life-changing leader must be aware of and alert to these. Before becoming part of a team, ask yourself if there are any doctrinal issues that might make you incompatible with other members. Something else to investigate before—and be aware of after—joining a team is the possibility of philosophical differences.

Some issues are not questions of right or wrong, but are simply based on a leader's or a church's perspective. You will never be in complete agreement with every person you work with, but there does need to be alignment on core doctrine and philosophy, as well as an awareness of the minor areas of difference. You must decide in advance which issues you can be flexible on and how you will handle differences of philosophy and doctrine without bringing division to the team or the church.

Even if you have studied the doctrinal and philosophical issues, there can still be a problem of inconsistency in leading according to those standards. If this arises, it may need to be addressed—but even in this, there must be a wise approach. Will you allow this situation to break a relationship? How can you address the issues without irreparably damaging the relationship? This requires a great deal of prayer and talking with others with whom you are in covenant relationship to seek wisdom and grace regarding which issues need addressing, which ones do not need addressing, and how to address those that do.

Another problem that can arise is disloyalty in attitude and action. Disloyalty never begins with acts of rebellion; it begins with thoughts and develops into attitudes. Harboring frustrations, resentment, offenses and bitterness will taint your thinking process and your decisions. Carefully guard your thoughts and do not allow negative attitudes to develop, as these can quickly escalate to actions that create disunity and discord on the team.

One source of disloyal thoughts can be judging the actions of others and questioning their motives. When you see someone do something that you believe is not right, it is easy to jump to a conclusion as to why they would do what they did. Everything seems obvious and clear-cut. The action is wrong, and it reveals their heart motives so clearly. Or does it? Remember, God is the only one who can look at the heart; therefore He is the only one who can rightly judge the heart and motive of a person. Do not allow yourself to lose relationship with someone over what you perceive as wrong actions and questionable motives. Remember that you do not have the full picture. There may be factors behind the scenes of which you are unaware and issues at stake that you do not know. Treat the person the way you would want to be treated—give him or her the benefit of the doubt.

Another problem in relationships can arise when one person is praised and rewarded, while you are criticized. You serve as hard as they do and pour your heart into your service just as much as they do, but they always get noticed and praised, and you remain unseen and unheard. Some people get all the face time in the pulpit, while you are relegated to overseeing the custodians. You may work longer hours, sacrifice more of your life, and yet receive less attention than some who seem to give less. This is a breeding ground for offenses and the kind of bitterness that destroys relationships. Listen to Matthew 6:1-4:

> Be especially careful when you are trying to be good so that you don't make a performance out of it. It might be good theater, but the God who made you won't be applauding. When you do something for someone else, don't call attention to yourself. You've seen them in action, I'm sure—"playactors" I call them—treating prayer meeting and street corner alike as a stage, acting compassionate as long as someone is watching, playing to the crowds. They get applause, true, but that's all they get. When you help someone out, don't think about how it looks. Just do it—quietly and unobtrusively. That is the way your God, who conceived you in love, working behind the scenes, helps you out (*THE MESSAGE*).

Never forget that you are serving God, not man. Serve with your whole heart—and refuse to allow the hurt of being overlooked to separate you from the friend who is serving with you.

Let's look back at one sentence again: "Some people get all the face time in the pulpit, while you are relegated to overseeing the custodians." Our Christian culture has been affected by the culture of the world in which we live. We find it very easy to be position-conscious. Some positions—usually the ones that receive more of the above-mentioned praise and reward—are considered more important than others. We have established an unspoken Christian hierarchy. The fivefold ministry gifts are at the top, and the rest of the areas of service fall in place in a descending order of value. Not only can this undermine relationships, but it also is an affront to God, who placed you in the position where you serve. God is not concerned with your title and your position. He is concerned with you and your obedience to Him. Obedience is the first priority, and position is simply an expression of an area of service to which He has called you. Read Matthew 20:25-28, keeping in mind that obedience is the first priority:

> But Jesus called them to Himself and said, "You know that the rulers of the Gentiles lord it over them, and those who are great exercise authority over them. Yet it shall not be so among you; but whoever desires to become great among you, let him be your servant. And whoever desires to be first among you, let him be your slave—just as the Son of Man did not come to be served, but to serve, and to give His life a ransom for many."

The president of a large missions organization had served for more than 15 years in that role when he decided it was time to step aside and allow someone else to fill that position. However, he was not ready to retire and wanted to continue to serve in the organization—so he asked if he could serve in the prayer ministries department. On his first day in his new position, he showed up early and was earnestly at work when everyone else in the office arrived. He had just left his "corner office" position, with all the prestige that entailed, and moved into a much smaller workspace. When his co-workers found him, he had chosen a place in the corner—actually in a closet, set up a portable TV tray on which to work, and was passionately pursuing the vision of the organization to continue spreading the gospel. He was working in a closet instead of a corner office, yet serving with equal passion and fervor as he had when he held the higher position. That is the heart of a servant. That is the heart God honors.

Another problem we can face when serving on a team is overestimating our own abilities and ministry. Scripture warns against comparing ourselves with others, and yet it is a tendency we all have. Unfortunately, we usually come out a winner in the internal comparison, and it is frustrating when those we perceive as having less speaking ability or less pastoral ability are advanced over us. If you honestly feel you have more abilities than are being utilized, go to the person over you and ask them to help you grow in your skills and gifts. Go with the heart of a learner, and ask your supervisor to help you look at yourself more accurately instead of with the great grace we often show ourselves when evaluating our own weaknesses.

One of the most common problems faced in relationships is unmet expectations. Many young leaders look at the Paul/Timothy relationship described in the Bible and desire to have a Paul who will mentor them and lead them into ministry. It's good for new leaders to seek out that kind of relationship; however, the expectations they place on their mentor can be unrealistic. Lead pastors have many needs demanding their time and attention, and it is impossible to adequately meet every need that is placed before them. Even though no offense is meant, the young Timothys may feel disappointed—and that disappointment can lead to feelings of rejection and can result in a huge rift in the relationship. So be realistic about the expectations you place on others. No matter who they are, they will eventually disappoint you in one way or another. Just as a husband cannot meet every need that his wife has, or a wife meet every need that her husband has, no relationship can ever meet your every need. Be patient and allow your Paul to be human, to possibly make mistakes, and to not be able to be all you want him or her to be.

TIMOTHY RELATIONSHIPS

Speaking of Paul/Timothy relationships—the third type of covenant relationship—you will also have your own young Timothys whom God has placed in your life for you to raise up. Serve them and believe in them. Cultivate the relationship and help them to process the issues discussed above as they become part of your team—even as you are processing these issues for yourself (see 1 Tim. 1:1-2,18; 2 Tim. 2:1).

PASTOR AND CONGREGATION RELATIONSHIPS

Finally, there is a covenant relationship between the senior pastor and the congregation. This is a covenant of love, respect and honor, built on a shepherd's heart. A pastor does not lead because of his gifting and skill. He does not lead because of his great oratorical abilities or wise decision making. A pastor leads to shepherd God's people—recognizing that they are God's people, not his own. The leader must love, serve and care for the people as God does—and he must be always looking at what is best for the people, not what is best for his own ministry.

John 10 demonstrates Jesus' heart for His people: "I am the good shepherd. The good shepherd gives His life for the sheep. . . . As the Father knows Me, even so I know the Father; and I lay down My life for the sheep. . . . Therefore My Father loves Me, because I lay down My life that I may take it again. No one takes it from Me, but I lay it down of Myself. I have power to lay it down, and I have power to take it again. This command I have received from My Father" (John 10:11,15,17-18).

TEAM MEMBERS' RELATIONSHIPS

The covenant relationships made between members of a team are vital for the success of the extended relationships on the team. If there are rifts between individual team members, the relationship of the team as a whole is adversely affected. It is each team member's responsibility to work hard to keep his or her relationships strong and secure—to allow no disagreements, jealousy, offenses or hurt to separate him or her from anyone else on the team.

The lead pastor must also remember that the relationships on the team will be influenced by how he or she leads. If the lead pastor models strong relationships, the rest of the team will develop strong relationships. However, if the lead pastor isolates himself from others or struggles with trusting and developing covenant relationships with others, that will be reflected in the team. Developing covenant relationships must be a priority for every pastor and every leader.

TWELVE LEADERSHIP COVENANTS

As you think about the people God has set in your life, consider your relationships with them and the commitments you have made to them. When you make a covenant with someone, you are not making light promises that are easily said and easily forgotten. You are making deep and lasting commitments that will change your life. This covenant will change the way you think, the way you act, and the way you pray. It will change how you use your time, your talents and your gifts. Consider this step carefully before you take it, because it is serious and life-changing. It is also incredibly rewarding. You will experience the blessing and richness of relationships that forever change your life. When you make a covenant today, you are making these 12 promises—these 12 covenants—with those whom God has set in your life.

1. I MAKE A COVENANT OF COMMITMENT

I choose to be knit together with you by a deliberate, binding decision, so as to be joined together with one heart and soul. This is the commitment

Jonathan made when he decided to stand beside and support David, the man destined to take Jonathan's place on the throne of Israel (see 1 Sam. 18:1). It is the commitment of a person who is willing to give up personal ambition and success to serve the call of God on the life of a friend.

2. I MAKE A COVENANT OF FAITHFULNESS
There is nothing you have done or will do that will make me stop loving you. My leadership style and gifting may be different from yours, but I am dedicated to loving and serving you as a person and as a leader. I will be a faithful friend in all seasons of your life and ministry. I will be the Proverbs 17:17 friend who loves at all times.

3. I MAKE A COVENANT OF PRAYER-INTERCESSION
I pledge to pray for you regularly, believing that our God will build a hedge around you—protecting you at all times—and will meet all the needs in your life and ministry. I will be the friend who stands in the gap on your behalf (see Ezek. 22:30) and intercedes for your family, your health, your ministry and your finances.

4. I MAKE A COVENANT OF TRANSPARENCY
I promise to strive to become a more open person, disclosing my feelings, struggles, joys and hurts to you as well as I am able. The degree to which I will share with you implies that I cannot make it without you, that I trust you with my problems and my dreams, and that I need you. I will be honest with you, and I expect you to be honest with me. I will trust our relationship enough to take the risk, realizing that it is by "speaking the truth in love" that we grow up in every way into Christ who is the head (Eph. 4:15). I will use wisdom and love in expressing truth to you (see Prov. 17:10; 29:5; 27:6; 27:17).

5. I MAKE A COVENANT OF SACRIFICE
Anything I have—my time, my energy, my insight or my possessions—is at your disposal if you need it, to the limit of my resources. I give these to you in a priority of covenant over other, non-covenant demands. As a part of this availability, I pledge my time on a regular basis, whether in prayer or in an agreed-on meeting time. I consider that the gifts God has given me for the common good should be liberated for your benefit. If I should discover areas of my life that are under bondage, hung up or truncated by my

own misdoings or by the scars inflicted by others, I will seek Christ's liberating power through His Holy Spirit and through my covenant partners, so that I might give to you more of myself.

I will put aside personal goals and ambitions in order to give whatever is necessary to make you successful. I will not wait until it is convenient to me to serve you, but I will act when you have the need—willingly, cheerfully and ungrudgingly giving of my life to help at your moment of need (see 1 John 3:16).

6. I MAKE A COVENANT OF LOYALTY

I will give you my strength; you can rely on me to be there for you and to always support you. I give you my steadfastness—for good or for bad, I am not leaving. You are stuck with me. I give you my love, not from obligation only, but because of a commitment of love to you. I affirm my trust in you, and if a situation arises that seems in conflict with that trust, I will give you the benefit of the doubt. I covenant to be sensitive to you and to your needs to the best of my ability. If in prayer I discern a need, I will also pray for sensitivity and wisdom in ministering to your need—sometimes speaking, sometimes challenging and sometimes simply praying.

7. I MAKE A COVENANT OF CONFIDENTIALITY

I promise to keep whatever you share with me within the confines of the relationship, so that we can cultivate an atmosphere of openness. I maintain confidentiality not only with regard to the words that are spoken, but also in the spirit and heart of the things shared. If I perceive the need to bring another leader into a situation for your sake, I will first come to you. If it appears that trust has been breached, I will come directly to you so that we can speak with each other and validate our trust in each other (see Matt. 5:23-24; 18:15-16).

8. I MAKE A COVENANT OF RESTORATION

I will be faithful to confront you if you fall into sin or deception, desiring to see you restored to spiritual health and the place God has for you. I will fulfill Galatians 6:1-4 in your life:

> Brethren, if a man is overtaken in any trespass, you who are spiritual restore such a one in a spirit of gentleness, considering yourself lest you also be tempted. Bear one another's burdens, and so

fulfill the law of Christ. For if anyone thinks himself to be something, when he is nothing, he deceives himself. But let each one examine his own work, and then he will have rejoicing in himself alone, and not in another.

9. I MAKE A COVENANT OF INTEGRITY

All of my actions and words to you will be actions and words of integrity. I will never talk behind your back, undermine your leadership, or speak negatively of you or your family. I will not use our relationship for my personal or ministry gain or benefit. Even when my expectations are disappointed, I will not give up my trust in you (see 1 Kings 9:4; Job 31:6; Pss. 7:8; 25:21; 78:72).

10. I MAKE A COVENANT OF HONOR

My loyalty to you will be extended to your family. I will pray for, love and serve them as I pray for, love and serve you. If a need arises, I will do all in my power to bless them and help them to meet that need. I will serve your children as David served Mephibosheth, not waiting for them to come to me, but seeking them out to serve their needs before they ask (see 1 Sam. 20:14-16,29; 2 Sam. 4:4; 21:7; 9:1-13).

11. I MAKE A COVENANT OF VISION

I will partner with you in seeing God's vision fulfilled in you, your family and your ministry. I will believe in your vision and encourage you in the vision, even if it is different from my vision. I will walk in cooperation with you and not in competition—not comparing our visions, our churches, our ministries or our lives.

12. I MAKE A COVENANT OF ENCOURAGEMENT

I will be someone who refreshes your spirit, lifts you up and strengthens you at all times. When you lose heart or become broken in spirit, I will be there to encourage you. I will be an Onesiphorus who seeks to love and refresh you when others are ashamed or embarrassed by you (see 2 Tim. 1:16).

I will be an Epaphroditus to you—a brother, fellow worker and fellow soldier who will minister to you in your time of need and will abundantly bless you when you feel most discouraged (see Phil. 2:25-29; 4:18). I will be a Barnabas to you, giving all I have to be an encourager to you, believing in you when others do not, and standing behind you when others leave you (see Acts 4:36-37; 15:36-40).

I will be careful to watch and discern when you are going through personal failure, when you are going through prolonged battle and warfare, when you are physically ill, when you are under satanic attack, when you are experiencing life's contradictions, and when you have family problems. In those times, I will be there as a covenant friend to "commend you to God and to the word of His grace, which is able to build you up" (Acts 20:32).

PRAYER FOR OUR COVENANT FRIENDS

Father, I thank You that no weapons formed against us as leaders will prosper. Every tongue raised against us will be cast down. Rumors and gossip will be turned aside. Let us dwell in the shadow of the Most High God, and we will be delivered from terror, darts of doubt and diseases (see Ps. 91:5-6). Set Your angels about us (see Ps. 91:11) and no power of the enemy shall harm us (see Luke 10:19).

Lord, let us have a discerning mind to prioritize the precious minutes in the day. Let us discern what is most important and be guarded against the tyranny of the urgent (see 2 Cor. 11:14; 1 John 4:1).

Renew us in the Holy Spirit. Let us wait and mount up with wings like eagles (see Isa. 40:27-31). Keep us holy in every way (see 1 Pet. 1:16). Protect us when we are tired and hard-pressed. Let us be a protection to each other in mutual accountability (see Jas. 4:7). As we draw near to You, draw near to us (see Jas. 4:8).

Lord, I lift up the hands of my brother or sister and their family. Place them in the shelter of the Most High to rest in the shadow of the Almighty. I will say of the Lord, You are their refuge and fortress. You will preserve their family time. You will cover their home. Your faithfulness will meet their financial needs in Christ Jesus (see Phil. 4:19). You will command Your angels to guard them as they travel and win the lost. You have said, "I will be with [them] in trouble; I will deliver [them] and honor [them]. With long life I will satisfy [them], and show [them] My salvation" (Ps. 91:15-16).

11

LEADERSHIP TENSIONS, TEMPTATIONS AND PRINCIPLES

A healthy church has many tensions—and when tensions cease to exist, so too does the vitality of the church. Life and ministry involve all kinds of people with their unique perceptions, concerns and problems. Diversity of opinion and varying cultural and religious traditions make tension inevitable.

Tension is not necessarily bad. Technically, it is "the stretching of two opposite forces while searching for a proper balance." The existence of tension is a fact of life. We must learn to handle positive, God-given tension with wisdom, rather than try to destroy it. This is done by carefully balancing truths that rest on opposite poles of any issue or situation.

Leaders will face a number of different tensions as they lead the church. These tensions are felt on many different levels and in many different leadership teams. There is the tension of whether to place our emphasis on the corporate church or on the individual believer. We must also make decisions about focusing on general or specific ministry—we are torn between wanting to minister to the obvious needs in the local church and community and also feeling called to serve the universal Church. Then there is tension between the desire to be relevant and on the cutting edge and the need to keep doctrinal and traditional roots. Trends are just that—strong interests at that moment. It is important to stay current with the issues and interests of the culture so that we can relate the gospel to people in a way they can understand. Traditions are great, but we should not allow them to impede us from making changes that will help us serve people better.

Of course, we must be careful, in our efforts to communicate the gospel in culturally relevant ways, that we do not distort its message. We might change some lights or décor, but doctrine and principles in the Bible should not be compromised. In making sure we stay true to biblical principles, we as leaders could face the tension of balancing the Word and the Spirit, sound theology and perceived fanaticism, healthy intellectualism and emotionalism. If emotionalism is out of control, we should remember the warning: "If we use all the steam for the whistle on the train, there will be no steam left to move the train."

One defining characteristic of leaders is their ability to see the future—to have a God-sized vision. Because the church follows the leaders as they receive God's vision for their future, there is tension for the leaders between the ability to think and perceive things as the leader and the ability to perceive things the way the average person in the congregation would. In pursuing the God-vision, leaders must balance a faith perspective that pushes ahead with a willingness to rest in the Holy Spirit and allow God to do His part in His time. When we have so much faith for the vision, we can easily try to press forward and enlarge the vision. But sometimes, the church is in a season of needing nurturing and strengthening. People would rather stay where they are than stretch into new levels of vision. We need to be in sync with the Spirit and learn how He wants to lead the church in each season.

Leadership involves managing people. One of the most common tensions I see among leaders is between developing close friendships within the leadership team and maintaining more of a working relationship with co-laborers in the ministry. This leads to tension between leading with authority that earns respect and leading with a sterner, dominating attitude, which could be perceived as manipulation. Similarly, when it comes to discipleship, there is tension between mentoring leaders by using strong guidelines, convictions and principles and encouraging leaders to develop their own convictions, philosophy and ministry techniques. Leaders do need to have people in their lives who can be brutally honest with them and can strengthen their hands in ministry. They must also learn to handle God-given tensions by carefully balancing the truths of God's Word. As biblical tensions are properly handled, the church will be brought closer to a place of maturity.

OVERCOMING MINISTRY TEMPTATION

To promote the highest end of the ministry, the servant of God must begin by examining himself. Plato once said, "An unexamined life is not worth living." Leaders, especially the lead pastor, must continually bring their lives before God and His Word to see if there are any issues that need to be addressed.

> Therefore take heed to yourselves and to all the flock, among which the Holy Spirit has made you overseers, to shepherd the church of God which He purchased with His own blood (Acts 20:28; see also Acts 26:14-16; 1 Cor. 9:26-27).

Along with his or her message and methods, the messenger as a person is important. Leaders can be excellent in their leadership but bring a reproach on Christ and His church with their personal conduct.

Leaders must continually be on guard against spiritual dry rot. Dry rot is a disease that destroys fibers in wood, eventually reducing boards or even entire trees to a mass of dust. Without spiritual seasoning or Holy Spirit preserving, the servant of God is in danger of spiritual decay. It is not always noticeable at first. Spiritual dry rot may take root in every level of a leader's life and ministry. The temptations toward spiritual decay are numerous and devious. We must always be on guard.

Gregory the Great once said, "He who is required by the necessity of his position to speak the highest things is compelled by the same necessity to exemplify the highest things." We have received a high calling—and therefore stand in a dangerous place.

As Martin Luther said, "Prayer, meditation, and temptation make a minister." The longer a person is in the ministry, the more receptive he or she may become to certain hidden temptations. Let us consider a few of the temptations all leaders will encounter sooner or later.

First, there is the temptation to become an administrator of things rather than serving people out of love and calling. One can become mechanical and robotic with the things of God—becoming a professional minister, more interested in the letter of correct theology than in ministering to people. Mechanical leadership can lead to the attitude that one can coast with one's own spiritual maturity—that leadership is equal to maturity. We may become blinded by our own success and ministry accomplishments. Or we could be tempted to function in ministry out of learned habits and legal principles, instead of living out the life of Christ that comes only by abiding in Him. In our hurried daily lives, we are in danger of losing our souls and the secret known by Paul: "To live is Christ" (Phil. 1:21).

Remember these words from Emily Herman: "There is an altar in men—a deep and majestic place—where the soul transacts with its God, and life is cleansed and kindled with unearthly flame.... It is the altar that makes the man."[1] Don't allow the things of God to become too familiar so as to become presumptuous about sacred things (see 1 Sam. 3:12-14). Put a high premium on the presence of God and on the things of God. Don't replace the precious with the lesser or the second best or a less expensive substitute. In 1 Kings 14:26-27, the leaders replaced stolen shields of gold with shields of bronze. Compared to gold, bronze is cheap. A casual glance might show the appearance to be the same, but the substance is changed. Bronze may be of utility to some, but it is a sign of lesser value, a debasing of the highest ideal, a cheap substitute for the best. God gave us His best. Let us do the same.

Leaders face other temptations in ministry as well. They may seek material security as the basis for joy and happiness. They may be tempted to take satisfaction in the failure of another leader. Usually, this is motivated by an ungodly jealousy. Jealousy amplifies our sinful human nature. We are tempted to find fulfillment or success in someone else's shortcomings, because we think their failure makes us look better by comparison.

Sometimes we react against truth because of who proclaims the truth. Or we use people for personal gain, ministry status or goal accomplishment. We might begin to think that it is all right to excuse little sins, habits and shortcomings because of our stress and sacrificial lifestyle.

We can be tempted to become hardened and distrustful toward people because of disappointments and disillusionment. All Asia turned against Paul, yet he ended his last epistle with a statement of love and trust for people. We are called to do the same.

We may also be tempted to evaluate our ministry by worldly standards rather than from a Kingdom perspective. If we measure ministry success by numbers, buildings and budgets, instead of by the spiritual quality and maturity of the people, then we will never be satisfied or fulfilled in ministry, and we will quickly burn out.

I'm sure we all identify with many of these temptations, whether out of personal experience or knowledge of others' struggles. The ministry was never intended to provide us with a safe place or a comfortable living. We are called to the fellowship of Christ's suffering on the cross. Temptations can only be overcome successfully by abiding in the living Christ and eating the living Word of God.

Do not lose heart if you have yielded to some of these temptations in the past. Today is a new day—a day of victory!

*What lies behind us and what lies before us are tiny matters
compared to what lies within us.*
OLIVER WENDELL HOLMES

PRINCIPLES THAT SUSTAIN A CHURCH

The church Christ is building will withstand the attacks of the enemy. The winds, rains and floods will not move the true church from its solid-rock foundation. The Matthew 7:24-25 description of a house built on a right foundation can represent a church built on right principles. Principles sustain a church when emotions or excitement cannot.

Every church wants to be exciting and to stay exciting, but life does not sustain this ideal. Every church has up times and down times—times of revival and times of dryness. When a lead pastor builds the church on principles, dry seasons do not hinder progress. People with principles obey the written Word of God with or without excited emotions. A lead pastor who wants to be on the cutting edge might use hype to keep people involved when emotions are down and the cloud of excitement has lifted, but principles guarantee longevity.

The word "principle" comes from root words meaning "first" and "leader." One synonym is "precept." Precepts are respected methods of operation or guidelines that shape an organization. A principle is a guiding force—a comprehensive and fundamental law, doctrine or assumption. By contrast, a trend is a current style or preference—something temporary. We can never build something lasting on temporary, passing whims of human nature. Styles and trends change constantly with the culture. Principles, however, never change. A method, technique or process of doing something will change from one style of leader to another, but the principles underlying those methods should remain the same.

The principles on which we build the church are based on God's eternal values as seen in His Word. They are an extension of God's character as applied in any circumstance at any time. We get these principles from biblical history and basic theology as presented in both the Old and New Testaments. Certain biblical models—such as the tabernacle of Moses, the

Levitical priesthood, the conquest of Canaan and the training of the 12 disciples—are evidence of these principles. God's principles must become our convictions. These convictions must conquer us and become our value system for living.

It's important to discern the difference between principles and methods. A principle is an extension of biblical truth. Truth does not change. A method is an extension of personality, style, culture and spiritual genes. A method is the way to apply the truth, but it is not the truth. The following is an illustration of this difference:

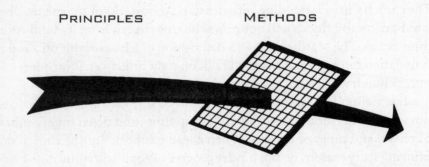

PRINCIPLES   METHODS

As principles pass through the grid of methodology, they may be weakened, strengthened, obscured, changed or even forgotten. We must use methods that are effective and easy to embrace culturally. At the same time, however, we must be careful not to compromise the integrity of truth in the name of relevancy, becoming so overly interested in communicating to our present culture that we end up making an idol out of communication or relevancy.

Leaders must continually evaluate and examine themselves to make sure they are not compromising godly principles because of a passion for success or quick growth. Dependence on methods at the expense of principles erodes the church's foundation and ultimately leaves everyone unsatisfied. We must be wary of trying to make methods better, more attractive and more tolerable to a humanistic, narcissistic and morally relativistic culture.

Leaders who are weak in biblical principles easily become prey to trends and spiritual fads. Truth is sought and applied on many levels, according to the maturity of the church. Therefore, what might seem trendy for one might be truth for another. A church lacking the solid foundation of basic principles has no secure way to evaluate spiritual fads and many other problems.

It is the responsibility of all church leaders to build on the rock-solid biblical principles that have been tried and proven by the Word of God. Leaders should continually ask themselves these questions: *Am I responding to truth or trend? Am I responding to personality or personal convictions? Am I responding for spiritual reasons or selfish reasons? Am I responding cautiously or hastily?* (See Pss. 85:11; 86:11; 117:2; Prov. 14:29; 23:23; 25:8; 29:20.)

Leaders are the helmsmen. Wherever they turn the wheel, the whole church goes. Therefore, leaders are responsible to make sure they are personally on the right biblical track before they fire up the ship's engine and go full steam ahead—possibly right into an iceberg!

INGREDIENTS THAT MOVE THE CHURCH FORWARD

Three ingredients move the church forward: (1) basic Bible doctrines, (2) biblical principles, and (3) methods. Picture a wheel with a hub, spokes and the rim.

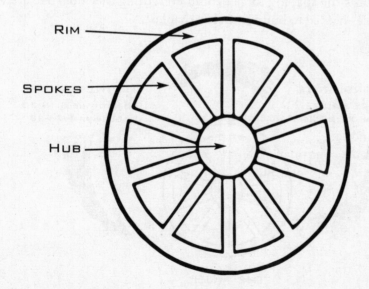

RIM

SPOKES

HUB

The hub represents the theological, unchangeable, basic doctrines of the Bible, which become the foundation for the church's statements of mission, purpose, vision and destiny, out of which all strategies are built.

The spokes represent the unchangeable principles, which become the expressions of truth in the church's principle statements, precepts, concepts and philosophy.

The rim represents the changeable styles, procedures and ideas for applying and communicating truth to the present times and culture. It represents the methods whereby truth is applied.

The leadership team is responsible for understanding the basic doctrines of the Word of God. Neglecting theology will make it impossible to establish strong principles. The stability of the local church is determined by the ability of the leaders to establish strong principles and sustain them in trendy times.

Leadership that builds on principles—rather than on hype, personality or fads—is truly an endangered species. Every leadership team needs to develop a theological motif—an overall emphasis—that may be spoken or unspoken but is the shaping force behind everything they do. Here are eight principles needed to build churches that last.

THE CORPORATE
EPHESIANS 2:20-22
COLOSSIANS 1:24-28

THE INDIVIDUAL
1 CORINTHIANS 6:19-20
COLOSSIANS 1:24-28

THE HUB:
ETERNAL PURPOSE OF GOD
MATTHEW 16:16-18
1 CORINTHIANS 12:12-30
EPHESIANS 4:12-16; 5:25-31

1. THE DYNAMIC HUB
Approach every consideration in this way: Work from the whole to the part, and from the part back to the whole. Remember that the body corporate exists to express the life of God in community, as well as to release and benefit individual believers. Each believer exists to express the life of God, as well as to benefit the corporate good.

2. THE OBJECTIVE RULES THE SUBJECTIVE
Subjectivity without biblical truth is dangerous, because its roots are in us—our experiences, moods, gifting or spiritual biases. Subjectivity can be confused with prophetic feelings or the voice of the inner man, when in reality it is simply a strong opinion, view or desire. We must allow the Word of God to have preeminence in all things. Subjective thoughts and ideas cannot be allowed to prevail.

3. THE CLEAR INTERPRETS THE OBSCURE
The Bible has a very simple, forthright redemptive message. When a teacher or preacher uses confusing types, shadows or metaphors to establish an obscure plan of God, that teacher is violating Christ's model. When Christ established His mission, vision and strategy, He preached a clear message from clear biblical passages.

4. THE MAJOR EMPHASIS RULES THE MINOR
The major emphases of Scripture are easily found throughout the Bible. When leaders begin to slip away from the major truths to focus on minor truths, they run the risk of imbalance and possible spiritual shipwreck. The apostles' doctrine should be the foundation for pastoral preaching and local church theology.

5. PROVEN BASICS COME BEFORE UNPROVEN SUCCESS IDEAS
Many aggressive leaders desire to be innovative and on the cutting edge. Consequently, willingness to take risks and explore new truths and new methods may become a snare to the leader. All unproven success ideas should be taken with a grain of salt. It is better to build slowly with the proven principles of God's Word and proven church patterns than to risk it all in the name of innovation. We need to commit ourselves to God's theological non-negotiables:

- The glory of God is the chief end of all men and women.
- The preaching of the gospel is the preaching of the Kingdom.
- The Scriptures are the only normative authority for believers.
- Sin, salvation and eternal death are eschatological realities.
- God desires all to be saved from sin and eternal death.
- God is the supreme Ruler over His Church—His servants. Everything is done in submission to Him.

6. THE PRINCIPLE OF THE CROSS

The cross is the hermeneutical filter through which all truths from Genesis to Revelation must pass. If you cannot get your truth through the cross, then you must let it go. Anything the cross confirms or fulfills must be accepted as truth.

> Therefore we also, since we are surrounded by so great a cloud of witnesses, let us lay aside every weight, and the sin which so easily ensnares us, and let us run with endurance the race that is set before us, looking unto Jesus, the author and finisher of our faith, who for the joy that was set before Him endured the cross, despising the shame, and has sat down at the right hand of the throne of God (Heb. 12:1-2).

> And being found in appearance as a man, He humbled Himself and became obedient to the point of death, even the death of the cross (Phil. 2:8).

> And by Him to reconcile all things to Himself, by Him, whether things on earth or things in heaven, having made peace through the blood of His cross. And you, who once were alienated and enemies in your mind by wicked works, yet now He has reconciled in the body of His flesh through death, to present you holy, and blameless, and above reproach in His sight (Col. 1:20-22).

The French theologian John Calvin once said, "In the cross of Christ, as in a splendid theater, the incomparable goodness of God is set before the whole world. The glory of God shines, indeed, in all creatures on high and below, but never more brightly than in the cross." The whole Bible looks to and from the cross with an ultimate victory in mind. We might endure our own crosses more joyfully if we could perceive correctly the crown awaiting us.

> Finally, there is laid up for me the crown of righteousness, which the Lord, the righteous Judge, will give to me on that Day, and not to me only but also to all who have loved His appearing (2 Tim. 4:8).

The Bible derives its full meaning from the cross. To leave the cross out would be like taking the sun out of the sky or the heart out of the body. To understand the cross and all its redemptive ramifications is to understand real, authentic Christianity.

Any leader who violates the clear message of the cross violates not just a part, but the whole of the gospel. As we build Christ's Church, we must keep the cross central. Count Zinzendorf, a prominent leader in the Moravian Church, said that he owed much of his spiritual fervor to a picture of the crucifixion with a simple inscription at the bottom: "All this for thee, how much for me." The cross is the fountainhead of life— the message of hope for all nations. It is the key that unlocks true spiritual blessings for the Church. The cross will be popular long after the latest trend, new lights and updated décor fade away. We must teach the cross dearly, continually and passionately.

One reason the cross must stay central is that its message helps us establish a perspective on life in which the self, with all its rights and demands, is truly on the cross—and the Lord Jesus is the center of existence. Sacrifice, surrender and total consecration are a few of the simple but strong truths of the cross—as are suffering, severance, separation, shame and glory. The resurrection life of God could only be released in the death of Christ on the cross. Giving up life opens a new way of living—life in the supernatural!

> But God forbid that I should boast except in the cross of our Lord Jesus Christ, by whom the world has been crucified to me, and I to the world (Gal. 6:14).

> Most assuredly, I say to you, unless a grain of wheat falls into the ground and dies, it remains alone; but if it dies, it produces much grain (John 12:24).

7. THE TEAM PRINCIPLE

When we understand the nature of God, we will grasp the team principle more clearly. God is triune. The Father works with the Son, the Son with the Holy Spirit, and the Holy Spirit with the Word of God. As an extension of that nature, Jesus worked with the 12, and the 12 worked with the 70.

The team principle is seen throughout the Scriptures. Moses attempted to lead and judge Israel by himself, but then formed teams to help carry the responsibility (see Exod. 18). Jesus had a team of 12 disciples with Him to help meet the needs of the crowds and go into cities and villages spreading the good news (see Matt. 10:5-15; Luke 10:1). The apostles formed teams to meet the overwhelming need in the Early Church. They assigned a team to preach the word of God and a team to distribute food and goods to the community (see Acts 6:1-3). Any time we violate the team principle, we violate a principle in the Word of God. Pride would like to elevate one person above another, but the kingdom of God is established on humility—honoring one another. To work as a team is to work with the blessing and wisdom of God.

8. THE BIBLICAL VISION MANDATE

The vision of the leadership team must comprehend the scope of God's plan and purpose. A clear biblical vision should have at least four main elements:

- *The kingdom of God is the mission.* Christ's objective was nothing less than the absolute eternal rule of God in the heavens, on earth, in the human heart and in the Church. Mature Christians are to take the rule of Christ into the home, workplace, classroom and all facets of business. When people catch a kingdom vision, they become excited: *We are taking the rule of Christ to the world!* Kingdom vision produces kingdom faith and kingdom thinkers.

- *The cross and resurrection of Christ are the source of Kingdom vision.* Through Christ come the many supernatural resources needed to accomplish God's vision. Forgiveness, grace, peace, joy and other virtues flow from the cross. At the cross we activate the faith to go into the entire world and preach the gospel. We leave our burdens at His feet and pick up His burden, which is not a burden at all, but the strength and power we need to live like Jesus and share His love.

- *The church is the vehicle through which the Kingdom is established.* The church exists to fulfill God's will. Its mission is to promote the kingdom of God. When pastors and leaders gain a Kingdom mindset, they motivate people to serve and sacrifice.

- *The Second Coming is the motive that keeps the vision sure.* The prospect of Jesus' eventual return brings with it the possibility of rewards and the reality of accountability.

Other areas—such as authority, holiness, the Holy Spirit, commitment and serving, the presence of God, and unity of leadership—are also principles in the Word of God. The wise leader will search out God's principles in all these areas in order to lay a solid foundation for the church.

Life-Changing Leaders
Have a Balanced Ministry

A church can walk in the paths of the Lord only if it is taught properly. Before moving the people forward, leaders need to lay down the track—to chart the course. The church grows as it follows the Word of God. Leaders are to teach God's Word to the people. As Moses instructed Israel, inspiring and stimulating people by teaching the Word of God and laying out His statutes and ordinances, we as leaders today need to instruct God's people to follow a godly path (see Exod. 18:20; Isa. 2:2-3).

Leaders must become people of the Word, totally baptized in the living Word of God and able to communicate it. In 1 Corinthians 11:23, Paul says, "For I received from the Lord that which I also delivered to you." First he received. Then he delivered. To be productive leaders, we must have the ability to receive a word from the Lord and to deliver that word to the church. Isaiah 33:18 asks, "Where is the receiver?" (*KJV*). That question is still relevant today. Where are the receivers? Where are those who receive a fresh word—fresh revelation—by the Spirit of God?

Receiving from the Lord comes as we seek revelation and listen to what the Holy Spirit wants to reveal to us as we study the Word. In 2 Timothy 2:15, Paul urges Timothy to "be diligent to present yourself approved to God, a worker who does not need to be ashamed, rightly dividing the word of truth." Study is work. It is labor. Like craftsmen making something worthy of praise, we must put effort into becoming those who rightly divide the Word of Truth. We must rely on study and research, use proper hermeneutics, and listen to the Spirit.

If we lean on revelation without diligent study and proper hermeneutics, we risk passing over the biblical basis on which the revelation is grounded. Proverbs 27:7 says, "To a hungry soul every bitter thing is sweet." Around the world today, any erroneous cultic doctrine tastes sweet to spiritually hungry people. We need to be leaders who carefully search the Scriptures and listen to the voice of God—instructing, inspiring and stimulating the people with the pure Word of God. Proverbs 25:2 says, "It is the glory of God to conceal a matter, but the glory of kings is to search out a matter." Our responsibility is to do the searching—and let the Holy Spirit do the revealing.

Break open the storehouse of your spirit and bring out the treasure both old and new to feed the people of God (see Ps. 30:1). When you seek God with the depths of your soul, your instruction will reflect the same depth of feeling, thought and judgment. Superficial instruction, routine professionalism and shallow preaching will not move people to the God-vision. Hear the fresh call of the Holy Spirit to study His Word with passion and diligence so that you can proclaim the true, living Word of God—line upon line; here a little, there a little.

PRIORITIZING THE
WORD OF GOD

In Acts 6:2, the apostles wrestle with the problem most of us face today: serving too many tables instead of serving the Word of God. It is not seemly, desirable or right that we should give up or neglect the Word of God in order to attend tables. We must ask ourselves what tables we are serving at the expense of the Word of God. The table of administration? The table of counseling? Recreation? Relationships? All of these are good things, but if the cost of attending to them is neglecting the Word of God, then they will in due season dilute our Word ministry.

Feeding the Word of God to the congregation is the central task and responsibility of all leaders. Every leader should be a person of the Word. The apostles realized that they were not serving the people best by giving them natural food. So they made an adjustment: "We will give ourselves continually to prayer and to the ministry of the word" (Acts 6:4). They knew that their ministry was to serve people by feeding them the Word of God. Sometimes it is difficult to give up a kind of service that we enjoy in order to get back to our primary function. But if we are obedient to God's call, we will find great fulfillment and satisfaction in the ministry He has designed us to flourish in.

We as leaders are called to feed the flock of God with the Word of God:

> So when they had eaten breakfast, Jesus said to Simon Peter, "Simon, son of Jonah, do you love Me more than these?"
>   He said to Him, "Yes, Lord; You know that I love You."
>   He said to him, "Feed My lambs."
>   He said to him again a second time, "Simon, son of Jonah, do you love Me?"
>   He said to Him, "Yes, Lord; You know that I love You."
>   He said to him, "Tend My sheep."
>   He said to him the third time, "Simon, son of Jonah, do you love Me?" Peter was grieved because He said to him the third time, "Do you love Me?"
>   And he said to Him, "Lord, You know all things; You know that I love You."
>   Jesus said to him, "Feed My sheep" (John 21:15-17).

Jesus uses two verbs to instruct Peter about how he is to lead God's people. One of those verbs, in the Greek, is *bosko*, meaning "to feed, nourish or provide food" for the sheep. This speaks of the ministry of preaching, teaching, training and prophesying. The second verb is *poimaino*, which means "to act as a shepherd, to tend the sheep, or to watch over and care for the sheep." This speaks of the ministry of counseling, relating, visiting, loving and caring. The balanced ministry of leaders includes both *bosko* and *poimaino*. We cannot be only a *poimaino* leader and neglect the *bosko*. Nor can we be a *bosko* leader and neglect the *poimaino*. We must combine the two. The following verses illustrate the necessity of balanced ministry:

> Therefore take heed to yourselves and to all the flock, among which the Holy Spirit has made you overseers, to shepherd the church of God which He purchased with His own blood (Acts 20:28).

> Shepherd the flock of God which is among you, serving as overseers, not by compulsion but willingly, not for dishonest gain but eagerly (1 Pet. 5:2).

> And I will give you shepherds according to My heart, who will feed you with knowledge and understanding (Jer. 3:15).

"I will set up shepherds over them who will feed them; and they shall fear no more, nor be dismayed, nor shall they be lacking," says the LORD (Jer. 23:4).

Let us not neglect the ministries of teaching and relating to people. Jesus, our model leader, masterfully balanced both sides of ministry. He taught the people, and then He spent time healing them, eating with them and answering their questions, showing that He cared. The Church is precious to God. We need to feed His people with great care and love—not just by lecturing.

Here are some practical, helpful hints for your Word ministry:

- Do not throw out classical systems of theology just because they are old.

- Follow logical order in establishing your theology, constructing your view with a solid biblical basis. This will have a great deal of influence upon your preaching ministry.

- Establish a proper skill of biblical exegesis. Be aware that your primary assumptions regarding the Word of God will dramatically affect your results. The method of determining the definition of a word in the Bible is the biblical usage of that word—not the linguistic meaning or cultural context only.

- Guard against developing an atomistic approach to the Bible—addressing only certain parts of the Word of God rather than the whole Word of God. Don't stay in a rut by trying to make a whole theology out of one atom.

- Find the necessary key principles of biblical interpretation for the Scriptures you are studying. Take time to use hermeneutics.

- Develop a thorough understanding of what happened on the cross, viewing the atonement, the suffering of Christ, the vicarious aspects of it, the surrendering aspects, and the theological aspects. What really happened on the cross?

- Develop a greater awareness of biblical metaphors and images. Learn how to develop an occasional use of gospel handles. A gospel handle is a text that might not explicitly contain the gospel message, but where you can see gospel principles.

The chief aim of preaching is to lift up Christ and proclaim the gospel. The gospel can be explained and illustrated using Scriptures where the gospel principle is evident, even if the word "gospel" is not mentioned. Learn how to use a single word from a text, such as "mountain," "grace," "law," "man" or "lift." Use a phrase, such as "cut it off," "lift it up" or "pull forward." Or use a whole sentence: "He stayed two more days in the place where He was" (John 11:6). You can preach an entire sermon based on this one sentence: *Why does God delay? Is God late?*

Most of us use Twitter or texting. Those methods of communication force us to convey a message in a very limited number of words or symbols. How much meaning can be inferred from a single tweet? Take the time to pick apart a word or phrase from Scripture with even more intention than you would give to seeking out the meaning of a tweet. Sometimes a text, such as Isaiah 22:23-25, will offer a metaphor we can use in explaining the gospel. Here we see the redemption of Jesus fixed as a nail in the wall—the picture of Christ fixed as a peg. So is the redemptive work of God fixed—immovable. Leaders need to develop an exemplary feeding ministry more than any other gift. The authority to lead is found in the ability to feed.

LEADERS MUST TEACH THE IMPORTANCE OF RELEASING RESOURCES

The fulfillment of every local church dream involves three parts: the leadership, the mission and the resources. A vision does not just materialize. It takes strategy, resources and hard work. Moses was called to the top of a mountain to receive God's vision for the people: a divinely ordered tabernacle for worship. To bring the vision into reality, tangible things were needed: gold, silver and precious stones (see Exod. 34:4; 35:4-9). Or in today's terms: money. Every leader must deal successfully with the challenge that money presents. Some leaders have a vision larger than their finances—they may have great faith for spiritual dreams and visions, but they struggle when it comes to financing the vision.

To shrink back from boldly preaching on finances is to fail at bringing the vision to fulfillment. Paul stated in Acts that he did not shrink back but boldly spoke the whole counsel of God: "For I have not shunned to declare to you the whole counsel of God. . . . Therefore watch, and remember that for three years I did not cease to warn everyone night and day with tears" (Acts 20:27,31). To fail to declare the whole revelation—

including matters of finance—to the church will rob it of divine blessing and cause it to fall short of the divine vision.

We must preach the giving of resources with faith and a proper doctrinal balance. Giving of financial resources is part of the message of the Bible. When we do not proclaim the full message, we cheat people out of the blessing they will receive when they give. One of every seven verses in the New Testament speaks of money. Various reports indicate that Americans spend roughly 50 percent of their waking hours thinking about money—how to get it, spend it and use it. We must give people a biblical perspective on money.

Our enemy the devil is a blatant liar. He tries to guilt-trip leaders concerning money. He questions motives and condemns actions leaders take to raise funds for the work. Yes, there are leaders who misuse money and the people from whom they get that money, and God will judge our hearts and ministries. Most leaders do not misuse people or money, but the devil would like to keep leaders in a place of fear and doubt, so that the vision will stay on the drawing board—unfulfilled and unprofitable. We as God's servants must expose Satan's blatant lies—including the lie that God will take more than He will give. God is not a miserly penny pincher. He is Lord over all the wealth of the universe. He is the Lord of abundance. God is not in the depriving business, but in the blessing business.

Every believer has a financial responsibility before God and the local church to pursue the God-ordained vision. The leadership team sets the attitude toward giving in the church. If the pastor and leadership team display a liberal, faith-filled and joyful attitude toward giving, then the church will have the same attitude. The liberality or stinginess of our attitude toward giving has far-reaching effects: "There is one who scatters, yet increases more; and there is one who withholds more than is right, but it leads to poverty" (Prov. 11:24).

God wants to trust His leaders with wealth and abundance. As righteous leaders with integrity, we never need to stoop to coercion or manipulation of God's people. We want to stimulate and motivate God's people, but we must do it God's way. We must lift up the Word of God as the right way of thinking about money. Here are a few examples of what the Scripture says on the subject:

> Honor the LORD with your possessions, and with the firstfruits of all your increase; so your barns will be filled with plenty, and your vats will overflow with new wine (Prov. 3:9-10).

Give, and it will be given to you: good measure, pressed down, shaken together, and running over will be put into your bosom. For with the same measure that you use, it will be measured back to you (Luke 6:38).

And you shall remember the LORD your God, for it is He who gives you power to get wealth, that He may establish His covenant which He swore to your fathers, as it is this day (Deut. 8:18).

And all these blessings shall come upon you and overtake you, because you obey the voice of the LORD your God (Deut. 28:2).

Thus says the LORD, your Redeemer, the Holy One of Israel: "I am the LORD your God, who teaches you to profit, who leads you by the way you should go" (Isa. 48:17).

The Bible makes it clear that riches are from the Lord. He is the God who prospers us and blesses us for a purpose. Riches are for our enjoyment and for building the kingdom of God. The obvious unabashed goal of many North American Christians is to hoard wealth so that retirement will be bliss. There is nothing wrong with planning for our financial future, but we must make sure that the kingdom of God receives abundantly from our hand now. Billy Graham once said, "If a man gets his attitude toward money straight, it will help straighten out almost every other area of his life." When the people of God are taught to order their financial lives according to the Word of God, blessing follows. We must learn to trust God's ability to meet abundantly all our material needs. We need to set our hearts on God and not on riches, as the psalmist reminds us: "If riches increase, do not set your heart on them" (Ps. 62:10).

Leaders must be confident in God's Word and bold in faith to proclaim it. From that position, they can then teach the people to give in faith and put all that they have at God's disposal. Leaders must also warn the people concerning the misuse of money. "But those who desire to be rich fall into temptation and a snare, and into many foolish and harmful lusts which drown men in destruction and perdition. For the love of money is a root of all kinds of evil, for which some have strayed from the faith in their greediness, and pierced themselves through with many sorrows" (1 Tim. 6:9-10). As leaders, we have the responsibility to teach God's people to abandon selfish ambitions to achieve wealth and prosperity. People must develop a kingdom philosophy—a kingdom worldview. He who lays up treasures for himself is not rich toward God (see Luke 12:15-20).

The kingdom worldview about finances starts with recognizing that Jesus is the Lord over our finances. To acknowledge Jesus as Savior is to make a commitment based on grace—on what He can do for us. To acknowledge Him as Lord is to make a commitment based on obedience—on what we can do for Him (see Luke 6:46). The rich young ruler backed away from discipleship because Jesus would have assumed lordship over his finances (see Matt. 19:16-22). Any concept we teach concerning the lordship of Christ that ignores or slights Christ's right to totally control people's material possessions is superficial and inadequate. Money is a trust from God and must be earned and managed according to scriptural principles.

God is looking for people who will obey His principles of finance and demonstrate to a skeptical and unbelieving world that God lives and "that He is a rewarder of those who diligently seek Him" (Heb. 11:6). The tithe is the foundation for financial blessing in the life of the believer and in the local church. Giving must begin with the tithe. Leaders who move the church forward teach the principle of tithing.

THE TITHE IS THE FIRST OF OUR WAGES AND THE FIRST OF OUR INCREASE

"And you shall answer and say before the LORD your God: '. . . and now, behold, I have brought the firstfruits of the land which you, O LORD, have given me.' Then you shall set it before the LORD your God, and worship before the LORD your God. . . . When you have finished laying aside all the tithe of your increase in the third year—the year of tithing—and have given it to the Levite, the stranger, the fatherless, and the widow, so that they may eat within your gates and be filled, then you shall say before the LORD your God: 'I have removed the holy tithe from my house'" (Deut. 26:5,10,12-13; see also Prov. 3:9-10).

THE TITHE ACKNOWLEDGES THAT ALL WE HAVE HAS COME FROM THE GOODNESS OF GOD

"Beware that you do not forget the LORD your God by not keeping His commandments, His judgments, and His statutes which I command you today. . . . And you shall remember the LORD your God, for it is He who gives you power to get wealth, that He may establish His covenant which He swore to your fathers, as it is this day" (Deut. 8:11,18).

THE TITHE IS TO BE GIVEN WITH AN ATTITUDE OF WORSHIP

"Mary then took a pound of very costly perfume of pure nard, and anointed the feet of Jesus and wiped His feet with her hair; and the house was filled with the fragrance of the perfume" (John 12:3, *NASB*; see also 2 Cor. 9:7).

THE TITHE IS THE SACRED PORTION WE SET ASIDE AS THE LORD'S—IT IS HOLY

"Then you shall say before the LORD your God: 'I have removed the holy tithe from my house, and also have given them to the Levite, the stranger, the fatherless, and the widow, according to all Your commandments which You have commanded me; I have not transgressed Your commandments, nor have I forgotten them'" (Deut. 26:13; see also Lev. 27:30).

THE TITHE IS NOT TO BE USED FOR PERSONAL NEEDS

"I have not eaten any of it when in mourning, nor have I removed any of it for an unclean use, nor given any of it for the dead" (Deut. 26:14; see also Lev. 27:30).

THE TITHE IS TO BE GIVEN AS AN ACT OF SPIRITUAL OBEDIENCE

"I have not eaten any of it. . . . I have obeyed the voice of the LORD my God, and have done according to all that You have commanded me" (Deut. 26:14).

THE TITHE IS THE BASIS FOR RECEIVING GOD'S COVENANTAL BLESSINGS OR CURSES

Look down from Your holy habitation, from heaven, and bless Your people Israel and the land which You have given us, just as You swore to our fathers, "a land flowing with milk and honey." . . . He will set you high above all nations which He has made, in praise, in name, and in honor, and that you may be a holy people to the LORD your God, just as He has spoken" (Deut. 26:15,19; see also Mal. 3:8).

THE TITHE IS THE PROVISION FOR RELEASING MINISTRY IN THE LOCAL CHURCH

"I also realized that the portions for the Levites had not been given them; for each of the Levites and the singers who did the work had gone back to his field. So I contended with the rulers, and said, 'Why is the house of God forsaken?' And I gathered them together and set them in their place. Then all Judah brought the tithe of the grain and the new wine and the oil to the storehouse" (Neh. 13:10-12; see also Acts 28:10; 1 Cor. 9:9,13-14).

THE BLESSINGS OF THE TITHE ARE IN THE NEW TESTAMENT AS WELL AS THE OLD TESTAMENT

"Woe to you, scribes and Pharisees, hypocrites! For you pay tithe of mint and anise and cummin, and have neglected the weightier matters of the law: justice and mercy and faith. These you ought to have done, without leaving the others undone" (Matt. 23:23).

"There is one who scatters, yet increases more; and there is one who withholds more than is right, but it leads to poverty. The generous soul will be made rich, and he who waters will also be watered himself. The people will curse him who withholds grain, but blessing will be on the head of him who sells it" (Prov. 11:24-26; see also Matt. 6:1; 1 Cor. 16:1-2).

Tithes and offerings are part of biblical instruction. Leaders who move the church forward will teach and model the principle of giving resources to God's house. There is no vision fulfillment without resources.

LEADERS ARE INTERCESSORY PRAYER WARRIORS

Leaders are the front line of defense for the people. They build hedges around the church's relationship with God, their finances, their health, their relationships and their future. In the wilderness, Moses was such an intercessor for the people. His father-in-law, Jethro, described the position this way: "Stand before God for the people, so that you may bring the difficulties to God" (Exod. 18:19). Over and over, Moses prayed for Israel, interceding between the people and God. In Exodus 17:9-13, we see him interceding for the Israelites as they battled against Amalek. It was through Moses' intercession that the Amalekites were defeated.

Here is one of the great lessons of leadership: Most of our victories will come upon our knees, not on our office chairs. We must first learn to storm the throne of God before we can storm the gates of the enemy. Well-known preacher John Wesley said, "Bear up the hands that hang down, by faith and prayer; support the tottering knees. Have you any days of fasting and prayer? Storm the throne of grace and persevere therein, and mercy will come down."

Life-changing leaders catch a vision of the power of an intercessory leader! There is no person on earth mightier than one who knows how to prevail with God and how to free those treasures in His hand so that they shower His people with blessing. Intercessory leaders know how to rock the very fortresses of hell and the strongholds of Satan to set the captives free and bring them out into a full and blessed life.

Isaiah 59:16 says that God "wondered that there was no intercessor." An intercessor is one who intervenes between God and others, whether an individual, church, community or nation. Just as Abraham interceded for Sodom and Gomorrah because his nephew Lot was living in the city, so too intercessory leaders advocate the cause of another before God's throne.

We cannot learn how to become intercessors simply by reading books about prayer and intercession. We will never learn to intercede until we begin to pray and intercede. Each of us must have a daily, diligent discipline in the fear of God—spending time in unhurried waiting on God in the sanctuary and learning in the quiet place the wonderful ways of God. There are no shortcuts; we must wait on God. As we wait, God can begin to deal with those deep things within us that hinder the movement of His Spirit. In God's presence, we begin to break up the ground of our hearts. We remove the sins that have been hardening the heart: ingratitude, neglect, coldness, wrong thinking, pride, unforgiveness, slander, lying, jealousy and uncontrolled temper. We remove these by repentance, confession and cleansing. Then we begin to pray with heart—not just head. We pray with deep feelings.

God gives vision, but only as we spend time in the prayer room, waiting on Him. Intercession is not rushing into God's presence with a long list of things we want Him to do for us. Intercession is not bringing our pastoral problems before God so that we can get through with the business and onto something else. Intercession is the slow, painful process of waiting on God and hearing from God—spending time in His presence and being still before Him.

The phrases "praying in the quiet place" and "waiting on God" do not mean that we do not pray with passion. E. M. Bounds said, "Prayer ascends by fire. Flame gives prayer access as well as wings, acceptance as well as energy. There is no incense without fire; no prayer without flame." People of passionate prayer release the power of God and successfully reap the harvest. They are like the believers in Acts, who prayed and experienced a shaking as "they were all filled with the Holy Spirit, and they spoke the word of God with boldness" (Acts 4:31). A heart that is passionately pursuing God is positioned to receive a greater measure of the Holy Spirit, who empowers and shakes us to lead with wisdom and power. Passionate prayer works the impossible and sets new boundaries of possibility.

Intercession is not only spending time with God and understanding God, but also allowing God to put within the leader a spiritual burden for the congregation and for the vision. The pathway of the intercessor is a pathway of pain—not physical pain but spiritual pain. The more you pastor, the more pain you will feel—the pain of people's problems, the pain of poor decisions, the pain of relational hazards, and more. There is much pain in the leadership role. Only through intercession can that pain be turned to forgiveness and released to the congregation.

Intercession also opens leaders' eyes to begin to see clearly the vision for the church. We begin to discern those upon whom God has put a leadership call. We see new strategies for organizing resources to better pursue the mission and reach the lost. We realize that discernment is the mark of a mature church. We see into the spiritual realm as God sees. Just as Elisha prayed about his servant, "Open his eyes that he may see" (2 Kings 6:17), so we must ask God to open our eyes so that we can see the church the way He sees it.

Through intercession, the church is established and becomes a praise on the earth, as described in Isaiah: "I have set watchmen on your walls, O Jerusalem; they shall never hold their peace day or night. You who make mention of the LORD, do not keep silent, and give Him no rest till He establishes and till He makes Jerusalem a praise in the earth" (Isa. 62:6-7). It is through intercession that the anointing of God is released; and it is the anointing that breaks the yoke (see Isa. 10:27). Intercession is the force that touches the heart, moves the hand and changes the world.

It is the first job of leaders to pray and intercede. We are the people's representatives before God. Let us keep our hearts strong in spiritual flow and broken before the Lord so that we can advocate for God's people with power and authority, allowing the Spirit to pray through us.

LEADERS DARE TO DREAM

Hope deferred makes the heart sick,
but when dreams come true, there is life and joy.
PROVERBS 13:12 (*NLT*)

The future belongs to those who have dreams. All great men and women have been motivated by their God-given dreams. People who have a plan and the faith to live out their dreams truly live a life of excitement and fulfillment. God desires to help us develop our full potential and bring into reality our purpose in life. He has a definite life plan for every person, and He protects each of us visibly or invisibly for some exact task. That task will be the true significance and glory of the life that has accomplished it.

Our job is to use our time wisely, as Paul reminds us in Ephesians: "Live life, then, with a due sense of responsibility, not as men who do not know the meaning and purpose of life but as those who do. Make the best use of your time, despite all the difficulties of these days" (Eph. 5:15-16, *Phillips*). The *Amplified Bible* puts it this way: "Look carefully then how you walk! Live purposefully and worthily and accurately, not as the unwise and witless, but as wise (sensible, intelligent people), making the very most of the time [buying up each opportunity], because the days are evil." The only way we are going to fulfill our God-sized dream is if we wisely use the time we have and maximize every moment.

John Killinger tells the story of hearing W. Clement Stone, the Chicago financier and philanthropist, reply to the question, "How have you done so much in your lifetime?" Stone explained, "I have dreamed. I have turned my mind loose to imagine what I wanted to do. Then I have gone to bed and thought about my dreams. In the night, I have dreamed about them. And when I have arisen in the morning, I have seen the way to get to my dreams. While other people were saying, 'You can't do that, it isn't possible,' I was well on my way to achieving what I wanted." This is the awesome power of having a dream: It fuels a burning desire deep within that creates energy—and this energy propels leaders into action.

Leaders with a powerful vision or dream will energize everyone around them. What would you do with your life if you knew it was impossible to fail at what you attempted? God begins every potential miracle in your life with a faith picture born of the Holy Spirit. This invisible idea—this vision—will eventually give birth to a visible, tangible fulfillment. Our dreams and visions begin as undeveloped pictures deep within our hearts and minds—things we can see that God wants to do in the future. The more that leaders feed on the Word of God with understanding, the more focused they become. The purpose of God becomes progressively clearer as they articulate the biblical vision.

Vision creates a bright future, increases our motivation level, and supplies a mighty stimulus to work hard for fulfillment. Vision will start you on the way to your destiny. It seals destiny. As Socrates said, "We have a better chance of hitting the target if we can see it."

THE DREAM, THE DREAMER AND THE FINISHER

To dream is to anticipate what is coming to pass and to contemplate it with pleasure. It is to have a fond hope or aspiration for the future that allows the dreamer to face obstacles with the determination of a winner and to look beyond what is to bring about what should be.

If dreamers want to see their visions become reality, they must set specific goals by which to mark achievement. In fitness, there is an acronym that many trainers and athletes use in setting goals: S.M.A.R.T. It stands for Specific, Measurable, Achievable, Relevant and Trackable. Goals need to be "specific"—they need to be precisely explained. "Ride 20 miles in less than 45 minutes" is a specific goal.

"Measurable" means that the goal needs to have milestones. How many days will it take for you to ride that distance? You might start by estimating how many days it will take to ride 5 miles, then 10 and 15 miles within the given timeframe. "Achievable" refers to the feasibility of your goal. Is your plan attainable given your metron? "Relevant" again relates to your metron. Does your goal match God's vision for your life, or are you pursuing someone else's dream for you? Finally, a goal needs to be "trackable"—you should know when you have reached the goal. Jesus was able to say, "I have finished the work which You have given Me to do" (John 17:4). Paul said, "I have fought the good fight, I have finished the race, I have kept the faith" (2 Tim. 4:7). A dream without action is just wasted thought. Dreams and goals can be attained—with commitment, planning and hard work.

Every leader needs to become like Joseph in the kingdom of God. A man of strength, clear purpose and a clear destiny, Joseph is a prophetic picture of all who dream God's dreams and accordingly pay the price to make them reality. Let's take a look at the progression of Joseph's journey: "Now Joseph had a dream, and he told it to his brothers; and they hated him even more. . . . Then he dreamed still another dream and told it to his brothers, and said, 'Look, I have dreamed another dream. And this time, the sun, the moon, and the eleven stars bowed down to me'" (Gen. 37:5,9).

The days passed, and his brothers sold Joseph as a slave to some Egyptians. When it looked as if he was beginning to have some success in Egypt, Joseph was wrongfully accused of inappropriate behavior with the ruler's wife. He was thrown in jail and left to wonder how his vision was going to become real. But in time, God gave him favor with the leaders of the jail—and of the nation—and elevated Joseph to second-in-command of Egypt. After years of waiting and wondering when he would experience the reality of his dream, Joseph saw its fulfillment when his brothers came to Egypt and bowed before him, asking for food. The Bible records that "Joseph remembered the dreams which he had dreamed about them" (Gen. 42:9).

Joseph's dreams were God-given and his future was God-governed. Vision and dreams many times focus only on the end result—the advancement promised. The tests, pain, trials, sorrow, hardships, delays and disappointments are usually not in the dream. As the saying goes, "Happy are those who dream dreams and are ready to pay the price to make them come true." Joseph paid the price. He worked hard in Potiphar's house and in jail. He was diligent to do whatever was asked of him with excellence. He was committed to the vision for his life that he had received, and he was determined to overcome every obstacle that stood between him and the fulfillment of that vision.

A dream is a mission statement in life—a determined goal that is God-inspired, resulting in kingdom extension and kingdom fruitfulness. The Lord will inspire the heart of leaders with a vision for His purpose. This vision or dream deserves and demands focus—keeping our eye on the goal. We will never accomplish our vision without strong desire. Visualization will fuel the fire of our God-birthed vision.

Our greatest example of a finisher is Jesus: "The author and finisher of our faith, who for the joy that was set before Him endured the cross, despising the shame, and has sat down at the right hand of the throne of God" (Heb. 12:2; see also Ps. 101:3; Matt. 6:22). Jesus could see the goal and He absolutely loved what He was pursuing. Great achievers learn to replay memories of their past triumphs and pre-play pictures of their desired successes. God invites us to call on Him to give us vision and understanding, promising to answer us and show us "great and mighty things" that we do not know (Jer. 33:3; see also Job 32:8). When we pursue God, He gives us the desires of our heart (see Ps. 37:4).

Desire is the starting place of achievement. As you move toward the vision God gives you, surround yourself with wholesome relationships that are in unity with your dream. You can lose motivation for the dream by being around faithless, small-minded and world-centered people, as Proverbs reminds us: "He who walks with wise men will be wise, but the companion of fools will be destroyed" (Prov. 13:20). Dare to reach for the companionship of great thinkers. Invest in good books. In particular, read autobiographies of great men and women who accomplished their dreams—absorb their spirit and the victorious attitudes that have driven them to success. Get inspired by their sacrificial living and their never-give-up attitude. Absorb, absorb, absorb! Read books that stretch your thinking capacity and push your thinking as a visionary.

Leaders need to be dreamers—people of rare gifting for intensity and focus, who will dedicate their entire lives to the dream. We will always move in the direction of our most dominant thought. Use your imagination—that invisible machine inside your mind that has the power to create God-given vision and high-definition pictures of destiny. Let the dream become the dominant passion in your life; allow it to fill every available space within and crowd out every distraction and all adversity. A specific target—a specific faith goal—will allow team members to pull all their strength together toward a unified vision. Remember that "where there is no vision, the people perish" (Prov. 29:18, *KJV*).

Leaders must not only dream great dreams, but they must also make plans to bring them to pass. They need to be finishers. King Solomon, who built the most splendid temple and enjoyed a beautiful dwelling place, wrote these words about dreams: "For a dream cometh through the multitude of business" (Eccles. 5:3, *KJV*). Scripture also tells us that "any enterprise is built by wise planning, becomes strong through common sense, and profits wonderfully by keeping abreast of the facts" (Prov. 24:3, *TLB*). Many leaders have great dreams, but no plans to bring them to reality.

Most people plan more for a one-week vacation than they do for their life journey! Create blueprints for the dream God has given you. God loves a planner; He respects people who think enough of their dreams to create plans for their attainment. Noah had a plan for the ark. Moses had a plan for the tabernacle. "Commit your work to the LORD, and your *plans* will be established" (Prov. 16:3, *ESV*, emphasis added). God cannot bless what you do not plan. Start moving in the direction of your dream, and let God guide and bless your steps.

LEADERS ARE FINISHERS

Leaders are called to be finishers who achieve the dream. So let's rise up today and begin to dream great dreams with God. D. L. Moody gave his sons some great advice upon his deathbed: "If God be your partner, make your plans big!" Let us not give in to mediocrity. Let us not give up in the midst of discouragement or severe testing. As the poet Henry Wadsworth Longfellow wrote, "Great is the art of beginning, but greater is the art of finishing." We are called to finish the vision totally.

Finally, let's turn to one more example of a visionary who finished his course: the apostle Paul. Paul finished without sinking. He lived his dream. He died with satisfaction. He could triumphantly say, "I did my best! I served faithfully!" Paul poured his life out: "For I am already being poured out as a drink offering" (2 Tim. 4:6). He successfully triumphed over obstacles in his race: "I have fought the good fight, I have finished the race, I have kept the faith" (2 Tim. 4:7). He kept the faith in the midst of quitters: "For Demas has forsaken me, having loved this present world, and has departed for Thessalonica—Crescens for Galatia, Titus for Dalmatia" (2 Tim. 4:10).

Through it all, Paul kept his eyes on the true Judge who sees all things past, present and future (see 2 Tim. 4:8). He cultivated a forgiving spirit and did not blame others for his trials (see 2 Tim. 4:16). The secret to Paul's strength was his conscious awareness that God always stood with him. He was never alone! Even as he wrote his letter to Timothy, when everyone except Luke had left him, Paul knew that God was and had always been his companion: "But the Lord stood with me and strengthened me, so that the message might be preached fully through me, and that all the Gentiles might hear. Also I was delivered out of the mouth of the lion. And the Lord will deliver me from every evil work and preserve me for His heavenly kingdom. To Him be glory forever and ever. Amen!" (2 Tim. 4:17-18).

I want to run and finish the way Paul did! Let us all become like Paul in his passion and perseverance in living out his dream.

Success is to be measured not so much by the position one has reached in life as by the obstacles which he has overcome while trying to succeed.
BOOKER T. WASHINGTON

LEADERSHIP TEAMS BUILD
AND SUSTAIN TRUST

We live in a culture of distrust. People have been disappointed by their government leaders, their church leaders and their business leaders. This distrust of leaders, coupled with our society's disillusionment with church and religious institutions, creates a serious challenge for life-changing leaders. A leader cannot lead without first earning the trust of the people—and once earned, that trust must be carefully guarded and protected.

TRUST DEFINED

A trustworthy person is a person in whom others can place their confidence and rest assured that the trust will not be betrayed. A trustworthy person is someone who keeps their word, who fulfills assigned responsibility, and who will not let others down. Trust is the assured reliance on the character, ability, strength or truth of someone or something in which one places confidence. During political races, you would think that trust must be based on the amount of money spent or the number of words and promises spoken, but those things have little effect on trust. Trust is not based on the eloquence of speeches or the greatness of promises made. It is based on who a person is—on the character that they exhibit in their day-to-day lives.

A TRUSTWORTHY PERSON IS RELIABLE

Our English word "trust" comes from a word meaning help or confidence. Trust is having complete confidence and faith in a person based on how they have behaved in the past. Trust relies on someone because they have proven themselves to be reliable. A wonderful picture of trust is an infant lying peacefully in his mother's arms. The baby does not cognitively think about the character traits of his mother, her education, maternal skills and knowledge, or her experience in mothering. The baby simply trusts that the mother who has always cared for and held him will continue to do so.

A TRUSTWORTHY PERSON IS A SOURCE OF SECURITY

To trust someone is to confide in them and to lean upon them for support. A person you trust is a person you can run to for refuge, emotionally or physically, knowing that he or she will be a place of security. As a father, I have heard the trust in my daughter's voice when she calls on the phone to say, "I have a problem." Why does she call me? Because she knows that I will be there for her no matter what the problem is. She knows she can turn to me for support and security.

A TRUSTWORTHY PERSON IS HONEST AND SINCERE

Trust is a firm belief in the honesty of another and the absence of suspicion regarding that person's motives or practices. There is no fear in a relationship of trust. When you prove yourself to be a trustworthy person, others do not need to fear your motives. They do not need to wonder if you are doing one thing now to earn their trust but will turn around and do something different later. They know that how you act toward them now is the same as how you will act tomorrow and the next day and the next.

A TRUSTWORTHY PERSON IS FAITHFUL TO HIS OR HER WORD

Trust believes not only that a person is capable of doing what they have promised, but also that they actually will do it. A trustworthy person does not promise one thing and then do another. As Dr. Seuss says in *Horton Hears a Who!*, trust "meant what it says and says what it meant. Trust is faithful one hundred percent."[1]

We may laugh at quoting a children's book, but the truth of that simple statement needs to be lived every day of our lives. When we say something, we need to mean it. We cannot make promises just to get people off our back or because it is convenient to do so. We need to mean every word—and we need to say what we mean. We cannot couch our statements in half-truths and vague suggestions; we must speak clearly and truthfully. We must be faithful, one hundred percent.

Trust is dependence on both the intention and the ability or strength of someone to accomplish what they say. Can you see a little boy watching his mother attempt to move a couch by herself? He watches her first push and then pull, stop to wipe the sweat off her forehead, and then push again. Finally he speaks up: "I will do that, Mommy." His mother can trust his character—he truly desires to help her, with no ulterior motives; however, she cannot trust him to accomplish his promise. As a little boy, he does not have the strength to accomplish what she as a grown woman cannot do. Be careful as a leader not to make promises that you do not have the ability to keep.

Are you a trustworthy person? Can people rely on what you say? Do you fulfill Psalm 15:4: "They always do what they promise, no matter how much it may cost" (*GNB*)?

Are you a trustworthy person who can be relied upon in all areas of responsibility? When those over you assign you an area of responsibility, do you fulfill all the duties with excellence? Can your pastor trust that if he gives you something to do, it will be done and done well?

Are you a trustworthy person who does not let down those who are over you? How about those whom you serve? Can you be relied upon? Are you one hundred percent faithful?

DEBUNKING SOME MYTHS ABOUT TRUST

TRUST IS NOT GIVEN BECAUSE OF YOUR POSITION

Some people feel that they can earn trust by reaching a position that is respected. If this were true, every president of the United States would be trusted completely. Trust does not come because of a title or a position, so you cannot use your title or position to demand trust. People are not going to trust you simply because you are the lead pastor or the youth pastor. They will trust you based on the proven track record of your character expressed in your daily life.

TRUST IS NOT GIVEN BECAUSE OF YOUR EXPERIENCE

Experience by itself does not make a person reliable. How many stories have we heard of people with great wealth, education or positions of power who were morally corrupt and unworthy of trust? We have all heard the quotation "Power tends to corrupt, and absolute power corrupts absolutely.

Great men are almost always bad men." The point here is not that power is evil, but that the power in itself does not engender trust. The character of a person must first be established; only a person of character and integrity is trustworthy.

TRUST IS NOT GIVEN BECAUSE OF YOUR SKILLS

You may have a great education and talent, and people may be in awe of you and have great respect for your abilities. That does not necessarily mean that they trust you. You can be an awesome orator—the best preacher to arise since Charles Spurgeon or Billy Graham—but that does not guarantee trust. You could be the greatest leader to step forth since Winston Churchill, and people still might not trust you. Trust is not based on what you can do or how great you may feel you are.

TRUST IS NOT GIVEN BECAUSE YOU ASK FOR IT

How often have you heard the statement "You have to trust me on this"? Although it is requested by people from car salesmen to politicians, trust is not given on demand. You cannot go to your Bible study or your youth group and demand that people trust you. Doing so would actually create more distrust than trust, because human nature is wary of those who demand trust. Ken Blanchard stated, "The key to successful leadership today is influence, not authority." You must earn trust, not demand it.

THE IMPORTANCE OF TRUST

Without trust, there will be little teamwork. When people do not trust those around them, they put walls of protection around themselves and filter all interaction through a screen of skepticism. A team that operates without trust cannot accomplish its full potential. There will be a lack of energy and passion, and an inability to fulfill the team's purpose.

Before you think that this could never happen to you and your team, remember that everyone is capable of actions and words that cause people to lose trust in them. Anyone can do things that undermine his or her reliability and dependability. Once that happens, no matter how gifted you are, no matter how right your doctrine is, and no matter how great your leadership may be, nothing can compensate for that lack of trust. No leader can allow trust to be lost and assume that skill, experience or position will compensate for his or her lack of trustworthiness.

BE A PERSON WHO TRUSTS

A vital foundation to earning others' trust is to exhibit trust-producing behaviors. The more a leader demonstrates trust in others, the more others will place their trust in him or her. Creating an environment of mutual trust is critical to true leadership. We must aim to be trustworthy. We must also be willing to risk trusting other people—to be vulnerable to having our trust betrayed and yet be willing to take that chance. We cannot earn trust without giving trust. So where must our trust lie?

TRUST BETWEEN YOU AND GOD

All trust begins between you and God. Trust is the vital element in the very beginning of each believer's life in Christ. We believe in—or trust—Jesus, and it is that trust that enables us to claim God's promise of salvation. Trust involves heartfelt confidence in God, leaning on God, and resting in God. It is giving to God our present problems and our future plans.

Our experience of placing our trust in God should increase our capacity to trust others and should encourage us to build trust within our relationships. Proverbs 3:5-6 declares, "Trust in the LORD with all your heart, and lean not on your own understanding; in all your ways acknowledge Him, and He shall direct your paths." You can trust completely and wholeheartedly because your trust is placed in One who is completely trustworthy. Psalm 18:30 promises, "As for God, His way is perfect; the word of the LORD is proven; He is a shield to all who trust in Him" (see also Job 13:15; Ps. 26:1).

TRUST AMONG LEADERS

Trust among leaders is based on the shared values the leaders adhere to and the relationships they build with one another over time. Trust is the glue that holds those relationships together; when trust is violated, the relationships break down. A united team is a team that is built on trust. This trust must be intentionally cultivated. Putting leaders in a room together and calling them a team does not make them trust one another. Trust must be built over time; it is developed in the context of shared life experiences and demonstrations of trustworthiness. A leader must work with his team and build trust among them.

TRUST BETWEEN LEADERS AND FOLLOWERS

Followers trust leaders when they believe that they will not be taken advantage of or betrayed by the leader, and that they will not be abused because of their trust in the leader. A common complaint about untrustworthy leaders is that they were "fleecing the flock"—taking from their followers for their own benefit. In contrast, we see Paul asking the Corinthians: "Did I take advantage of you by any of those whom I sent to you?" (2 Cor. 12:17). He reminds them how he came, not for their possessions, but for them—to serve them and love them—comparing himself to a parent who gives everything for the benefit of his children (see vv. 14-21).

As a leader, you must prove yourself trustworthy before others will feel secure placing their trust in you. You must be looking out for their best, not your own. Seek to do what is best for the people, not what builds your own ministry. There is a reason God called those who lead His people "shepherds." A shepherd's focus is to nurture and care for the sheep, not to rule over them. A trustworthy leader will nurture and care for the people, building trust between himself and them.

That trust must go both ways. You must trust your people if you expect them to trust you. You must believe the best of them and give them the benefit of the doubt instead of questioning their motives. Believe in them and their dreams, and encourage them. A trustworthy leader can never allow an "us versus them" mentality to arise between themselves and the people they lead. Instead there must be mutual trust and mutual respect.

TRUST BETWEEN LEADERS AND THE CHURCH

When leaders trust the church as an organization to be caring and to watch out for them, the relationship is productive and positive. Here I am differentiating between the church as the people of God and the church as an organization. There are those who serve the church body while receiving a salary from the church entity, and there are those who serve the church body in a volunteer capacity.

It is important for a church administration to operate honorably in their interactions with all their staff, both paid and volunteer. They must serve their staff just as the staff serves the church, and they must look out for their best interests. In 1 Timothy 5:18, Paul cites the Old Testament principle of not muzzling the ox while it is treading the grain. The church entity must care for those who serve and support them in their ministry.

TRUST BETWEEN FOLLOWERS AND THE CHURCH

The congregation—those who believe in and love the church—must have trust in the church's doctrines and leadership integrity, and in how the church will handle people in all walks of life. The leaders must demonstrate integrity in all their interactions with and relating to the church, and they must act with consistency. Inconsistent leadership breeds insecurity in the people and creates distrust. Leaders must lead with care and wisdom. It is easy to think that the people will forgive one mistake, one unwise decision or one error in judgment. Even when there is forgiveness, the long-term impact cannot be avoided. Mistakes, whether large or small, lead to a distrust of the leader's ability or wisdom or character. A breach in relationship can be created by one mistake, but it takes more than one good decision to repair the damage. So be careful, get counsel, pray earnestly, and walk prudently.

TRUST IN THE FUTURE

Trust requires a forward, hopeful view of future possibilities, not a backward view of past differences. Forgive the past. One of my assistants used to joke that if I ever learned to count past "one" when enumerating her mistakes, she would be in trouble. Counting other people's mistakes and always remembering their past are practices that breed distrust. They create an atmosphere in which people are hesitant, unsure and mistrusting. Learn to forgive people's mistakes and look forward to the potential of what they can be.

This focus on the future does not apply only to individual relationships, but also to the call of God on your life. You must trust God with your future plans, turning every area of your life over to Him. You cannot live in the past, contemplating what would have happened if you had made different decisions. Neither can you live wishing to return to the past, when things were different and better. Trust requires you to adapt to change. Perhaps your leaders have moved you to a different position that you feel hesitant about. Maybe doors you thought would open have remained locked. Do not dwell on it.

Look ahead to the future. Trust God's hand in your life. You may only see how you were wronged in the past—how others mistreated you or misused you, how someone else took the recognition for something you accomplished, or how someone undermined what you had built—but you cannot look back at those things with regret, resentment or bitterness. Look instead to God. You may see the past through the lens of others' mistreatment of you, but instead look at it through the eyes of God, with a focus on what He is building in and through you. Trust God who is working through the past and leading you toward a new future.

THE TRUST POWER OF LEADERSHIP

First Corinthians 4:1-2 states, "Let a man so consider us, as servants of Christ and stewards of the mysteries of God. Moreover it is required in stewards that one be found faithful." Faithfulness and trustworthiness are required in leaders. To establish oneself as trustworthy and build trust with others, three things are needed: character, communication and respect.

LEADERSHIP CHARACTER THAT BUILDS TRUST

A trustworthy leader must have integrity. When there is a gap between what people anticipate and what actually happens, distrust begins to arise. There must be honesty in a leader's words and consistency in a leader's actions. If the leader makes a quick decision, and then changes his mind the next day and revokes that decision, it raises questions in the people's minds. A trustworthy leader must never betray the trust invested in them by duplicity or instability.

A trustworthy leader must be honest and open. The people must have confidence that they can take a leader's words at face value and be assured that the leader has both the ability and the intention to fulfill his promises. There must be straightforwardness, not ambiguity, from the leader.

A trustworthy leader must be truthful. Leaders must be accurate in everything they say, not misleading others either through omitting or adding to the truth. They must always present things with an authentic and genuine perspective. Edwin Dummer stated, "Man's life would be wretched and confined if it were to miss the candid intimacy developed by mutual trust and esteem."

A trustworthy leader must keep his or her promises. Trust is built on kept promises and is destroyed by broken promises. People must be able to depend upon their leader, knowing that he or she will be faithful to do all that was promised.

A trustworthy leader is consistent. Trust takes time to build through visible actions, true words and reliable behavior repeated over and over. It is built on predictability. Leaders who are dependable and consistent in their leadership will find that those they lead are secure and confident. Crises do not faze them because they have seen the leaders' proven track record and are reassured of a positive outcome to the situation.

A trustworthy leader delegates well. Leaders should use delegation as a tool to train others and increase their skills and abilities. They need to know when and how to hand over responsibility to others and let them grow through the experience. A trustworthy leader never takes others' success and credits it to him- or herself; instead, he or she is quick to offer praise and acknowledgement for a job well done, awarding others for their responsibility.

The tendency of many leaders is not to delegate as much as they should, but to do things themselves so that they can make sure everything is done "right." A trustworthy leader has learned to trust those he or she manages and allow them to grow in their responsibility—not micro-managing, but carefully guiding and training. When a leader delegates, he or she needs to make sure not to delegate only the unwanted tasks but also those areas that are challenging and enjoyable.

LEADERSHIP COMMUNICATION THAT BUILDS TRUST

A trustworthy leader builds trust by creating a culture of transparency. Transparency creates openness, and openness precedes trust. Openness is created when you expose your vulnerabilities and trust people not to take advantage of you or use that vulnerability against you. This must be done carefully and wisely. Complete openness in all areas of your life is not possible, nor is it wise. You must be strategically open in the areas where you are attempting to garner trust.

A trustworthy leader builds trust through straight talk. People need to know where they stand with you. If your staff or leadership team is always guessing about what your position is and what you really mean by your statements, it will breed insecurity in the team and weaken its effectiveness. You need to speak clearly and with purpose. There can be no question when you finish as to what you meant to communicate. It is a good idea to end a conversation with a one- or two-sentence summary of your main point for those listening to take away with them. If they forget everything else that was said, those two sentences can govern their actions because they were stated simply and pointedly.

This does not mean being abrupt and rude; some people use the excuse of "straight talk" to justify communicating harshly. That is not talking straight; it is using your tongue to create hurt. Talking straight is to speak simply and to the point with graciousness. The attitude behind straight talking must always be one of grace, applying Colossians 4:6: "Be gracious in your speech. The goal is to bring out the best in others in a conversation, not put them down, not cut them out" (*THE MESSAGE*).

A trustworthy leader builds trust by asking for others' input. Show your respect for others by asking them for their perspective. Give them ownership in the process by allowing them to speak into it. When they do, do not simply shrug off their comments or refute them as not practical or applicable, but listen carefully and ask questions. An idea you initially set aside as not being helpful may be applied later in the process to accentuate your plan. Never write off an idea at the outset. Give it time. Listening to others—really listening to understand—will create a spirit of trust.

A trustworthy leader builds trust by sharing information. Give honest feedback to others, but give it respectfully and graciously. Do not approach them with a judgmental or critical attitude, but speak with sincerity and respect. Also, learn how to share your thought process as you make decisions. There needs to be wisdom and balance in what you communicate and to whom you communicate, but letting your leaders be part of the process will help them to trust the final decision and to take ownership of it.

We were looking for a building to house our second campus—something on the west side of the city, about 30 minutes away from our main campus. This was not a light decision; we were taking it very seriously and proceeding very cautiously. The eldership team discussed the matter thoroughly and then took the issue to our larger church leadership team. We clearly communicated the vision, the need and the available opportunities, and we asked team members for their prayer and for their input—and they gave it. When a property opened up that fit our needs, the leadership team passionately stepped in to see the vision accomplished and the building readied for a new service. They did so because they had been part of the process. They had watched the search for a building take place and had prayed over the potential opportunities. When a decision was made, they had already taken ownership of the vision and were one hundred percent on board.

A trustworthy leader builds trust by admitting when he or she makes mistakes. Reality check—people usually know when you have made a mistake, so hiding it only makes them wonder what else you are concealing. John Maxwell stated, "A man must be big enough to admit his mistakes, smart enough to profit from them, and strong enough to correct them."

Making mistakes is a normal part of life; everyone makes them. Unfortunately many of us are insecure enough that we try to hide our mistakes so we can appear perfect. The problem is that we aren't perfect—and everyone knows it except us. When the Duke of Wellington was informed of a mistake he had made, his adamant reply was: "There is no mistake; there has been no mistake; and there shall be no mistake." The best way to build trust is not to adamantly proclaim that there is no such thing as a mistake, but to admit the mistake, learn from it, and move forward.

A trustworthy leader builds trust by maintaining confidentiality. Do people feel comfortable confiding in you? If they tell you something, can they know that it is safe and will never be shared with another? When you break confidence to share something with a person, that person will begin to wonder if you have broken their confidence as well. If you told them something that was supposed to be confidential, what is to keep you from doing the same with their confidences? Every time you break confidentiality, the person you share with will mistrust you a little more. They may act pleased that you have trusted them with this secret information, but they will be less inclined to share their secrets with you, lest you treat them as you have just treated someone else.

A trustworthy leader builds trust by not criticizing others. If you are always criticizing others to a friend or a fellow leader, that person will begin to wonder what you say about them when they aren't around. A critical spirit breeds an environment of mistrust. An oft-quoted verse exhorts: "Do to others as you would have them do to you" (Luke 6:31, *NIV*). A person who freely criticizes others will soon find themselves at the other end of the criticism. The manner in which you treat other people will turn back toward you. If you speak encouraging and uplifting words about others, this is what people will speak back to and around you. If you are free with your criticism, others will feel free to criticize you.

A trustworthy leader builds trust by being approachable and open. Live with a heart of compassion toward all whom you encounter. Be caring and empathetic. Have an understanding attitude toward whatever is said to you rather than reacting with judgment. Show genuine interest in people. Have you ever been in a conversation with a person who gives you their undivided attention while you are talking? They look you in the eyes, focus on you, listen to every word you say, and then ask you questions to follow up on or better understand what you said. They do not try to think of what they want to say while you are talking, but they listen intently—as if you were the only person on earth—and by so doing, they communicate that they are genuinely interested in everything you say. That is a person whom others want to be around—whom others trust. Be that person!

A trustworthy leader builds trust by being discreet. A discreet person is one who acts prudently and wisely. A quick search for the word "discretion" in the book of Proverbs shows us an individual who is quick to listen and gain understanding (see Prov. 1:4-5); who seeks wisdom and avoids evil (see Prov. 2:10-12); who seeks wisdom, understanding and knowledge (see Prov. 3:19-23; 8:12); and who is slow to anger but quick to forgive (see Prov. 19:11).

LEADERSHIP RESPECT FOR PEOPLE BUILDS TRUST

To respect someone is to view them as having great worth and therefore treat them with high regard. You cannot pretend to respect those you do not; the truth will show through in little ways—and no one trusts or respects those who do not respect and trust them. Remember, the people you are working with or relating to may have some serious character flaws. They may create problems for you every time you turn around—but they are still created by God in His image and deserve to be treated with respect.

An anthropologist went to live among a tribal group in Africa to study them for a year. She found a people living primitively, engaging in superstitious rituals, and practicing strange customs that seemed foolish to her. But she quickly realized that unless she respected them and valued them, she could learn nothing from them. The more she studied them with an attitude of respect, the more she learned—and the greater her respect for them became. Respect has nothing to do with a person's position or title, or with their financial worth or standard of living. Respect has to do with the fact that God created them and loved them enough to die for them— so how dare we regard them so lightly and value them so little?

A trustworthy leader demonstrates respect by acknowledging skills in others. God has made each person unique, and each person has unique skills and abilities. Value the gifts and talents of the people God has entrusted to your leadership. Do not compare them with one another and value them on a sliding scale, but value all of them for the gifts God has put in them. Those gifts are not in flawless vessels. You can have a person on your team who is greatly gifted with music but is terrible with relationships. Do not disregard a person's skill because of his or her other flaws. Instead, help your team member to grow in those areas where he or she is weaker, while affirming those areas that are stronger.

A trustworthy leader demonstrates respect by giving people room to grow and to learn new skills. If you have an individual with great gifts but lacking in certain areas, you do not want to put them in a position where those weaknesses will destroy them, but you can value their gift while at the same time providing discipleship for them to grow and overcome the flaws that hinder them.

Be proactive in providing growth opportunities for people. It is easy to find someone who is greatly skilled in one area and to use them exclusively in that area of skill without allowing them the opportunity to grow in other areas. But God has made people multi-faceted, and as leaders we need to help our team members develop all areas of their life, not just the ones that are beneficial to us right now. Allow them opportunities to learn, to study, and to discover and develop other strengths they may have.

A trustworthy leader demonstrates respect by embracing vulnerability. We make ourselves vulnerable when we put our trust in people and relinquish control of the outcome. When trust is broken, we feel let down and betrayed. If we allow our emotions to cause us to react against that betrayal instead of prayerfully asking God how we should respond, we can negatively affect the outcome and continue a downward spiral of mistrust. When someone betrays us or hurts us, we should never respond immediately. Instead, we should take the hurt to God and ask Him how we should respond. When we respond to a betrayal with God's grace, the outcome can be increased trust instead of broken relationship.

A trustworthy leader demonstrates respect by helping people to improve their leadership. Motivate people and inspire them. Stimulate people intellectually. Cultivate high emotional intelligence on your team. Research says that 85 percent of the most successful leaders have the ability to bring out the best in themselves and others. They have the ability, the capacity and the skill to manage their own emotions, as well as the emotions of others and a group's "emotional intelligence."

Emotional intelligence is the ability to identify, assess and control the emotions of yourself, others and groups. Understanding and accurately perceiving emotions, non-verbal signals and facial expressions are must-have skills. We lead with emotions, touch other peoples' emotions, and we react or respond with emotions. You must develop the ability to recognize your emotions, understand what they are saying to you, and realize how your emotions affect others and your perception of others.

A trustworthy leader demonstrates respect by managing expectations. What do you as a leader expect from those you are working with and those you are working for? Ask yourself, *Why am I doing what I am doing, and how does it affect our organization?* Don't create expectations you cannot fulfill. Remove false expectations. People generally have higher expectations for their leaders than they do for themselves—and some of these expectations are simply unrealistic. If someone considers you to be trustworthy, then by accepting that trust you become accountable for a satisfactory outcome or result. Make sure that you communicate clearly what you are able to deliver, so that trust is not broken by disappointment or disillusionment.

Trust must be earned and then protected at all costs. Without trust, the leadership process is empty. Our experience of placing our trust in God should increase our capacity to trust and encourage us to build trust within our relationships and our leadership. The more a leader exhibits trust-producing behaviors, the more a person will put trust in his or her leadership. Creating an environment of trust is the heart of true leadership. We must aim for trustworthiness in our leadership.

LIFE-CHANGING LEADERS MOVE THE CHURCH FORWARD

As Moses was building his leadership team in the wilderness, he was instructed to select a particular kind of person to stand with him and help bear the load. Those he chose were to be able leaders. The original Hebrew text describes these leaders as having strength, power or might. They were to be firm and warlike, and to display courage and valor: "Moreover you shall select from all the people able men, such as fear God, men of truth, hating covetousness; and place such over them to be rulers of thousands, rulers of hundreds, rulers of fifties, and rulers of tens" (Exod. 18:21; see also Num. 11:17,25; 2 Sam. 17:10).

Moses was instructed to pick leaders who feared God, who revered God. Fearing God and proper living are closely related—almost synonymous. Leaders are to have a healthy respect for God and live a holy life. They are to consistently keep their promises and be people of their word and of integrity. Moses was to choose people who hated covetousness, who were not moved by financial gain. He looked for those who had the spirit of wisdom, because wisdom is needed in every area of leadership and in every area of life. These leaders needed to be people who were mature, respected and proven in their ministry. They were to have a reputation that was established and accepted by the people.

Moses' responsibility was to provide leaders the congregation could respect, trust and follow without fear. The church today needs such qualified leadership to lead her to the victories of tomorrow. Where are these qualified leaders to be found? Should they come from within the house or be imported from a college or another like-minded church? If current leaders choose to train emerging leaders who are in the church, what methods should be used? What qualifications should the leader possess?

The Bible is the handbook for all who train leaders and endeavor to build healthy local churches. The Bible contains all the concepts and principles for raising up local leaders that we should use today in training leaders at all levels.

One of the greatest leadership development models in Scripture is Paul training Timothy. In Philippians 2:20, Paul refers to the leader he had raised up for the Ephesian church: "I have no one else like Timothy, who genuinely cares about your welfare" (*NLT*). Other translations say, "like-minded" (*KJV*), "of equal soul" (*EBR*), or "takes a genuine interest in your welfare" (*NIV*). In other words: "For I have no one else as near to my own attitude as my son, Timothy. There is no one else of kindred spirit, no one so like-minded."

Paul was in prison. His ministry was limited, so he had to trust someone. That someone was his son-in-the-faith, Timothy. No one except Timothy would handle problems, people and pressure the same way Paul himself would handle them. Timothy was a man of proven character and ministry, and a true son in the gospel to Paul. He had what Paul called a "kindred spirit." He was like-minded and equal in soul.

Leaders have the responsibility to gather potential leaders and to develop them to be good leaders for the congregation. First Chronicles 12:22 says, "Day by day men came to David to help him, until there was a great army like the army of God" (*NASB*). When you gather great leaders, you have the beginnings of a great church. Your leaders will have the ability to carry on the work of God in every department of the church, just as you would lead—and even better—as the Holy Spirit anoints each member of the team.

RISKS IN GATHERING LEADERS

Jesus prayed all night before choosing the Twelve (see Luke 6:12-13)—and with good reason. When you gather leaders, you take a risk. This is one of the necessary risks of being a leader. Fervent prayer is the only wise approach!

YOU RISK GATHERING IMPOSTER LEADERS

Acts 28:3 says, "But when Paul had gathered a bundle of sticks and laid them on the fire, a viper came out because of the heat, and fastened on his hand." Paul had gathered sticks to build a fire to warm himself, but in the sticks there was a snake. As soon as the fire heated the snake, it struck out and attached itself to Paul's hand. When we gather leaders, we take the chance that in a pile of sticks there may be one snake. That snake may eventually attach itself to your hand and poison you and your ministry.

Paul shook off the snake (see v. 5), and we can do the same. Isaiah 11:1-3 speaks of judging not by the natural eye or the natural ear. We must pray all night, like Jesus, who prayed for discernment in choosing the right leaders. If Samuel had chosen the next king of Israel without discernment, he would have completely missed David. But he was sensitive to the voice of God, which led him to the right leader out of Jesse's seven sons (see 1 Sam. 16:1-13). We must be careful to use discernment when choosing leaders. It is possible to have more sticks than snakes, although at times it seems we have chosen more snakes than sticks.

YOU RISK GATHERING UNTESTED LEADERS

Paul chose John Mark, who failed him in a time of pressure: "Now when Paul and his party set sail from Paphos, they came to Perga in Pamphylia; and John, departing from them, returned to Jerusalem" (Acts 13:13). Later, "Paul insisted that they should not take with them the one who had departed from them in Pamphylia, and had not gone with them to the work" (Acts 15:38). Mark failed the team in a time of crisis. He vacillated and turned back. He let Paul down. He revealed a character flaw. After his character was developed, he was restored to the leadership team—but not before causing Paul pain.

Leaders take this kind of risk in choosing leaders who are untested and unproven. We might be surprised. We might be disappointed. However, we should never be so disappointed that we refuse to restore a leader who has let us down. We must keep developing them, even when we see their glaring weaknesses. The account of his abandoning Paul and the team is not the final word on Mark: "Get Mark and bring him with you, for he is useful to me for ministry" (2 Tim. 4:11).

YOU RISK GATHERING UNSTABLE AND UNFAITHFUL LEADERS

David had Ahithophel (see 2 Sam. 15:12; 16:21; 17:23); Paul chose Demas: "Luke the beloved physician and Demas greet you" (Col. 4:14).

Demas was changed by Paul's presence for a short time. He was magnetized by Paul's engaging ministry, but as soon as he was away from that magnet, he went back to his own character and denied the way of Christ (see 2 Tim. 4:10). Demas is a prime example of a disciple whose wavering impulse caused him to surrender the passion of sacrifice and sink in the swirling waters of the world.

YOU RISK GATHERING DISLOYAL LEADERS

Absalom was gifted with remarkable beauty, commanding presence, natural dignity, extraordinary graces, charm and eloquence (see 2 Sam. 14:25). Yet a treacherous nature was within him. Absalom had unresolved offenses that resulted in his hating and betraying David. His ego, pride and selfishness led him to believe that he could have anything he wanted, and that he was a better leader than the great King David, his father. His disloyalty inspired a murderous plot toward his own family (see 2 Sam. 15). He was willing to attack David so that his own egotistical spirit could be satisfied.

YOU RISK GATHERING LEADERS WHO WILL EXPLOIT THE LOCAL CHURCH

A final risk is that you might gather leaders who will exploit the local church for their own purposes and will not care for the flock as a true shepherd would. The leader we all want has an uncomplaining heart that trusts God's ways, His unexplained dealings with the soul, and His ordering of life. This kind of leader is rare.

SIGNS OF STICK-LIKE LEADERS

We need leaders who are birthed into the main elements of the local church's vision, principles and philosophies. They need to be grafted into the vision of the house (see Prov. 29:18); the principles of the house (see 1 Chron. 15:13; 2 Chron. 4:20); and the philosophy, standards, doctrines, procedures and spirit of the house.

We read that Abraham's servants, who became warriors, were born, raised and trained in his own house (see Gen. 14:14). The birthing process for team members requires a spiritual identification with the local church. As the vision and principles of the local church are set forth, they must be assimilated into the team member's spirit, not just his or her mind. A spiritual illumination must take place, resulting in a teachable spirit and a changed leader.

The Holy Spirit will illuminate the minds of leaders as they form teams on all levels. The Lord will lay on the heart of the lead pastor and other leaders those people whom they should train and raise up in the local church. Look for stability of character—someone with a settled, untroubled and unoffended heart. One positive identification mark is faithfulness in all areas of living—faithfulness in small things, in natural things, and in things belonging to others: "He who is faithful in what is least is faithful also in much; and he who is unjust in what is least is unjust also in much. Therefore if you have not been faithful in the unrighteous mammon, who will commit to your trust the true riches? And if you have not been faithful in what is another man's, who will give you what is your own?" (Luke 16:10-12). Qualified potential leaders are faithful. They have proven their faithfulness by managing their finances well and by doing the right, small things consistently.

Another marker of a qualified leader is humility. A humble leader will respond properly when corrected. If pride is involved, there will continually be reaction and irritation as you try to train a leader who will not take correction. Watch for those who are willing to serve in menial areas, not just in the areas they prefer. Leaders should show a willingness to serve in any area of the church that has need. Those who manipulate themselves into a place of leadership without serving are leaders who will mutilate the Body of Christ.

A high level of personal integrity is of utmost importance. Leaders must take their words seriously. Those you want on your team will have a proven record of following through on the promises they make.

Leaders who have identified with the spirit of the leadership and the spirit of the house also respond to the preaching and teaching from the pulpit. If a leader does not take notes, say amen, smile or show some other kind of response, surely there should be some discussion about the person's love for the preaching.

As leaders are birthed in the local church, they will display a genuine love for people. They'll stay after services and mingle. People will want to be with these leaders, gathering around them at all public events, potlucks, small-group meetings and leadership meetings. The leader's sensitivity to the needs of others engenders in others a love for that leader. If a person is pushing for promotion and recognition, that ambition will come out in little ways before it is clearly manifested. Notice if prospective leaders are always siding with people who make wrong decisions or who promote wrong concepts. If they regularly justify themselves and shift blame away from themselves, this should warn you not to put them in a leadership position.

When gathering potential leaders, choose people who have successful family and occupational relationships. Watch out for those who show an inability to keep confidences and who are hasty in their decision making. If people continue to make poor judgment calls and poor decisions even after they have been warned and taught concerning those areas, they will ultimately hurt the church. Those who are emotionally unstable in situations that cause pressure will also cause problems in the church. Consider the potential leader individually, and also consider the leader's family. Emotional instability will cause pressure in both the home and the leadership area.

All potential ministry team members must encounter the revealing fire of God. Fire shows forth the true nature of the potential leader. Until a leader goes through the fire, he or she is an unknown factor in the leadership team (see Lev. 1:7-17; Matt. 3:11-12; 1 Cor. 3:13; 1 Pet. 1:7; Heb. 12:28-29).

LEADERS HANDLE CONFLICTS
IN THE CHURCH

There will always be conflict in the local church. All churches in every part of the world experience the devastating effects of disagreement, discord and conflict. The Early Church described in the New Testament encountered several such problems—and survived. In most churches, the main problem usually relates back to an unresolved leadership conflict or an unresolved congregational conflict. God has provided us with the keys we need to handle conflicts and hard cases, just as He gave Moses the ability to handle the various conflicts that arose within the nation of Israel.

We have the anointing of the Holy Spirit and the wisdom of God to enable us to deal rightly with the tough situations that will inevitably arise. Leaders who do not know how to approach conflicts will allow little fires to burn continually in the church. Qualified leaders are able to exercise sound judgment in all matters: "And let them judge the people at all times. Then it will be that every great matter they shall bring to you, but every small matter they themselves shall judge" (Exod. 18:22).

Webster's dictionary defines "conflict" as "a striking together, a contest; to fight, contest, to clash, incompatibility; to be in opposition, sharp disagreement; emotional disturbance resulting from a clash." The Greek word we often translate as "conflict" is *agon*. *Agon* was used to identify the place where the Greeks assembled for the Olympic games and watched athletic contests. The term came to mean "struggle" or "combat." *Agon* is translated five different ways in the New Testament: "conflict" (Phil. 1:30), "contention" (1 Thess. 2:2, *KJV*), "fight" (1 Tim. 6:12), "race" (Heb. 12:1), and "agony" (Luke 22:44).

We have all encountered conflict in some capacity. Whether it is a disagreement among the leadership team or a church member who disagrees with a leader's decision, conflict is disturbing. Conflict can make us hard or soft, bitter or better. It can make us lose confidence and be hesitant to take initiative when we see trouble, because we are afraid of what might happen. But conflict also strengthens our character. The more conflict we experience, the more we will pray, learn the Word of God, and keep humility as the canopy over our lives.

Conflict makes us examine and purify our motives. It reveals faults and flaws in us and in the church that we would not have been aware of if a disagreement had not shaken us up and forced us to closely examine our philosophy and principles. Conflict teaches us spiritual endurance and spiritual carefulness. Sometimes it even jolts us into the will of God. Not all conflict is negative. There are times when the Lord shakes the church, allowing conflict to come so that He can make needed changes.

Conflict is a sister to contention. These two dwell together and grow together whenever they are not handled properly. Contention can lead to separation, as it did in the Early Church: "Then the contention became so sharp that they parted from one another" (Acts 15:39; see also Prov. 18:18; 23:29; 1 Cor. 1:11). The word "contention" implies quarreling, especially rivalry or wrangling as in the church at Corinth. It can also mean having sharp feeling or emotion toward someone, which affects our irritation level. Contention carries with it the idea of strife—of being a lover of strife. It signifies an eagerness to contend. Where there is contention and conflict there is also strife and discord (see Prov. 6:16-19).

The following are eight common sources of leadership conflict:

1. When there is inconsistency in the practicing of biblical principles that have been clearly established in the local church.

2. When the leadership violates standards and attitudes taught to the people.

3. When leadership presumptuously declares a vision or direction from the Lord and then aborts the work in order to move in another direction without explanation.

4. When leadership avoids, procrastinates or ignores the need to confront those who are sowing seeds of contention, and then does not properly handle the problem.

5. When leaders violate their personal standards and wisdom in choosing unqualified leadership to serve the people, thus causing great confusion.

6. When leaders handle an explosive or complex situation in haste, without prayer and without considering the ramifications of their actions or decisions.

7. When leadership does not consistently practice the principle of forgiveness as taught in Matthew 18:21-35, thus allowing offenses to grow in the church and among the leaders.

8. When leaders violate the spirit of team ministry by acting independently of the elders or leadership team in making major decisions that will affect the whole body.

Leaders who move the church forward are those who successfully handle conflicts. In Acts 15, we see three basic principles that were used by the leadership in approaching conflicts. First, we see the principle of effective communication with an honest heart and a teachable spirit (see Acts 15:1-4,6). Second, we see the principle of the leadership coming together to consider the matter before they spoke to the congregation (see Acts 15:6). Third, we see the principle of gathering all the facts from the parties involved (see Acts 15:4,12).

These three principles are applicable to any conflict in the local church. Effective communication takes a lot of time and a lot of work. Gathering facts can be tedious and painful; but without all the facts, we risk multiplying the conflict rather than solving it. Root problems must be dealt with, not just manifestations of a problem. Here are some practical tips for handling conflicts in the leadership team or in the local church: (1)Refrain from hasty decisions. (2) Remember that you are dealing with real people and with human failure. You are not at war with people, but with a spiritual adversary—the devil. (3) Discipline your carnal impulses and negative reactions, and instead love looking for the best in people. (4) Exercise grace in every action and don't repeat half-truths.

We may have past failures in relationships with other team members. It is a fact of life that not all relationships go smoothly. Sometimes we remember people the wrong way. We think of the last conflict we had with them or the last thing they said to us that was not as wholesome as it should have been. We may judge people for their past failures in relationships—or for their responses to our failures. Sometimes we make hasty judgments about other leaders' decisions or procedures.

When you feel as if your leadership is being threatened, handle those vain imaginations in light of the truth of your calling. If you are operating in your metron, you can successfully deal with disagreements, knowing that you are within the confines of the lines God has drawn for you. Be confident in your metron and allow some differences in methodology.

THREE LESSONS FROM JESUS IN HANDLING CONFLICT

The foot-washing service described in John 13 provides insight into handling conflicts. Three significant things happened in this chapter: First, Jesus laid aside His garments (see v. 4). Mature servants are willing to lay aside their reputation or status to deal with a problem. Many times we have to set aside our titles and our positions in order to speak lovingly to others; we do not want these things to intimidate the people we deal with, nor should we attempt to hide behind them. Mature leaders know that in dealing with conflict, they must expose themselves and be deeply sincere and honest with people.

Second, Jesus girded Himself with a towel (see v. 4). This is the outfit of a servant. True leaders will gird themselves with a servant's attitude. All leadership should be underneath, pushing up. Leaders should take the servant's mentality and the servant's attitude continually—in every situation. Even when you are right but you have been accused of wrong, take the servant's attitude. When you are in a place where you can retaliate, take the servant's attitude. When you are in a place where you can bring vengeance on someone, take the servant's attitude. Remember that the robe of the leader is not the white collar or the title; it is the servant's towel.

Third, Jesus washed the disciples' feet (see v. 5). This is the function of a servant. In this action, we see Christ's humility and how unselfish He was concerning His own reputation. True humility expresses itself not in unfavorable comparisons of ourselves with others, but in wholehearted devotion to the interests of others. First Peter 5:5, in the *Concordant Literal Translation,* says, "Tie on humility like a dress fastened with string." Jesus showed the disciples how to minister to one another and how to prepare themselves for conflicts that would arise within the team and within the church. We can do this only when we wear the servant's towel.

Washing one another with a humble spirit and the power of the Holy Spirit is essential to relationships within the leadership team. Washing by the Holy Spirit is the evidence of maturity and the key to team success. We are responsible to lay aside our garments while washing. We are responsible to clothe ourselves with a servant's towel. We are responsible to wash our brothers and sisters even when they initially reject us and do not want us to wash them (like Peter, who did not want Christ to wash his feet—see John 13:6-9).

We are responsible to wash ourselves first, to make sure we speak from a clean heart and spirit (see Ps. 51:2,7; John 9:7; Acts 16:33). Many conflicts must be washed from our hearts and from the leadership team. We sometimes bruise one another with our tongues, passing on half-truths or saying things that harm one another. These things need to be washed out of our spirit, and washed from the leadership and from the church.

At times we hold and hide resentments that stem from past offenses or disappointments. We must release these in the power of the Holy Spirit and ask the Lord Jesus to heal us. Leaders must set the example of being a servant with a humble spirit—being washed ourselves, washing others, and responding to those who come to wash us. One of the great signs of humble leaders is their receptivity to other leaders who point out their blind spots. Blind spots cause us to stumble and make wrong decisions. As we form a leadership team, it is with the help of others that these blind spots can be washed out of our lives to save us from destruction.

Maturity is evidenced when a problem is encountered without overreaction, retaliation, criticism, taking it personally, or allowing a fixation on that issue to develop. May the Holy Spirit give each of us the kind of spirit that allows us to wash one another and build a strong team in spite of the conflicts we endure.

CONCLUSION

My desire is that you will become a great leader who forms strong teams that in turn build a life-changing church. Vision becomes reality when the team factor is a reality. It's a simple principle: A healthy leadership team is a prerequisite to a healthy, growing church. And it all starts with you.

The most important leader is you. You have a direct relationship with people and leaders. You have the power to shape people. You are the one who must take ownership of your area and become the best leader and the best team player. It is the team that makes the church life-changing, not the lead pastor. The leader's importance and reputation are greatly diminished if the team is bad. Churches do well because of all the unnamed people who lead them. Without that greatness, there are no great churches.

With you in the mix, what does a person become? Do you model self-lessness, loyalty, integrity, unity, a strong prayer life and commitment to the vision? Shaping power is in the influence of touch, modeling and mentoring. People will serve and make a difference because of you.

Leadership is more than a mindset; it is a behavior set. You are a leader. That means everyone around you has to become better and you have to understand that you are an important role in their life. The character and quality of you the leader make you the valuable person on whom the entire church is being built.

In this book, I have laid out practical strategies for building and maintaining teams that will in turn change lives. My hope is that you will increase your capacity to lead and fulfill the great vision God has in mind for you and your church with a life-changing team behind it. You're never too young to be great and you're never too old to be better! The best is yet to come!

ENDNOTES

Chapter 2: Life-Changing Local Churches
1. Charles Colson, *The Body* (Dallas, TX: Word Publishing, 1992), p. 65.
2. Ibid.

Chapter 3: Life-Changing Lead Pastor Profile
1. Thomas Gillespie, "The Laity in Biblical Perspective," citied in Ralph D. Bucy, ed., *The New Laity* (Waco, TX: Word Books, 1978).
2. For more information about the California Psychological Inventory, see www.cpp.com.
3. Kent M. Keith, "Paradoxical Commandments of Leadership," published in *The Silent Revolution: Dynamic Leadership in Student Council* (1968).

Chapter 4: Life-Changing Leadership Teams
1. Howard A. Snyder, *The Problem of Wine Skins* (Downers Grove, IL: InterVarsity Press, 1975).
2. Bill Hull, *The Disciple-Making Pastor* (Grand Rapids, MI: Baker Books, 2007), p. 109.
3. Gene Edwards, *A Tale of Three Kings* (Carol Stream, IL: Tyndale, 1992).

Chapter 5: Life-Changing Eldership Teams
1. Don Basham, "Giving Praise and Encouragement," *New Wine*, vol. 11, no. 6, June 1979, p. 4.

Chapter 6: Leaders Who Build the Church
1. William Law, "Upon Christian Perfection," *The Works of the Reverend William Law, M.A.* (London: J. Richardson, 1726), p. 29.
2. Larry Crabb, *Real Church* (Nashville, TN: Thomas Nelson, 2009), pp. xiii-xiv.
3. Ibid., p. xix.

Chapter 7: Life-Changing Leadership Team Integrity
1. William E. Schmidt, "For Town and Team, Honor Is Its Own Reward," *The New York Times*, May 25, 1987.
2. *The Pryor Report*, vol. 6, no. 1A, 1989.
3. Cited in John Maxwell, *Ethics 101: What Every Leader Needs to Know* (New York: Hachette, 2008).

Chapter 8: Life-Changing Servant Leadership
1. John Stott, *The Cross of Christ* (Downers Grove, IL: InterVarsity Press, 2006), p. 178.

Chapter 11: Leadership Tensions, Temptations and Principles
1. Emily Herman, *Christianity in the New Age* (London: Cassell and Company, LTD, 1919), p. 214.

Chapter 13: Leadership Teams Build and Sustain Trust
1. Dr. Seuss, *Horton Hears a Who!* (New York: Random House, 1954).

CONTACT INFORMATION

Twitter: @frankdamazio
Facebook: **Pastor Frank Damazio**

Pastor Frank online:
(blogs, sermon notes, pastor-leader resources)
www.frankdamazio.com

Send inquiries to:
9200 NE Fremont St.
Portland, OR 97220
503.255.2224
www.frankdamazio.com

PROVEN STRATEGIES FOR BUILDING A WORLD-IMPACTING CHURCH

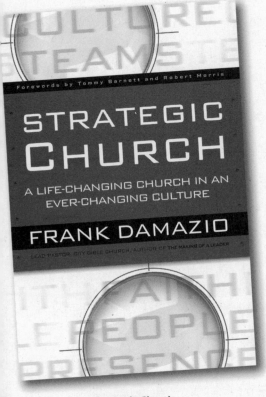

Strategic Church
Frank Damazio
ISBN 978-0-8307-63764
ISBN 0-8307-6376-7

There's no shortcut to having a strong church. It takes a vision, time, work and a divine strategy. *Strategic Church* will give you the tools to build and equip a strong, relevant, life-changing local church as you follow God's vision. Whether you're a lead minister, small-group leader, worship pastor or church member, you'll find clear and proven principles in this book to help you thrive as a builder of Christ's Church.

"*Strategic Church* is a manifesto and a handbook for building Jesus' Church. It will inspire you, inform you, and propel you to make God's vision a reality."
JUDAH SMITH
Lead Pastor, City Church, Seattle, Washington

"*Strategic Church* will help you understand how to mobilize people to pray, how to relate to culture, and so much more. It's a must-read for every leader who is serious about building a church that sees lives being transformed."
DARLENE ZCHECH
Songwriter and Co-pastor, Hope Unlimited Church